ISBN 978-1-334-34723-8
PIBN 10708399

1 MONTH OF
FREE
READING

at
www.ForgottenBooks.com

By purchasing this book you are eligible for one month membership to ForgottenBooks.com, giving you unlimited access to our entire collection of over 1,000,000 titles via our web site and mobile apps.

To claim your free month visit:
www.forgottenbooks.com/free708399

English
Français
Deutsche
Italiano
Español
Português

www.forgottenbooks.com

Mythology Photography **Fiction**
Fishing Christianity **Art** Cooking
Essays Buddhism Freemasonry
Medicine **Biology** Music **Ancient**
Egypt Evolution Carpentry Physics
Dance Geology **Mathematics** Fitness
Shakespeare **Folklore** Yoga Marketing
Confidence Immortality Biographies
Poetry **Psychology** Witchcraft
Electronics Chemistry History **Law**
Accounting **Philosophy** Anthropology
Alchemy Drama Quantum Mechanics
Atheism Sexual Health **Ancient History**
Entrepreneurship Languages Sport
Paleontology Needlework Islam
Metaphysics Investment Archaeology
Parenting Statistics Criminology
Motivational

RAILWAY RETURNS

FOR

ENGLAND AND WALES,

SCOTLAND,

AND

IRELAND.

For the Year 1873.

Pursuant to the Act 34 & 35 *Vict. cap.* 78.

WITH SUMMARY TABLES FOR UNITED KINGDOM

For each Year from 1854 to 1873, &c.

Presented to both Houses of Parliament

LONDON:

PRINTED BY GEORGE EDWARD EYRE AND WILLIAM SPOTTISWOODE,

PRINTERS TO THE QUEEN'S MOST EXCELLENT MAJESTY.

FOR HER MAJESTY'S STATIONERY OFFICE.

1874.

[C.—1035.]   *Price* 1s. 1d.

CONTENTS.

Statistical and Commercial Department, Board of Trade,   R. VALPY.
    Whitehall, June 1874.

SUMMARY TABLE for UNITED

LENGTH of LINES, CAPITAL, PASSENGERS CONVEYED,

YEAR.	LENGTH OF LINE OPEN FOR TRAFFIC AT THE END OF EACH YEAR.			CAPITAL AUTHORISED.			CAPITAL PAID UP.						
	Double or more.	Single.	TOTAL.	By Shares and Stock.	By Loans and Debenture Stock.	TOTAL.	Ordinary.	Guaranteed.	Preferential.	Loans.	Debenture Stock.	TOTAL.	Per Mile of Line open.
	Miles.	Miles.	Miles.	£	£	£	£	£		£	£	£	£
1854	6,103	1,950	8,053	276,000,577	92,383,731	368,384,308	166,030,906	49,277,952		70,660,036		286,068,794	35,523
1855	6,153	2,183	8,336	280,628,621	94,343,345	374,971,966	169,605,442	52,518,026		75,161,241	*(Cannot be given for these years.)*	297,284,709	35,703
1856	6,266	2,444	8,710	282,890,751	94,877,156	377,767,907	173,446,109	56,789,558		77,359,419		307,595,066	35,315
1857	6,357	2,682	9,039	288,013,644	99,038,090	387,051,734	178,624,394	58,126,627		78,406,237		315,157,258	34,866
1858	—	—	9,542	292,248,276	100,434,479	392,682,755	181,837,781	61,854,547		81,683,179		325,375,507	34,099
1859	—	—	10,002	285,434,181	98,282,170	383,716,351	184,560,019	63,555,179		80,628,116	5,619,614	334,362,928	33,480
1860	6,690	3,743	10,433	298,685,142	100,729,685	399,414,827	190,790,867	67,873,840		81,888,546	7,276,874	346,180,127	33,368
1861	6,893	3,972	10,865	322,369,654	107,503,292	429,872,946	193,591,991	73,784,336		87,144,443	7,806,568	362,327,338	33,349
1862	7,009	4,542	11,551	336,777,276	111,819,462	450,596,738	197,077,589	87,792,380		89,983,373	10,665,096	385,218,438	33,349
1863	7,270	5,052	12,322	355,700,795	119,298,750	474,999,545	204,597,257	97,496,291		89,641,525	12,480,729	404,215,902	32,804
1864	7,402	5,387	12,789	390,413,187	130,109,197	520,522,384	214,947,054	104,647,626		95,075,392	13,049,541	425,719,613	33,288
1865	7,503	5,786	13,289	432,889,245	143,402,418	576,291,663	219,596,196	124,263,475		97,821,097	13,795,375	455,476,143	34,275
1866	7,711	6,143	13,854	466,151,633	154,412,773	620,564,406	228,345,622	134,455,096		105,065,863	14,105,594	481,872,184	34,782
1867	7,844	6,403	14,247	481,447,440	161,406,968	642,853,408	233,023,854	148,209,387		110,392,559	15,687,117	502,262,387	35,254
1868	—	—	14,623	455,895,068	159,550,550	615,445,618*	224,133,427	28,391,336	134,940,707	108,428,905	25,286,500	511,680,855	34,979
1869	—	—	15,145†	449,087,873	160,180,060	609,287,653	226,788,183	25,203,671	130,553,969	101,729,396	34,504,570	518,779,761§	34,254
1870	—	—	15,537†	437,963,372	158,215,010	596,178,382	229,292,150	56,188,320	122,508,764	90,713,779	51,220,860	529,906,873§	34,106
1871	8,338	7,038	15,376	451,898,906	163,827,962	615,726,890	230,234,058	64,552,793	108,406,620	82,995,545	67,282,535	552,651,551	35,943
1872	8,512	7,302	15,814	472,419,873	172,169,480	644,589,353	239,039,089	63,004,313	114,780,361	66,224,217	85,981,511	569,047,346‡	35,984
1873	‡‡ 8,687	7,395	16,082	497,922,723	178,763,863	676,686,586	244,449,905	66,187,541	121,989,528	85,888,314	99,855,120	588,320,308	36,574

* The authorized capital of several companies, having merely a nominal existence, has been omitted in 1868 and subsequent years.
† Number of miles constructed. ‡ Including 37,855l. Capitalised Rentcharge. § Stock and Share Capital received.
‡‡ See also Table No. 2 a., p. 64.

KINGDOM in each Year from 1854 to 1873.

GROSS and NET RECEIPTS, and WORKING EXPENSES.

NUMBER of PASSENGERS conveyed exclusive of Season Ticket Holders.	GROSS RECEIPTS.										WORKING EXPENDITURE.		NET RECEIPTS.		
	FROM PASSENGER TRAFFIC.††		FROM GOODS TRAFFIC.		TOTAL FROM TRAFFIC.			MISCELLANEOUS.		TOTAL from all Sources.					YEAR.
	Total.	Proportion to Total Receipts.	Total.	Proportion to Total Receipts.	Total.	Per Mile of Line open.	Per Train Mile.	Rents, Tolls, Navigation, Steamboats, &c.	Proportion to Total Receipts.		Total.	Proportion to Total Receipts.	Total.	Proportion to Total paid up Capital.	
No.	£	Per Cent.	£	Per Cent.	£	£	s. d.	£	Per Cent.	£	£	Per Cent.	£	Per Cent.	
111,180,165	10,344,964	50·68	9,970,770	49·32	20,315,734	2,510	5 6½								1854
118,567,170	10,694,790	49·73	10,812,809	50·27	21,507,599	2,580	5 9½								1855
129,315,196	11,376,337	49·11	11,789,156	50·89	23,165,498	3,660	5 11½								1856
128,971,240	11,888,319	49·18	12,286,292	50·83	24,174,611	3,674	5 9½					Cannot be given for these years.			1857
139,141,135	11,697,906	48·83	12,258,845	51·17	23,956,751	2,511	5 6								1858
140,757,394	12,537,493	48·70	13,206,009	51·30	25,743,502	2,574	5 6								1859
163,435,678	13,065,756	47·13	14,680,866	52·87	27,766,622	2,661	5 5				13,187,368	47	14,579,254	4·19	1860
173,721,189	13,326,475	46·65	15,238,880	53·85	28,565,355	2,629	5 5				13,843,337	46	14,722,018	4·06	1861
180,429,071	13,911,985	47·76	15,216,573	52·24	29,128,558	2,522	5 4½				14,268,409	49	14,860,149	3·86	1862
204,635,075	14,521,528	45·61	16,634,869	53·39	31,156,397	2,529	5 4				15,027,234	48	16,129,163	3·99	1863
229,272,166	15,684,040	46·11	18,331,524	53·89	34,015,564	2,660	5 3				16,000,308	47	18,015,256	4·23	1864
251,862,715	16,572,051	46·17	19,318,062	53·83	35,890,113	2,701	5 1½				17,149,073	46	18,741,040	4·11	1865
274,293,668	17,396,925	45·58	20,768,429	54·42	38,164,354	2,755	5 4				18,811,673	49	19,352,681	4·02	1866
287,968,113	17,935,634	45·43	21,544,365	54·57	39,479,999	2,771	5 3½				19,848,952	50	19,631,047	3·91	1867
‖	‖	—	‖	—	‖	—	—	‖	—	‖	‖	—	‖	—	1868
313,759,053	18,811,504	44·06	23,263,817	52·15	41,075,321	2,712	5 9½	1,620,606	3·80	43,695,927	20,780,078	49	21,915,849	4·23	1869
336,545,397	19,301,911	43·52	24,115,159	53·50	43,417,070	2,794	5 1½	1,661,078	3·68	45,078,148	21,715,535	48	23,362,613	4·41	1870
375,230,754	20,622,560	43·18	26,484,978	54·17	47,107,538	3,064	5 3	1,785,222	3·65	48,892,780	23,152,860	47	25,739,920	4·66	1871
422,974,823	22,287,555	41·87	29,016,559	54·50	51,304,114	3,244	5 4½	1,931,896	3·63	53,235,510	26,277,840	49	26,957,670	4·74	1872
455,320,188	23,853,892	41·51	31,821,529	55·11	55,675,421	3,462	5 7½	2,066,579	3·58	57,742,000	30,752,848	53	26,989,152	4·59	1873

‖ Cannot be given for this year, several Companies having omitted to make the necessary returns.
†† Including Receipts from Season Tickets, Carriages, Horses, &c., and Post Office Mails.

SUMMARY TABLES FOR ENGLAND AND WALES,

No. 1.—AMOUNT of ORDINARY, GUARANTEED, and PREFERENTIAL STOCK and SHARE CAPITAL, classed

RATE per CENT. of DIVIDEND PAID.	Years.	ENGLAND AND WALES.			SCOTLAND.		
		Ordinary.	Guaranteed.	Preferential.	Ordinary.	Guaranteed.	Preferential.
		£	£	£	£	£	£
Capital of New Companies the Lines of which were in course of construction, and no Dividend earned	1870	1,919,259	39,512		253,282	60,000	
	1871	1,506,140	—	173,363	75,724		
	1872	2,172,303	—	192,732	281,096	—	—
	1873	2,602,131	—	186,598	450,667	—	—
Capital of Constructed Lines upon which no Dividend was Paid	1870	22,275,964	12,097,894		6,641,054	458,661	
	1871	25,586,956	133,584	6,371,231	2,658,499	—	546,458
	1872	24,418,080	—	6,512,147	2,582,568	—	600,266
	1873	25,520,934	153,635	6,098,479	6,051,056	—	668,614
Dividends Paid: Not exceeding 1 per Cent.	1870	18,339,244	14,640		325,834	—	
	1871	679,590	—	4,709,183	4,528,536	—	75,000
	1872	8,978,194	—	347,810	1,570,043	—	—
	1873	8,542,694	—	1,514,607	973,813	—	95,291
Exceeding 1 and not exceeding 2 per Cent.	1870	5,633,353	183,170		1,049,711	2,419,573	
	1871	9,106,478	—	21,540	938,868	—	—
	1872	4,808,104	101,180	5,043,173	3,604,268	—	80,292
	1873	639,360	101,180	5,302,133	311,694	—	218,030
„ 2 and not exceeding 3 per Cent.	1870	7,685,352	325,400		129,276	1,623,762	
	1871	16,009,397	2,221,700	682,870	86,147	—	2,647,749
	1872	1,403,701	2,535,924	315,400	242,520	602,125	1,625
	1873	14,737,890	2,221,700	568,820	473,532	602,534	2,684,800
„ 3 and not exceeding 4 per Cent.	1870	27,145,298	11,982,317		6,396,948	2,811,504	
	1871	11,609,334	9,074,851	5,222,189	227,454	1,993,651	1,876,751
	1872	24,759,083	8,068,204	5,007,069	240,222	1,266,526	8,029,810
	1873	16,411,902	8,600,432	5,672,323	7,614,754	966,826	8,179,465
„ 4 and not exceeding 5 per Cent.	1870	14,523,158	89,131,879		449,544	12,705,126	
	1871	22,450,650	31,594,201	66,185,020	418,249	4,218,294	9,119,516
	1872	10,698,841	34,338,870	68,687,893	6,835,543	2,633,489	8,805,734
	1873	9,116,979	36,677,213	72,660,233	6,451,189	2,994,789	6,676,869
„ 5 and not exceeding 6 per Cent.	1870	6,408,875	10,838,834		4,034,260	2,205,318	
	1871	17,307,349	9,367,109	1,694,330	11,178,161	1,117,793	1,214,170
	1872	28,082,841	8,842,109	1,996,914	1,418,753	512,343	728,170
	1873	16,274,685	9,457,309	2,442,675	185,950	522,343	728,170
„ 6 and not exceeding 7 per Cent.	1870	64,960,371	1,078,302		125,500	3,003,455	
	1871	14,412,307	80,654	641,690	21,000	1,891,333	1,112,122
	1872	2,988,865	98,937	471,860	4,761,060	2,047,583	1,398,122
	1873	34,247,457	80,654	641,860	125,500	1,891,333	1,112,122
„ 7 and not exceeding 8 per Cent.	1870	18,817,365	808,070		312,582	396,355	
	1871	51,560,603	518,573	227,500	382,583	396,355	—
	1872	54,732,166	140,000	397,500	293,583	240,000	—
	1873	51,807,941	518,573	227,500	272,583	240,000	—
„ 8 and not exceeding 9 per Cent.	1870	1,754,386	—		—		
	1871	2,188,477	—	—	—		
	1872	32,594,629	819,143	—	40,000		
	1873	2,225,192	—	—	40,000		
„ 9 and not exceeding 10 per Cent.	1870	2,166,387	435,840		37,000		
	1871	19,107,500	1,190,370	385,840	—		
	1872	2,800,920	50,000	385,840	—		
	1873	19,242,170	490,570	279,165	—		
„ 10 and not exceeding 11 per Cent.	1870	302,175	—		—	200,000	
	1871	—	—	—	37,000	200,000	
	1872	—	—		37,000	200,000	
	1873	—	—		37,000	200,000	
„ 11 and not exceeding 12 per Cent.	1870	2,660,300	—		—		
	1871	315,000	—	50,000	—		
	1872	290,000	37,725	—	—		
	1873	3,800,846	—	165,000	—		
„ 12 and not exceeding 13 per Cent.	1870	—			—		
	1871	3,213,899	44,275		—		
	1872	3,355,300	2,000	50,000	—		
	1873	631,580	39,125	—	—		
TOTAL	1870	194,591,487	126,935,858		19,754,991	25,883,754	
	1871	195,048,690	54,225,517	86,364,756	20,552,221	9,817,436	16,591,766
	1872	201,583,027	55,084,092	89,408,338	21,906,656	7,502,066	19,644,019
	1873	205,801,711	58,340,391	95,709,893	22,987,788	7,417,825	20,363,361

Note.—The separate amounts of Guaranteed and Preferential

SCOTLAND, AND IRELAND, FOR THE YEARS 1870 to 1873.

according to the Rate per Cent. of Dividend Paid, in each of the Years 1870, 1871, 1872, and 1873.

IRELAND.			UNITED KINGDOM.			Years.	RATE per CENT. of DIVIDEND PAID.
Ordinary.	Guaranteed.	Preferential.	Ordinary.	Guaranteed.	Preferential.		
£	£	£	£	£	£		
499,453	—		2,671,994	99,512		1870	Capital of New Companies the Lines of which were in course of construction, and no Dividend earned.
534,448	—	33,380	2,116,307	—	206,743	1871	
580,361	1,455	—	3,033,760	1,455	192,732	1872	
449,834	1,575	3,560	3,502,632	1,575	140,158	1873	
2,349,858	1,616,393		31,266,876	14,172,948		1870	Capital of Constructed Lines upon which no Dividend was Paid.
1,853,469	43,150	1,029,581	30,098,934	176,734	7,947,270	1871	
2,791,228	—	1,086,472	29,791,876	—	8,198,885	1872	
2,539,094	—	620,946	34,111,084	153,635	7,388,039	1873	
125,352	—		18,790,430	14,640		1870	Dividends Paid: Not exceeding 1 per Cent.
—	—	115,880	5,208,126	—	4,900,063	1871	
119,178	—	122,950	10,667,415	—	470,060	1872	
22,128	—	420,223	9,538,635	—	2,030,121	1873	
1,023,346	122,250		7,706,310	2,724,993		1870	Exceeding 1 and not exceeding 2 per Cent.
438,378	—	122,950	10,483,724	—	143,790	1871	
—	—	—	8,412,372	101,180	5,123,465	1872	
365,380	—	245,003	1,316,484	101,180	6,765,166	1873	
796,763	—		8,611,391	1,949,162		1870	„ 2 and not exceeding 3 per Cent.
1,388,730	—	45,300	17,484,274	2,221,700	3,375,919	1871	
366,899	—	162,015	2,013,120	3,138,049	479,040	1872	
680,800	—	—	15,892,222	2,824,234	3,253,620	1873	
2,157,175	1,814,795		35,699,421	16,608,616		1870	„ 3 and not exceeding 4 per Cent.
123,806	100,000	1,715,578	11,960,594	11,168,502	8,814,518	1871	
1,317,840	100,000	1,785,700	26,217,145	9,484,780	14,822,579	1872	
720,490	100,000	1,982,585	24,747,146	9,667,258	15,884,373	1873	
6,980,902	2,028,854		21,953,604	108,865,859		1870	„ 4 and not exceeding 5 per Cent.
3,418,470	366,700	2,171,207	26,382,369	36,179,195	77,475,743	1871	
3,490,050	366,700	2,343,642	21,024,434	37,339,059	79,737,269	1872	
3,824,645	327,750	2,283,557	19,392,813	39,999,752	81,620,659	1873	
652,223	290,180		11,096,058	18,334,332		1870	„ 5 and not exceeding 6 per Cent.
5,978,023	—	306,922	34,458,583	10,484,902	3,215,422	1871	
5,076,022	—	307,925	34,577,616	9,354,452	3,083,009	1872	
5,150,157	—	310,900	21,610,792	9,979,652	3,481,745	1873	
—	—		65,085,871	4,081,757		1870	„ 6 and not exceeding 7 per Cent.
557,828	—	—	14,991,185	1,971,987	1,753,812	1871	
1,000,000	—	—	8,749,925	2,146,520	1,869,982	1872	
—	—	—	34,372,957	1,971,987	1,753,982	1873	
—	—		19,129,947	1,204,425		1870	„ 7 and not exceeding 8 per Cent.
—	—	—	51,943,186	914,928	227,500	1871	
557,828	—	—	55,583,577	380,000	397,500	1872	
1,557,828	—	—	53,638,352	758,573	227,500	1873	
—	—		1,754,386	—		1870	„ 8 and not exceeding 9 per Cent.
—	—	—	2,183,477	—	—	1871	
—	—	—	32,634,629	819,143	—	1872	
350,000	—	—	2,615,192	—	—	1873	
350,000	—		2,558,387	435,840		1870	„ 9 and not exceeding 10 per Cent.
350,000	—	—	19,457,500	1,190,570	385,840	1871	
350,000	—	—	2,650,920	50,000	385,840	1872	
—	—	—	19,242,170	490,570	279,165	1873	
—	—		302,175	200,000		1870	„ 10 and not exceeding 11 per Cent.
—	—	—	37,000	200,000	—	1871	
—	—	—	37,000	200,000	—	1872	
—	—	—	37,000	200,000	—	1873	
—	—		2,660,300	—		1870	„ 11 and not exceeding 12 per Cent.
—	—	—	315,000	—	50,000	1871	
—	—	—	290,000	37,725	—	1872	
—	—	—	3,800,846	—	165,000	1873	
—	—		—	—		1870	„ 12 and not exceeding 13 per Cent.
—	—	—	3,213,899	44,275	—	1871	
—	—	—	3,855,300	2,000	50,000	1872	
—	—	—	631,530	39,125	—	1873	
14,935,672	5,872,472	5,540,098	229,282,150	158,692,084	108,496,620	1870	TOTAL.
14,635,147	509,850	5,540,098	230,284,058	64,552,793	108,496,620	1871	
15,549,406	468,155	5,708,004	239,039,089	68,004,313	114,760,361	1872	
15,660,856	429,325	5,866,774	244,449,805	66,187,541	121,939,528	1873	

Capital cannot be distinguished for the Year 1870.

SUMMARY TABLES FOR ENGLAND AND WALES,

No. 2.—Amount of Loans and of Debenture Stock, classed according to t h

RATE per CENT. of INTEREST PAID.	Years.	ENGLAND AND WALES.		SCOTLAND.	
		Loans.	Debenture Stock.	Loans.	Debenture Stock.
		£	£	£	£
Not receiving any Interest -	1870	8,000	—	—	—
	1871	161,616	743,174	—	—
	1872	59,200	404,342	—	—
	1873	49,000	742,366	—	—
Interest Paid: Not exceeding 1 per Cent. -	1870	—	—	—	—
	1871	—	—	—	—
	1872	—	—	—	—
	1873	—	—	—	—
Exceeding 1 and not exceeding 2 per Cent. - -	1870	—	46,915	1,400	—
	1871	—	46,915	1,400	—
	1872	—	46,915	1,400	—
	1873	—	46,915	1,400	—
„ 2 and not exceeding 3 per Cent. - -	1870	205,415	31,910	6,500	73,537
	1871	—	—	6,500	—
	1872	—	360,643	28,015	73,538
	1873	—	31,910	20,265	73,538
„ 3 and not exceeding 4 per Cent. - -	1870	21,457,878	16,292,926	9,273,066	1,427,584
	1871	26,212,321	24,360,024	10,443,096	1,559,137
	1872	22,607,609	37,010,467	10,436,101	2,143,111
	1873	18,194,524	45,701,265	11,011,906	2,361,094
„ 4 and not exceeding 5 per Cent. - -	1870	49,466,859	29,144,952	4,712,866	1,369,839
	1871	37,187,052	34,967,658	3,485,969	1,817,286
	1872	26,209,447	38,461,742	2,805,983	2,162,713
	1873	20,902,203	41,907,238	2,204,685	2,684,608
„ 5 and not exceeding 6 per Cent. - -	1870	658,602	1,282,472	8,760	—
	1871	542,870	1,482,251	8,160	—
	1872	288,360	2,072,454	8,160	—
	1873	239,810	2,297,678	—	—
„ 6 and not exceeding 7 per Cent. - -	1870	19,206	—	—	—
	1871	21,516	—	—	—
	1872	—	—	—	—
	1873	—	—	—	—
„ 7 and not exceeding 8 per Cent. - -	1870	31,975	—	—	—
	1871	35,700	—	—	—
	1872	36,600	18,000	—	—
	1873	36,600	18,000	—	—
TOTAL - -	1870	71,842,935	46,799,175	14,002,592	2,870,960
	1871	64,111,075	61,600,022	13,945,125	3,376,373
	1872	49,201,716	78,374,563	13,279,659	4,379,362
	1873	39,422,137	90,745,362	13,238,256	5,119,240

SCOTLAND, AND IRELAND, FOR THE YEARS 1870 to 1873.

Rate per Cent. of Interest Paid, in each of the Years 1870, 1871, 1872, and 1873.

IRELAND.		UNITED KINGDOM.		Years.	RATE per CENT. of INTEREST PAID.
Loans.	Debenture Stock.	Loans.	Debenture Stock.		
£	£	£	£		
—	—	8,000	—	1870	Not receiving any Interest.
—	—	161,616	743,174	1871	
—	—	59,200	404,342	1872	
100	—	49,100	742,366	1873	
...	—	—	—	1870	Interest Paid: Not exceeding 1 per Cent.
...	—	—	—	1871	
...	—	—	—	1872	
—	—	—	—	1873	
—	—	1,400	46,915	1870	Exceeding 1 and not exceeding 2 per Cent.
—	—	1,400	46,915	1871	
—	—	1,400	46,915	1872	
—	—	1,400	46,915	1873	
115,764	—	327,679	105,447	1870	„ 2 and not exceeding 3 per Cent.
14,500	—	21,000	—	1871	
14,500	—	42,515	434,181	1872	
14,500	—	34,765	105,448	1873	
1,483,022	567,689	32,312,966	18,288,149	1870	„ 3 and not exceeding 4 per Cent.
1,407,059	665,107	38,062,476	26,584,268	1871	
1,331,079	891,876	34,374,789	40,045,454	1872	
1,267,544	1,230,580	30,478,974	49,292,939	1873	
3,098,996	982,886	37,278,718	31,497,677	1870	„ 4 and not exceeding 5 per Cent.
2,448,717	1,687,088	43,071,738	38,421,927	1871	
2,256,474	2,335,710	31,271,904	43,960,165	1872	
1,820,987	2,759,938	24,927,875	47,351,779	1873	
171,473	—	833,835	1,282,472	1870	„ 5 and not exceeding 6 per Cent.
169,069	4,000	720,099	1,486,251	1871	
140,789	—	487,809	2,072,454	1872	
124,790	—	364,600	2,297,673	1873	
—	—	19,206	—	1870	„ 6 and not exceeding 7 per Cent.
—	—	21,516	—	1871	
—	—	—	—	1872	
—	—	—	—	1873	
—	—	31,975	—	1870	„ 7 and not exceeding 8 per Cent.
—	—	35,700	—	1871	
—	—	36,600	18,000	1872	
—	—	36,600	18,000	1873	
4,868,252	1,550,525	90,713,779	51,220,660	1870	TOTAL.
4,089,345	2,306,140	82,095,545	67,282,535	1871	
3,742,842	3,227,586	66,224,217	85,981,511	1872	
3,227,921	3,990,518	55,889,314	99,855,120	1873	

SUMMARY TABLES for ENGLAND and

No. 1.—CAPITAL. - - - - - -

	AUTHORISED CAPITAL.			PAID UP STOCK	
	By Shares and Stock.	By Loans and Debenture Stock.	TOTAL.	Ordinary.	Guaranteed.
	£	£	£	£	£
ENGLAND AND WALES - -	410,845,169	148,223,144	559,066,513	205,801,711	58,340,391
SCOTLAND - - - - -	60,408,649	20,770,707	81,179,356	22,967,738	7,617,825
IRELAND - - - - -	26,670,905	9,770,012	36,440,917	15,680,836	429,825
TOTAL UNITED KINGDOM -	497,923,723	178,763,863	676,686,686	244,449,805	66,187,541

No. 2.—TRAFFIC. - - - -

	Length of Line in Miles open on 31st December 1878.			PASSENGER TRAFFIC.				Holders of Season or Periodical Tickets.	GOODS (EXCEPT LIVE STOCK) TRAFFIC.		NUMBER OF MILES TRAVELLED BY TRAINS.		
	Double or more.	Single.	Total.	Number of Passengers conveyed (exclusive of Season and Periodical Tickets).					Minerals.	General Merchandise.	Passenger Trains.	Goods and Mineral Trains.	TOTAL.
				1st Class.	2nd Class.	3rd Class (including Parliamentary).	TOTAL.						
									Tons.	Tons.			
ENGLAND AND WALES	7,138	4,231	11,369	38,474,219	62,968,761	306,194,106	401,465,066	257,470	93,227,035 and 24,503,074*	44,967,591	73,724,510	88,592,176	†162,551,504
SCOTLAND - - -	1,046	1,564	2,612	3,963,619	5,409,963	30,060,596	37,512,796	37,707	18,875,783	6,097,161	10,276,513	13,282,517	‡23,510,082
IRELAND - -	501	1,600	2,101	1,894,116	3,960,634	10,497,506	16,342,506	19,402	512,550 and 545,061*	2,209,353	5,942,944	2,780,652	§9,465,863
TOTAL UNITED KINGDOM -	8,687	7,395	16,082	36,310,754	70,327,428	346,682,006	455,320,188	314,579	112,615,696 and 24,960,755*	53,284,004	94,944,067	99,305,695	‖197,354,749

* Not classified. † Including 1,244,612 miles travelled by mixed trains. ‡ Including 1,106,682 miles travelled by mixed trains.
§ Including 759,787 miles travelled by mixed trains. ‖ Including 3,105,087 miles travelled by mixed trains.

No. 3.—WORKING EXPENDITURE, NET RECEIPTS, AND ROLLING STOCK.

	Length of Line in Miles open on 31st December 1878.	WORKING EXPENDITURE. -								
		Maintenance of Way, Works, &c.	Locomotive Power (including Stationary Engines).	Repairs and Renewals of Carriages and Waggons.	Traffic Expenses (Coaching and Merchandise).	General Charges.	Rates and Taxes.	Government Duty.	Compensation for Personal Injury, &c.	Compensation for Damage and Loss of Goods.
	No.	£	£	£	£	£	£	£	£	£
ENGLAND AND WALES	11,369	4,519,007	7,640,741	1,952,608	7,209,732	943,462	904,551	462,517	300,685	196,551
		and 38,894l. not classified.								
SCOTLAND - - -	2,612	633,048	1,033,961	336,061	897,334	120,071	108,846	44,138	56,567	34,409
IRELAND - - - -	2,101	381,341	436,896	99,464	323,701	66,366	66,848	—	7,259	10,747
TOTAL UNITED KINGDOM -	16,082	5,983,396	9,119,600	2,388,123	8,430,767	1,129,919	1,079,845	506,455	364,509	231,707
		and 38,894l. not classified.								

WALES, SCOTLAND, and IRELAND in 1873.

No. 1.—CAPITAL.

AND SHARE CAPITAL.		CAPITAL RAISED BY LOANS AND DEBENTURE STOCK.			TOTAL CAPITAL paid up and raised by Loans and Debenture Stock.	SUBSCRIPTIONS TO OTHER COMPANIES.
Preferential.	TOTAL paid up Stock and Share Capital.	Loans.	Debenture Stock.	TOTAL raised by Loans and by Debenture Stock.		
£	£	£	£	£	£	£
95,709,593	359,851,495	39,422,137	90,745,362	130,167,499	490,018,994	15,256,398
20,363,361	50,768,994	13,238,256	5,119,240	18,357,406	69,126,420	1,517,145
5,866,774	21,956,455	3,227,921	3,990,518	7,218,489	29,174,894	477,322
121,939,528	432,576,874	55,888,314	99,855,120	155,743,484	588,320,308	17,850,847

No. 2.—TRAFFIC.

RECEIPTS (GROSS) FROM PASSENGER TRAFFIC.								RECEIPTS (GROSS) FROM GOODS TRAFFIC.				TOTAL Receipts from Traffic.	Miscellaneous Rents, Tolls, Navigation, Steamboats, &c.	TOTAL RECEIPTS FROM ALL SOURCES OF TRAFFIC.
RECEIPTS FROM PASSENGERS.					Excess Luggage, Parcels, Carriages, Horses, Dogs, &c.	Mails.	TOTAL Receipts from Passenger Traffic.	Merchandise.	Live Stock.	Minerals.	TOTAL Receipts from Goods Traffic.			
1st Class.	2nd Class.	3rd Class (including Parliamentary).	Holders of Season or Periodical Tickets.	TOTAL from Passengers.										
£	£	£	£	£	£	£	£	£	£	£	£	£	£	£
3,687,638	3,488,132	9,940,661	855,024	17,921,455	1,890,482	448,973	¶20,127,185	15,297,890	861,026	10,845,889	26,874,804	47,061,969	1,795,289	48,857,278
414,478	240,371	1,222,106	87,024	1,963,979	196,046	101,579	2,261,606	1,947,485	146,195	1,693,740	**3,810,829	6,072,485	235,353	6,207,788
271,158	306,215	587,821	36,919	1,202,113	103,214	99,774	1,405,181	872,481	197,683	65,383	1,135,396	2,540,997	35,987	2,576,984
4,373,274	3,984,718	11,750,588	978,967	21,087,547	2,119,694	644,326	¶23,353,392	18,047,756	1,144,760	12,608,462	31,821,529	55,675,421	2,066,579	57,742,000

¶ Including 2,326l. receipts from excess fares not classified.　　** Including 23,551l. receipts from " Goods Traffic " not classified.

No. 3.—WORKING EXPENDITURE, NET RECEIPTS, AND ROLLING STOCK.

WORKING EXPENDITURE.							ROLLING STOCK. On 31st December 1873.					
								CARRIAGES, WAGGONS, TRUCKS, &c.				
Legal and Parliamentary Expenses.	Steamboat, Canal, and Harbour Expenses.	Miscellaneous Working Expenditure not included in the foregoing.	TOTAL Working Expenditure.	TOTAL RECEIPTS, as given in the Traffic Return.	NET RECEIPTS.	Proportion per Cent. of Expenditure to Total Receipts.	Locomotives.	Carriages used for the Conveyance of Passengers only.	Other Vehicles attached to Passenger Trains.	Waggons of all kinds used for the Conveyance of Live Stock, Minerals, or General Merchandise.	Any other Carriages or Waggons used on the Railway, not included in the preceding Columns.	TOTAL No. of Vehicles of all descriptions for Conveyance of Passengers, Live Stock, Ballast, &c.
£	£	£	£	£	£		No.	No.	No.	No.	No.	No.
313,475	601,740	434,860	*25,813,377	48,857,278	23,043,901	53	9,586	26,421	7,390	249,117	4,228	281,356
68,998	86,224	66,469	†3,518,084	6,307,788	2,789,704	56	1,380	3,072	973	65,350	991	70,386
9,360	4,763	14,840	1,421,387	2,576,984	1,155,347	55	519	1,141	565	9,234	108	11,048
391,833	692,736	516,169	30,752,848	57,742,000	26,989,152	53	11,485	24,634	9,128	323,701	5,322	362,785

* Exclusive of 14,069l. received by the North London Company for working other lines.
† Exclusive of 7,087l. expended by the City of Glasgow Union for other Companies.

RAILWAY RETURNS.—1873.

No. I.—C A P I T A L, &c.

RETURN of the authorised SHARE and LOAN CAPITAL of the several RAILWAY COM-
PANIES in ENGLAND and WALES, SCOTLAND, and IRELAND, and of their PAID-UP
ORDINARY, GUARANTEED, and PREFERENTIAL CAPITAL, and DEBENTURE STOCK
or FUNDED DEBT, on the 31st day of December 1873, specifying the rate per
cent. of the Dividends for the year 1873 on each of the said Capitals ; showing
also the Loans outstanding on the 31st day of December 1873, classified according to the several rates per cent. of Interest; and the Capital subscribed to
other undertakings, whether such undertakings are on lease to, or worked by, the
subscribing Company, or are independent.

     A

No. 1.—AMOUNT of CAPITAL, &c., upon the

NAME OF COMPANY.	AUTHORISED CAPITAL.			PAID-UP STOCK AND			
				Ordinary.		Guaranteed.	
	By Shares and Stock.	By Loans and Debenture Stock.	Total.	Amount.	Rate of Dividend paid.	Amount.	Guaranteed Rate of Dividend.	Rate of Dividend paid.
	£	£	£	£	Per cent.	£	Per cent.	Per cent.
Aberdare - - - -	*Leased to the Taff Vale.*							
Abingdon - - - -	*Leased to the Great Western.*							
Alcester - - - -	50,000	16,650	66,650	3,332	Nil	—	—	—
Aldborough Pier and Railway -	40,000	13,000	53,000	1,370	Nil	—	—	—
Alexandra Park - - -	150,000	50,000	200,000	—	—	—	—	—
Anglesey Central - -	140,000	46,600	186,600	107,000	Nil	—	—	—
Aylesbury and Buckingham -	220,000	71,500	291,500	82,589	Nil	—	—	—
Bala and Dolgelly - - -	*Worked by the Great Western.*							
Bala and Festiniog - -	190,000	63,300	253,300	—	—	—	—	—
Banbury and Cheltenham Direct -	600,000	200,000	800,000	—	—	—	—	—
Barnoldswick - - -	*Worked by the Midland.*							
Barnstaple and Ilfracombe -	105,000	35,000	140,000	104,400	Nil	—	—	—
Bedford and Northampton - -	*Leased to the Midland.*							
Berks and Hants Extension -	*Worked by the Great Western.*							
Birkenhead (Vested jointly in Great Western and London and North Western.)	2,550,000	—*	2,550,000	1,941,505 134,316†	4 —	—	—	—
Birkenhead, Chester, and North Wales -	840,000	280,000	1,120,000	—	—	—	—	—
Birmingham and Lichfield Junction -	135,000	45,000	180,000	—	—	—	—	—
Birmingham West Suburban -	165,000	26,000	191,000	74,275	Nil	—	—	—
Bishop's Castle - - -	472,000	157,000	629,000	133,259	Nil	—	—	—
Bishop's Waltham - -	*Worked by the London and South-western.*							
Blyth and Tyne - - -	974,000	324,000	1,298,000	315,000	10	—	—	—
Bodmin and Wadebridge - -	22,500	13,000	35,500	27,393*	Nil	—	—	—
Bodmin, Wadebridge, and Delabole -	180,000	60,000	240,000	—	—	—	—	—
Bourton-on-the-Water - -	*Worked by the Great Western.*							
Brecon and Merthyr Tydfil Junction -	1,228,900	738,558 14,075*	1,981,533	264,360	Nil	—	—	—
Bridport - - - -	*Leased to the Great Western.*							

31st December 1873.—ENGLAND AND WALES.

Share Capital				Capital raised by Loans and Debenture Stock.					Total Capital paid up and raised by Loans and Debenture Stock.	Subscriptions to other Companies.	Remarks.
Preferential.			Total Paid-up Stock and Share Capital.	Loans.		Debenture Stock.		Total raised by Loans and Debenture Stock.			
Amount.	Preferential Rate of Dividend.	Rate of Dividend paid.		Amount.	Rate of Interest.	Amount.	Rate of Interest.				
£	Per cent.	Per cent.	£	£	Per cent.	£	Per cent.	£	£	£	
—	—	—	3,332	—	—	—	—	—	3,332	—	
—	—	—	1,370	—	—	—	—	—	1,370	—	
—	—	—	—	—	—	—	—	—	—	—	
—	—	—	107,000	40,000	5	—	—	40,000	147,000	—	
—	—	—	82,589	36,500	5	—	—	36,500	119,089	—	In addition to the capital received as per annexed statement, the sum of 28,919l. has been received.
—	—	—	—	—	—	—	—	—	—	—	
—	—	—	—	—	—	—	—	—	—	—	
—	—	—	104,400	—	—	—	—	—	104,400	—	
350,200	4½	4½	2,426,021	—	—	—	—	—	2,426,021	—	* Borrowing powers assumed in equal moieties by the "London and North Western" and "Great Western" Railway Companies. † Calls received on forfeited shares, in respect of which no dividend is paid. Act passed in 1873. No capital has yet been raised.
—	—	—	—	—	—	—	—	—	—	—	
—	—	—	—	—	—	—	—	—	—	—	
—	—	—	74,275	—	—	—	—	—	74,275	—	
86,750	5	Nil	220,009	88,000 1,700	5 6	—	—	89,700	309,709	—	
215,000 50,000	5 10	5 10	580,000	8,440 31,650 66,208 1,800	4 4½ 4½ 5	—	—	106,098	686,098	—	
—	—	—	27,393	8,000	Nil	—	—	8,000	35,393	—	* Of this amount 5,000l. was raised by creation of share capital in place of debenture loans.
—	—	—	—	—	—	—	—	—	—	—	
868,640	5	5†	1,133,000	—	—	708,208 14,075*	5 5	722,283	1,855,283	—	* Rentcharge Stock. † £5 per cent. on 52,900l. only —Rumney shares.

No. 1.—AMOUNT of CAPITAL, &c., upon the

NAME OF COMPANY.	AUTHORISED CAPITAL.			PAID-UP STOCK AND				
	By Shares and Stock.	By Loans and Debenture Stock.	Total.	Ordinary.		Guaranteed.		
				Amount.	Rate of Dividend paid.	Amount.	Guaranteed Rate of Dividend.	Rate of Dividend paid.
	£	£	£	£	Per cent.	£	Per cent.	Per cent.
Bristol and Exeter - - - -	4,248,417	1,177,511	5,425,928	2,022,460	6½	—	—	—
Leased to or worked by the Bristol and Exeter. { Devon and Somerset - -	272,700	536,000	808,700	259,582	Nil	—	—	—
West Somerset -	144,000	40,000	184,000	67,796	Nil	—	—	—
Bristol and North Somerset - - -	*Worked by the Great Western.*							
Bristol and Portishead Pier and Railway -	260,000	86,600	346,600	132,167	Nil	—	—	—
Capital of Portishead Dock Undertaking	255,000	85,000	340,000	52,780	Nil .	—	—	—
Bristol Port, Railway, and Pier - - -	125,000	41,000	166,000	125,000	Nil	—	—	—
Buckfastleigh, Totnes, and South Devon -	*Worked by the South Devon.*							
Buckinghamshire - - - -	*Leased to the London and North-western.*							
Buckley - - - - -	*Worked by the Wrexham, Mold, and Connah's Quay.*							
Burry Port and Gwendreath Valley - -	280,000	93,000	373,000	135,400	Nil	—	—	—
Bury St. Edmunds and Thetford - -	100,000	33,300	133,300	40,946	Nil	—	—	—
Calne - - - - -	*Worked by the Great Western.*							
Cambrian - - - - -	3,410,554	1,382,599	4,793,153	826,723	Nil	80,000 326,948	4½ 5	4½ 5
Cannock Chase and Wolverhampton - -	80,000	26,600	106,600	70,500	6	—	—	—
Canterbury and Herne Bay - - -	100,000	33,000	133,000	—	—	—	—	—
Cardiff and Ogmore Valley - -	100,000	33,300	133,300	—	—	—	—	—
Carmarthen and Cardigan - - -	300,000	93,300	393,300	29,000	Nil	—	—	—
Central Wales and Carmarthen Junction -	545,000	12,000	557,000	140,000 68,500* 68,000†	Nil Nil Nil	—	—	—
Cheshire Lines Committee - - - (Consisting of the Great Northern, Manchester, Sheffield, and Lincolnshire, and Midland Railway Companies.) Incorporated by "The Cheshire Lines Act, 1867."	—*	—*	—*	—	—	—	—	—
Chester and Holyhead - - - -	*Worked by the London and North-western.*							
Chichester and Midhurst - - -	190,000	63,000	253,000	76,352	Nil	—	—	—
Cleveland Extension Mineral - - -	170,000	56,000	226,000	—	—	—	—	—
Cockermouth, Keswick, and Penrith - -	259,000	85,000	344,000	234,000	6	—	—	—

SHARE CAPITAL.				CAPITAL RAISED BY LOANS AND DEBENTURE STOCK.					TOTAL CAPITAL paid up and raised by Loans and Debenture Stock.	SUBSCRIPTIONS TO OTHER COMPANIES.	REMARKS.
Preferential.			Total Paid-up Stock and Share Capital.	Loans.		Debenture Stock.		Total raised by Loans and Debenture Stock.			
Amount.	Preferential Rate of Dividend.	Rate of Dividend paid.		Amount.	Rate of Interest.	Amount.	Rate of Interest.				
£	Per cent.	Per cent.	£	£	Per cent.	£	Per cent.	£	£	£	
5,135	4	4	4,061,577	150,520	4	318,749	4	1,067,554	5,129,131	485,729	*Redeemable.
1,123,814	4	4		315,227	4¼	250,533	4¼				
400,045	4½	4½		3,500	4¼	26,025	4¼				
125,238	4½	4½		3,000	4½						
165,885*	4½	4½									
219,000	5	5									
12,000	5	Nil	271,582	—	-	165,598	5	535,465	807,047	6,895	
						369,867	6				
492	5	Nil	142,028	40,000	5	—	-	40,000	182,028	—	As at 15th February 1874.
21,540	5	4½									
52,200	5	5									
58,805	5	Nil	190,972	76,466	5	—	-	76,466	267,438	—	
—	—	—	52,780	—	-	—	-	—	52,780	—	Works in progress.
—	—	—	125,000	41,000	5*	—	-	41,000	166,000	—	* Interest not paid.
47,600	5	Nil	183,000	—	-	20,000	5	60,700	243,700	—	
						40,700	6				
—	—	—	40,946	7,900	4½	—	-	7,900	48,846	-	
1,425,260	5	Nil	2,658,931	600	5	676,192	4	1,364,210	4,023,141	—	
						687,418	5				
—	—	—	70,500	26,600	6	—	-	26,600	97,100	—	
—	—	—	—	—	-	—	-	—	—	—	
158,780	6	Nil	187,780	60,000	5	—	-	60,000	247,780	—	
112,000‡	5	5	508,500	—	-	—	-	—	508,500	—	Note.—Ordinary Shares.—This statement is taken from the accounts of the Llanelly Railway and Dock Company, when the Swansea and Carmarthen Lines were part of that Company's undertaking. A question of accounts will, however, arise as to cancelling a sum of 30,000l. * Preferred. † Deferred. ‡ First Preference Shares. ‖ Second Preference Shares.
120,000‖	5	Nil									
—	—	—	—	71,611	4½	—	-	158,607†	158,607	—	*The Capital is authorised to be raised and subscribed by the three owning Companies in equal proportions, and is shown in their separate returns. †The existing loans will be paid off as they fall due. The railway is not completed.
				86,996	4½						
—	—	—	76,352	—	-	—	-	—	76,352	—	
—	—	—	—	—	-	—	-	—	—	—	
25,000	5	5	259,000	28,650	4	—	-	75,250	335,250	—	
				20,900	4½						
				26,700	4½						

No. 1.—AMOUNT of CAPITAL, &c., upon the

NAME OF COMPANY.	AUTHORISED CAPITAL.			PAID-UP STOCK AND				
				Ordinary.		Guaranteed.		
	By Shares and Stock.	By Loans and Debenture Stock.	Total.	Amount.	Rate of Dividend paid.	Amount.	Guaranteed Rate of Dividend.	Rate of Dividend paid.
	£	£	£	£	Per cent.	£	Per cent.	Per cent.
Colchester, Stour Valley, Sudbury, and Halstead.	Leased to the Great Eastern.							
Coleford - - - - -	66,000	22,000	88,000	—	—	—	—	—
Coleford, Monmouth, Usk, and Pontypool -	Leased to the Great Western.							
Colne Valley and Halstead - - -	218,000	71,633	289,633	62,919	Nil	—	—	—
Cornwall - - - - -	1,375,060	458,000	1,833,060	574,394	Nil	799,600	4½	4½
Cornwall Minerals - - - -	775,000	250,000	1,025,000	315,290	Nil	—	—	—
Cornwall Minerals and Bodmin and Wadebridge Junction.	90,000	30,000	120,000	—	—	—	—	—
Corris - - - - -	15,000	5,000	20,000	15,000	4½	—	—	—
Corwen and Bala - - - -	Leased to the Great Western.							
Cowbridge - - - -	35,000	11,600	46,600	18,258	Nil	—	—	—
Cowes and Newport (Isle of Wight) -	50,000	16,500	66,500	29,965	Nil	—	—	—
Croesor and Portmadoc - - -	25,000	8,330	33,330	15,000	Nil	—	—	—
Cromford and High Peak - - -	Leased to the London and North-western.							
Crystal Palace and South London Junction -	Worked by the London, Chatham, and Dover.							
Culm Valley Light - - - -	25,000	8,000	33,000	4,752	Nil	—	—	—
Dare Valley - - - - -	Leased to the Taff Vale.							
Denbigh, Ruthin, and Corwen - - -	172,500	82,500	255,000	89,604	Nil	—	—	—
Devon and Cornwall - - - -	1,000,000	332,633	1,332,633	75,000	Nil	—	—	—
Devon and Somerset - - - -	Worked by the Bristol and Exeter.							
Didcot, Newbury, and Southampton Junction	600,000	200,000	800,000	—	—	—	—	—
Dowlais - - - - -	—	—	—	—	—	—	—	—
Dowlais Extension - - -	—	—	—	—	—	—	—	—
East and West Junction - - -	300,000	600,000	900,000	300,000	Nil	—	—	—
East Cornwall Mineral (Calstock to Callington)	60,000	20,000	80,000	30,000	Nil	—	—	—
East Gloucestershire - - -	Worked by the Great Western.							
East Lincolnshire - - -	Leased to the Great Northern.							
East London - - - -	Worked by the London, Brighton, and South Coast.							
East Norfolk - - - -	160,000	53,300	213,300	47,599	Nil	—	—	—
Easton and Church Hope - - -	30,000	10,000	40,000	20,250	Nil	—	—	—

31st December 1873.—ENGLAND AND WALES—*continued.*

SHARE CAPITAL.				CAPITAL RAISED BY LOANS AND DEBENTURE STOCK.					TOTAL CAPITAL paid up and raised by Loans and Debenture Stock.	SUBSCRIPTIONS TO OTHER COMPANIES.	REMARKS.
Preferential.			Total Paid-up Stock and Share Capital.	Loans.		Debenture Stock.		Total raised by Loans and Debenture Stock.			
Amount.	Preferential Rate of Dividend.	Rate of Dividend paid.		Amount.	Rate of Interest.	Amount.	Rate of Interest.				
£	Per cent.	Per cent.	£	£	Per cent.	£	Per cent.	£	£	£	
—	–	–	—	—	–	—	–	—	—	—	No steps have yet been taken to exercise the powers contained in the Coleford Railway Act.
65,580 23,680	5 5	Nil Nil	152,179	57,714	5	—	–	57,714	209,893	—	
—	–	–	1,373,994	16,952 94,276 43,028 500	4 4½ 4½ 4½	302,731	4½	457,487	1,831,481	—	
372,355	6	6	687,645	71,600	5	—	–	71,600	759,245	24,589	Line not yet open. The Contractor pays the interest on the Preference Capital and Debentures until the opening of the line for traffic.
—	–	–	—	—	–	—	–	—	—	—	
—	–	–	15,000	4,800	5	—	–	4,800	19,800	—	
—	–	–	18,258	—	–	—	–	—	18,258	—	
—	–	–	29,965	10,000	5	—	–	10,000	39,965	—	
—	–	–	15,000	8,000	5½	—	–	8,000	23,000	—	
—	–	–	4,752	—	–	—	–	—	4,752	—	
53,160	5	Nil	142,764	49,100 21,876	4 5	—	–	70,976	213,740	—	
85,000	5	Nil	160,000	2,500 39,241	4 4½	—	–	41,741	201,741	—	Line in course of construction.
—	–	–	—	—	–	—	–	—	—	—	This Railway being the private property of the Dowlais Iron Company, there is no Stock or Share Capital.
—	–	–	—	—	–	—	–	—	—	—	
—	–	–	—	—	–	—	–	—	—	—	
—	–	–	300,000	—	–	411,144 120,670 66,082	5 6 –*	597,896	897,896	—	* This amount does not bear interest until six months after the opening of the line, viz., 5th February 1874. * Rentcharge Stock.
30,000	6	Nil	60,000	15,000 5,000*	5 5	—	–	20,000	80,000	—	
19,110	6	Nil	66,709	—	–	—	–	—	66,709	—	
—	–	–	20,250	—	–	—	–	—	20,250	—	

No. 1.—Amount of Capital, &c., upon the

Name of Company.	Authorised Capital.				Paid-up Stock and			
	By Shares and Stock.	By Loans and Debenture Stock.	Total.	Ordinary.		Guaranteed.		
				Amount.	Rate of Dividend paid.	Amount.	Guaranteed Rate of Dividend.	Rate of Dividend paid.
	£	£	£	£	Per cent.	£	Per cent.	Per cent.
East Somerset - - -	*Worked by the Great Western.*							
Ely and Clydach Valleys - - -	33,000	11,000	44,000	—	—	—	—	—
Ely, Haddenham, and Sutton -	*Worked by the Great Eastern.*							
Ely Valley - - -	*Worked by the Great Western.*							
Evesham and Redditch - - -	*Worked by the Midland.*							
Evesham, Redditch, and Stratford-on-Avon Junction.	90,000	30,000	120,000	—	—	—	—	—
Exeter and Crediton - - -	*Leased to the London and South-western.*							
Exmouth Docks and Railway - -	60,000	15,000	75,000	60,000	Nil	—	—	—
Faringdon - - -	*Worked by the Great Western.*							
Festiniog - - -	176,186	42,000	218,186	86,186	4	—	—	—
Festiniog and Blaenau - - -	20,000	12,550	32,550	11,482	Nil	—	—	—
Forcett - - - - -	34,200	11,400	45,600	30,856	6	—	—	—
Forest of Dean Central - -	*Worked by the Great Western.*							
Freshwater, Yarmouth, and Newport -	130,000	43,000	173,000	1,260	Nil	—	—	—
Furness - - - - -	3,493,500	1,115,066	4,608,566	1,542,000	9½	10,000 / 495,600	2½ / 5	2½ / 5
Garstang and Knot End - - -	90,000	30,000	120,000	60,000	Nil	—	—	—
Gloucester and Dean Forest - - -	*Leased to the Great Western.*							
Gorsedda Junction and Portmadoc - -	20,000	6,666	26,666	11,004	Nil	—	—	—
Great Eastern - - - -	18,722,913	9,757,371	28,480,284	826,885 / 8,350,563	Nil / ½	23,750 / 669,675 / 109,600 / 3,563,210 / 105,000 / 761,817 / 80,654	3½ / 4 / 4½ / 5 / 5½ / 6 / 7	3½ / 4 / 4½ / 5 / 5½ / 6 / 7
Colchester, Stour Valley, Sudbury, and Halstead.	250,000	83,000	333,000	228,675	3¾	—	—	—
Ely, Haddenham, and Sutton -	36,000	12,000	48,000	36,000	1⅚	—	—	—
London and Blackwall - -	1,982,180	656,000	2,638,180	1,532,125	4½*	—	—	—
Lowestoft Railway and Harbour -	240,000	—	240,000	—	—	120,000 / 120,000	4 / 6	4 / 6
Lynn and Hunstanton - -	60,000	20,000	80,000	60,000	10	—	—	—
Mellis and Eye - - -	15,000	5,000	20,000	14,691	Nil	—	—	—

Leased to or worked by the Great Eastern.

31st December 1873.—ENGLAND AND WALES—*continued.*

Share Capital.				Capital raised by Loans and Debenture Stock.					Total Capital paid up and raised by Loans and Debenture Stock.	Subscriptions to other Companies.	Remarks.
Preferential.			Total paid-up Stock and Share Capital	Loans.		Debenture Stock.		Total raised by Loans and Debenture Stock.			
Amount.	Preferential Rate of Dividend.	Rate of Dividend paid.		Amount.	Rate of Interest.	Amount.	Rate of Interest.				
£	Per cent.	Per cent.	£	£	Per cent.	£	Per cent.	£	£	£	
—	-	-	—	-	—	—	-	—	—	—	Act passed in 1873.
—	-	-	—	—	-	—	-	—	—	—	
—	-	-	60,000	15,000	5	—	-	15,000	75,000	—	
35,000	5	5	121,186	12,000	5	—	-	12,000	133,186	—	In addition to paying interest on capital the Company paid 1,352*l.* for way leave, and 271*l.* for rent of lands.
—	-	-	11,482	12,550	5	—	-	12,550	24,032	—	
—	-	-	30,856	1,020 / 8,980	4½ / 5	—	-	10,000	40,856	—	
—	-	-	1,260	—	-	—	-	—	1,260	—	
42,000 / 265,000 / 298,000 / 227,500 / 8,325	4½ / 5 / 6 / 8 / 10	4½ / 5 / 6 / 8 / 10	2,888,425	229,658 / 223,564 / 43,105 / 2,690	4 / 4½ / 4½ / 4¾	259,315	4	758,332	3,646,757	181,003	*Note.* — 222,576*l.* has been received in anticipation of calls.
17,100	5	Nil	77,100	16,100	5	—	-	16,100	93,200	—	This railway is at present closed.
—	-	-	11,004	—	-	—	-	—	11,004	—	
916,454 / 3,117,177 / 58,109	4 / 5 / 6½	4 / 5 / 6½	18,582,594	120,520 / 1,385,652 / 2,078,812 / 216,684 / 4,000	4 / 4½ / 4½ / 5 / 5½	832,674 / 111,740 / 488,217 / 4,454,955	4 / 4½ / 4½ / 5	9,693,254	28,275,848	328,450	
30,250	5	5	258,925	—	-	—	-	—	258,925	—	
—	-	-	36,000	—	-	12,000	5	12,000	48,000	—	
250,055	*4½	*4½	1,782,180	142,480 / 82,880 / 14,825	4½ / 4½ / 5	323,770	4½	563,955	2,346,135	—	*Dividend guaranteed under the lease of the Line to the Great Eastern Railway Company for 999 years from the 1st January 1866.
—	-	-	240,000	—	-	—	-	—	240,000	—	
—	-	-	60,000	700	5	18,595	4½	19,295	79,295	—	
—	-	-	14,691	4,454	5	—	-	4,454	19,145	—	By a resolution of the Company the balance of the revenue is applied in reduction of the loan capital.

No. 1.—Amount of Capital, &c., upon the

| NAME OF COMPANY. | AUTHORISED CAPITAL. | | | PAID-UP STOCK AND | | | | |
| | By Shares and Stock. | By Loans and Debenture Stock. | Total. | Ordinary. | | Guaranteed. | | |
				Amount.	Rate of Dividend paid.	Amount.	Guaranteed Rate of Dividend.	Rate of Dividend paid.
	£	£	£	£	Per cent.	£	Per cent.	Per cent.
Great Eastern—*cont.*								
Northern and Eastern - -	1,180,400	307,800	1,488,200	847,800 / 264,730	5 / 6	63,000 / 3,910	5 / 6	5 / 6
Saffron Walden - - -	120,000	39,000	159,000	81,562	Nil	—	—	—
Tendring Hundred - -	50,000	16,633	66,633	23,250	Nil	—	—	—
Tendring Hundred Extension	105,000	34,667	139,667	76,000	Nil	—	—	—
West Norfolk Junction - -	75,000	25,000	100,000	74,998	2 1/16	—	—	—
Wivenhoe and Brightlingsea -	40,000	13,000	53,000	24,955	Nil	—	—	—
Great Marlow - - - -	18,000	6,000	24,000	8,280	Nil	—	—	—
Great Northern - - -	19,765,469	6,628,825	26,394,294	6,120,866 / 575,000 / 1,159,275 / 1,159,275 / 972,578 / 81,400 / 36,453 / 269,260	7½ / 7½ / 8½ / 6 / * / † / ‡ / §	—	—	—
East Lincolnshire - - -	600,000	*—	600,000	—	—	600,000	†6	6
Hatfield and St. Albans -	85,000	28,000	113,000	57,980	Nil	—	—	—
Holme and Ramsey - -	30,000	10,000	40,000	30,000	Nil	—	—	—
Horncastle - - -	48,000	13,000	61,000	48,000	7½	—	—	—
Muswell Hill Estate - -	70,000	—	70,000	70,000	Nil	—	—	—
Nottingham and Grantham Railway and Canal.	1,014,000	265,000	1,279,000	1,014,000	4 1/16	—	—	—
Royston and Hitchin - -	346,667	115,466	462,133	266,675	6	—	—	—
Spilsby and Firsby - -	25,000	8,333	33,333	25,000	Nil	—	—	—
Stamford and Essendine -	140,000	46,000	186,000	121,500	Nil	—	—	—
Wainfleet and Firsby - -	18,000	6,000	24,000	18,000	Nil	—	—	—
Extension to Skegness - See also the "Cheshire Lines Committee," "Midland and Eastern," and "Norwich and Spalding."	27,000	9,000	36,000	27,000	Nil	—	—	—
Great North of England, Clarence, and Hartlepool Junction.	*Leased to the North-eastern.*							
Great Western - - -	39,042,309	15,617,381	54,659,690*	12,301,284	6¼	16,208,309	5	5
Abingdon - - -	20,000	5,000	25,000	15,000	6	—	—	—
Bala and Dolgelly - -	180,000	58,900	238,900	168,830	2¼	—	—	—
Berks and Hants Extension -	298,000	99,000	397,000	108,725	2¼	—	—	—

Left margin labels: Leased to or worked by the Great Eastern. / Leased to or worked by the Great Northern. / Leased to or worked by the Great Western.

31st December 1873.—ENGLAND AND WALES—*continued.*

SHARE CAPITAL.				CAPITAL RAISED BY LOANS AND DEBENTURE STOCK.					TOTAL CAPITAL paid up and raised by Loans and Debenture Stock.	SUBSCRIPTIONS TO OTHER COMPANIES.	REMARKS.
Preferential.			Total Paid-up Stock and Share Capital.	Loans.		Debenture Stock.		Total raised by Loans and Debenture Stock.			
Amount.	Preferential Rate of Dividend.	Rate of Dividend paid.		Amount.	Rate of Interest.	Amount.	Rate of Interest.				
£	Per cent.	Per cent.	£	£	Per cent.	£	Per cent.	£	£	£	
—	—	—	1,179,440	—	—	—	—	—	1,179,440	—	
—	—	—	81,562	30,985	5	—	—	30,985	112,547	—	
4,010	6	Nil	27,260	13,800	5	—	—	13,800	40,560	—	
2,980	6	Nil	78,930	26,000	5	—	—	26,000	104,930	—	
—	—	—	74,998	—	—	25,000	5	25,000	99,998	—	
14,640	6	½	39,595	9,580	5	—	—	9,580	49,175	—	
9,720	5	4	18,000	2,500	5	—	—	2,500	20,500	—	
55,000	3½	3½	16,874,999	18,265	3¾	4,389,437	4	4,915,670	21,790,669	2,097,245	* Dividend deferred. † Bradford and Thornton shares —to be incorporated on the opening of the line. ‡ Halifax, Thornton, and Keighley shares—to bear dividend from 5th August 1876. § New Ordinary 1864 not bearing dividend. ‖ Westgate Station shares—dividend distributed by Great Northern.
69,980	4	4		334,090	4	53,000	5				
200,000	4½	4½		120,878	4½						
1,596,150	4½	4½									
4,557,262	5	5									
122,500	6½	6½									
—	—	—	600,000	—	—	—	—	—	600,000	—	* Borrowing powers (200,000*l.*) exercised by the Great Northern Railway Company. † Guaranteed by the Great Northern Railway Company.
—	—	—	57,980	23,000	5	—	—	23,000	80,980	—	
—	—	—	30,000	10,000	5	—	—	10,000	40,000	—	
—	—	—	48,000	13,000	4¼	—	—	13,000	61,000	—	
—	—	—	70,000	—	—	—	—	—	70,000	—	Open for traffic from 24th May to 31st July.
—	—	—	1,014,000	—	—	—	—	—	1,014,000	—	
—	—	—	266,675	—	—	—	—	—	266,675	—	
—	—	—	25,000	8,333	5	—	—	8,333	33,333	—	
18,500	5	5	140,000	—	—	8,400	4½	16,000	156,000	—	
						12,600	5				
—	—	—	18,000	6,000	5	—	—	6,000	24,000	—	
—	—	—	27,000	9,000	5	—	—	9,000	36,000	—	
5,999,497	5	5	34,509,090	119,775	3½	3,616,308	4	14,877,586	49,386,676	677,971	As at 31st January 1874. * This does not include some permissive powers, which have not as yet been exercised, in relation to the assumption of the borrowing powers of other Companies, and to the creation of Capital for the acquisition of or for subscribing towards the undertakings of other Companies; nor does it include Capital authorised to be raised jointly with other Companies.
				794,653	4	668,433	4½				
				3,149,493	4½	3,723,288	4½				
				233,126	4½	2,079,968	5				
				10,260	4½						
				482,282	5						
600	5	5	15,600	5,000	5	—	—	5,000	20,600	—	
—	—	—	168,830	11,100	4½	—	—	50,280	219,110	—	
				39,180	5						
50,000	5	5	158,725	23,150	4	—	—	99,000	257,725	—	
				6,000	4½						
				2,800	4½						
				67,050	5						

No. 1:—AMOUNT of CAPITAL, &c., upon the

NAME OF COMPANY.	AUTHORISED CAPITAL.			PAID-UP STOCK AND				
	By Shares and Stock.	By Loans and Debenture Stock.	Total.	Ordinary.		Guaranteed.		
				Amount.	Rate of Dividend paid.	Amount.	Guaranteed Rate of Dividend.	Rate of Dividend paid.
Great Western—*cont.*	£	£	£	£	Per cent.	£	Per cent.	Per cent.
Leased to or worked by the Great Western—cont.								
Bourton-on-the-Water	30,000	10,000	40,000	29,900	2¾	—	—	—
Bridport	85,000	21,600	106,600	64,431	⅜	—	—	—
Bristol and North Somerset	515,000	157,800	672,800	370,454	Nil	—	—	—
Calne	49,000	16,100	65,100	20,820	Nil	—	—	—
Coleford, Monmouth, Usk, and Pontypool.	160,000	50,000	210,000	160,000	5	—	—	—
Corwen and Bala	120,000	40,000	160,000	120,000	3½	—	—	—
East Gloucestershire	225,000	75,000	300,000	215,024	Nil	—	—	—
East Somerset	135,000	38,300	173,300	68,573	Nil	—	—	—
Ely Valley	83,000	27,300	110,300	35,000 48,000	*— 5	—	—	—
Faringdon	27,500	9,100	36,600	10,000	Nil	—	—	—
Forest of Dean Central	81,000	26,660	107,660	39,517	Nil	—	—	—
Gloucester and Dean Forest	254,000	83,470	337,470	254,000	5¼	—	—	—
Leominster and Kington (including the Presteign Branch.)	120,000	39,000	159,000	80,790	4	—	—	—
Llanelly Railway and Dock	364,000	121,000	485,000	200,000	5½	—	—	—
Llangollen and Corwen	90,000	30,000	120,000	90,000	3	—	—	—
Llynvi and Ogmore	955,000	317,800	1,272,800	269,020	3	130,920	5	5
Marlborough	51,000	15,000	66,000	30,830	1½	—	—	—
Milford	70,000	23,000	93,000	58,891	Nil	—	—	—
Much Wenlock and Severn Junction	68,000	16,000	84,000	24,050	Nil	—		—
Nantwich and Market Drayton	120,000	40,000	160,000	119,370	4½	—	—	—
Ross and Monmouth	160,000	53,000	213,000	79,325	Nil	—	—	—
Stratford-upon-Avon	82,500	26,700	109,200	64,787	7½	—	—	—
Vale of Llangollen	74,000	23,000	97,000	44,700	4	—	—	—
Wellington and Drayton	300,000	39,483	339,483	217,770	4½	—	—	—
Wellington and Severn Junction	60,000	10,000	70,000	59,862	5	—	—	—
Wenlock	125,000	41,500	166,500	*40,000 60,000	Nil 2½	—	—	—
Witney	50,000	33,000	83,000	37,044	Nil	—	—	—
See also "Birkenhead," "Hammersmith and City," "Ludlow and Clee Hill," "Shrewsbury and Hereford," "Tenbury," "Vale of Towy" "Victoria Station and Pimlico," "West London," and "Weymouth and Portland."								

31st December 1873.—England and Wales—*continued.*

Share Capital.				Capital raised by Loans and Debenture Stock.					Total Capital paid up and raised by Loans and Debenture Stock.	Subscriptions to other Companies.	Remarks.
Preferential.			Total Paid-up Stock and Share Capital.	Loans.		Debenture Stock.		Total raised by Loans and Debenture Stock.			
Amount.	Preferential Rate of Dividend.	Rate of Dividend paid.		Amount.	Rate of Interest.	Amount.	Rate of Interest.				
£	Per cent.	Per cent.	£	£	Per cent.	£	Per cent.	£	£	£	
—	-	-	29,900	200 500 9,300	4 4½ 5	—	-	10,000	39,900	—	
20,000	6	6	84,431	21,600	5	—	-	21,600	106,031	—	
—	-	-	370,454	—	-	124,500	5	124,500	494,954	—	Line opened 3rd September 1873.
—	-	-	20,820	11,600	5	—	-	11,600	32,420	—	
—	-	-	160,000	50,000	5	—	-	50,000	210,000	—	
—	-	-	120,000	40,000	4½	—	-	40,000	160,000	—	
—	-	-	215,024	73,400	4½	—	-	73,400	288,424	—	
51,680	5	5	120,253	36,250 2,050	4½ 5	—	-	38,300	158,553	—	
*—	-	-	83,000	11,100 1,000	4½ 5	15,000	4½	27,100	110,100	—	* Amount held by the Great Western Railway Company, on which no dividend is paid.
5,060	5½	Nil	15,060	7,500	5	—	-	7,500	22,560	—	
40,850	6	Nil	80,367	25,626	5	—	-	25,626	105,993	—	
—	-	-	254,000	10,600 14,300	4¼ 4½	—	-	24,900	278,900	25,000	
19,280	4½	4½	100,070	26,000	4½	—	-	26,000	126,070	—	
109,569 54,431	5 6	5 6	364,000	17,130 3,160 63,810 35,900	4 4¼ 4½ 5	1,300	5	*121,300	†485,800	—	* Including 300*l.* borrowed to meet a Debenture Bond falling due at the end of the year. † 808*l.* premium was also received on 6°/₀ Preference Stock.
—	-	-	90,000	30,000	4½	—	-	30,000	120,000	—	
184,940	5	5	584,880	33,671 126,769	4½ 5	300 13,778 36,364	4 4½ 5	210,882	795,762	—	Line worked by the "Great Western" Railway Company from 1st July 1873.
4,800	6	6	35,630	12,865 *2,100	5 5	—	-	14,965	50,595	—	*Rentcharge Stock.
—	-	-	58,891	6,400 8,600	4½ 5	—	-	15,000	73,891	—	
20,000 15,000	4½ 5	4½ 5	59,050	8,000	4½	—	-	8,000	67,050	20,000	
—	-	-	119,370	26,300	4½	—	-	26,300	145,670	—	
79,360	6	6	158,685	47,100	4½	—	-	47,100	205,785	—	
16,990	5	5	81,777	1,000 10,550 13,400	4 4¼ 4½	—	-	24,950	106,727	—	
26,500	5	5	71,200	23,000	4½	—	-	23,000	94,200	—	
—	-	-	217,770	6,100	4½	—	-	6,100	223,870	—	
—	-	-	59,862	2,830	4½	—	-	2,830	62,692	—	
25,000	5	5	125,000	4,258 30,771 †6,471	4½ 5 4	—	-	41,500	166,500	—	* Amount subscribed by other companies. † Rentcharge Stock.
12,150	5	Nil	49,194	16,000	5	—	-	16,000	65,194	—	

No. 1.—AMOUNT of CAPITAL, &c., upon the

NAME OF COMPANY.	AUTHORISED CAPITAL.			PAID-UP STOCK AND				
	By Shares and Stock.	By Loans and Debenture Stock.	Total.	Ordinary.		Guaranteed.		
				Amount.	Rate of Dividend paid.	Amount.	Guaranteed Rate of Dividend.	Rate of Dividend paid.
Gwendraeth Valleys - - -	£ 170,000	£ 56,600	£ 226,600	£ 100,000	Per cent. Nil	£ —	Per cent. —	Per cent. —
Halesowen and Bromsgrove Branch Railways	147,000	49,000	196,000	86,416	Nil	—	—	—
Hammersmith and City Railway - - Great Western and Metropolitan Railway Companies jointly in respect of.	340,000	113,000	453,000		—	141,260 179,884	5 5½	5 5½
Hammersmith Extension - - -	244,444	—	244,444	61,000	Nil	—	—	—
Harborne - - - -	100,000	33,000	133,000	50,850	Nil	—	—	—
Harrow, Edgware, and London - -	45,000	15,000	60,000	2,084	Nil	—	—	—
Hatfield and St. Albans - - -	Worked by the Great Northern.							
Hatfield Chase Warping and Improvement -	44,000	14,600	58,600	—	—	—	—	—
Hayling Railways - - - -	Worked by the London, Brighton, and South Coast.							
Hemel Hempstead and London and North-western.	190,000	63,200	253,200	35,130	Nil	—	—	—
Henly-in-Arden and Great Western Junction	30,000	10,000	40,000	—	—	—	—	—
Hereford, Hay, and Brecon - - -	355,000	140,000	495,000	187,280	1¾	—	—	—
Hexham and Allendale - - -	75,000	25,000	100,000	*75,000	Nil	—	—	—
Holme and Ramsey - - - -	Worked by the Great Northern.							
Horncastle - - - -	Worked by the Great Northern.							
Hoylake and Birkenhead Railway and Tram-way.	94,000	—	94,000	220	Nil	—	—	—
Hylton, Southwick, and Monkwearmouth -	50,000	16,600	66,600	15,697	Nil	—	—	—
Isle of Wight - - - -	196,360	146,300	342,660	109,150	Nil	—	—	—
Isle of Wight (Newport Junction) - -	134,000	44,600	178,600	68,142	Nil	—	—	—
Keighley and Worth Valley - -	Worked by the Midland.							
Kendal and Windermere - - -	Leased to the London and North-western.							
Kettering, Thrapstone, and Huntingdon -	Worked by the Midland.							
Kingsbridge - - - -	190,000	60,000	250,000	27,960	Nil	—	—	—
King's Lynn Docks and Railway -	135,500	45,160	180,660	59,408	Nil	—	—	—
Kington and Eardisley - - -	130,000	73,000	203,000	63,980	Nil	—	—	—

31st December 1873.—ENGLAND AND WALES—continued.

SHARE CAPITAL.				CAPITAL RAISED BY LOANS AND DEBENTURE STOCK.					TOTAL CAPITAL paid up and raised by Loans and Debenture Stock.	SUBSCRIPTIONS TO OTHER COMPANIES.	REMARKS.
Preferential.			Total Paid-up Stock and Share Capital.	Loans.		Debenture Stock.		Total raised by Loans and Debenture Stock.			
Amount.	Preferential Rate of Dividend.	Rate of Dividend paid.		Amount.	Rate of Interest.	Amount.	Rate of Interest.				
£	Per cent.	Per cent.	£	£	Per cent.	£	Per cent.	£	£	£	
—	—	—	100,000	33,300	5	—	—	33,300	133,300	—	
—	—	—	86,416	—	—	—	—	—	86,416	—	
—	—	—	321,144	14,000 / 32,800 / 23,300 / 1,000	4 / 4½ / 4½ / 5	—	—	71,100	392,244	—	
—	—	—	61,000	—	—	—	—	—	61,000	—	Line in course of construction.
—	—	—	50,850	*28,614	5	—	—	28,614	79,464	—	*Rentcharge Stock.
—	—	—	2,084	—	—	—	—	—	2,084	—	
—	—	—	—	—	—	—	—	—	—	—	
—	—	—	35,130	—	—	—	—	—	35,130	—	Line in course of construction.
—	—	—	—	—	—	—	—	—	—	—	Company incorporated under Act of 1873.
146,580	5	1¾	333,860	—	—	139,210	5	139,210	473,070	—	
—	—	—	75,000	5,367	5	—	—	5,367	80,367	—	*3,340l. of this Stock was issued at 50 per cent. discount.
—	—	—	220	—	—	—	—	—	220	—	No capital has been paid up beyond the 220l.; the amount requisite for paying deposit on purchase of the line, for purchase of rolling stock, for cost of constructing tramway, &c. having been simply received on loan, and up to date no shares or debentures have been issued in respect thereof; the amount of such loan is 53,627l.
—	—	—	15,697	—	—	—	—	—	15,697	—	Line in course of construction.
62,890	5	2	172,040	—	—	128,514	5	128,514	300,554	—	
—	—	—	63,142	13,550 / 11,360	5 / 6	—	—	24,910	88,052	—	Line not yet open for traffic.
—	—	—	27,960	—	—	—	—	—	27,960	—	
9,500	6	Nil	68,908	25,160	5	—	—	25,160	94,068	—	
1,488	5	Nil	65,418	—	—	52,800	5	52,800	118,218	—	

No. 1.—Amount of Capital, &c., upon the

Name of Company.	Authorised Capital.			Paid-up Stock and				
				Ordinary.		Guaranteed.		
	By Shares and Stock.	By Loans and Debenture Stock.	Total.	Amount.	Rate of Dividend paid.	Amount.	Guaranteed Rate of Dividend.	Rate of Dividend paid.
	£	£	£	£	Per cent.	£	Per cent.	Per cent.
Lancashire and Yorkshire *See also* the "North Union" and "Preston and Wyre."	22,377,958	7,354,853	29,732,811	13,334,594	7½	782,000 833,000 1,233,000 538,048 90,780 53,230 297,490 607,750 260,050 794,040 287,793	4 4½ 4½ 4½ 4½ minimum 5 5 5 5 28/125 6 6 minimum	4 4½ 4½ 4½ 7½ 5 5 5 5 28/125 6 7½
Lancashire Union	*Worked by the London and North-western.*							
Lancaster and Carlisle	*Leased to the London and North-western.*							
Launceston and South Devon	*Worked by the South Devon.*							
Leeds, Castleford, and Pontefract Junction	120,000	40,000	160,000	14,640	Nil	—	—	—
Leominster and Kington	*Worked by the Great Western.*							
Liskeard and Caradon	30,825	10,000	40,825	23,625	2½	—	—	—
Liskeard and Looe Union Canal	26,000	14,000	40,000	26,000	2½	—	—	—
Liskeard and Looe Union Canal	*Worked by the Liskeard and Caradon.*							
Llanelly Railway and Dock	*Worked by the Great Western.*							
Llanfyllin and Llangynog	45,000	15,000	60,000	438	Nil	—	—	—
Llangollen and Corwen	*Leased to the Great Western.*							
Llantrissant and Taff Vale Junction	*Worked by the Taff Vale.*							
Llynvi and Ogmore	*Worked by the Great Western from 1st July 1873.*							
London and Aylesbury	197,000	65,000	262,000	—	—	—	—	—
London and Blackwall	*Leased to the Great Eastern.*							
London and Greenwich	*Leased to the South-eastern.*							
London and North-western	47,449,148	20,277,517	67,726,665	30,921,694 171,355*	7½ 5	—	—	—
Leased to or worked by the London and North-western: Buckinghamshire	1,245,000	—*	1,245,000	1,245,000	†4	—	—	—
Chester and Holyhead	3,455,000	—*	3,455,000	—	—	2,100,000 725,000 630,000	2½ 5 5½	2½ 5 5½
Cromford and High Peak	227,700	92,825	320,525	127,700	3/10	—	—	—
Kendal and Windermere	175,000	56,000	231,000	—	—	111,700 49,820	8 6	8 6
Lancashire Union	530,000	175,000	705,000	530,000	5	—	—	—
Lancaster and Carlisle	2,991,130	463,333	3,454,463	2,420,300	12	—	—	—
Mold and Denbigh Junction	325,000	247,000	572,000	73,000 *76,000 †76,000	Nil Nil. Nil.	—	—	—

31st December 1873.—England and Wales—*continued.*

Share Capital. Preferential. Amount.	Preferential Rate of Dividend.	Rate of Dividend paid.	Total Paid-up Stock and Share Capital.	Capital raised by Loans and Debenture Stock. Loans. Amount.	Rate of Interest.	Debenture Stock. Amount.	Rate of Interest.	Total raised by Loans and Debenture Stock.	Total Capital paid up and raised by Loans and Debenture Stock.	Subscriptions to other Companies.	Remarks.
£	Per cent.	Per cent.	£	£	Per cent.	£	Per cent.	£	£	£	
—	-	-	19,161,775	95,501 2,719,000 57,300 30,300 250	3¾ 4 4½ 4½ 4¾	1,000 3,268,111	3½ 4	6,171,462	25,383,237	—	
—	-	-	14,640	—	-	—	-	—	14,640	—	The works have not yet been commenced.
7,200	5	5	30,825	9,550	5	—	-	9,550	40,375	—	
—	-	-	26,000	1,000 9,500 3,500	4 4½ 5	—	-	14,000	40,000	650	
—	-	-	438	—	-	—	-	—	438	—	Company incorporated by Act passed in 1873.
—	-	-	—	—	-	—	-	—	—	—	
315,400 1,817,858 899,155 9,000,643 183,400 220,840	2½ 4 4½ 5 6 10	2½ 4 4½ 5 6 10	43,530,345	19,700 75,075 4,201,993 642,260 42,350 8,595	3½ 3¾ 4 4½ 4½ 5	36,700 14,341,543	3½ 4	19,368,216†	62,898,561	3,183,028	* Stour Valley Stock entitled to two-thirds ordinary "London and North-western" dividend. † Including 1,005,815*l.* of Loan Capital of Lines leased to or amalgamated with the "London and North-western" and for the interest on which sum the Company is liable.
—	-	-	1,245,000	—	-	—	-	—	1,245,000	—	* Borrowing powers merged in those of the "London and North-western" Company. † Guaranteed by the "London and North-western" Railway Company.
—	-	-	3,455,000	—	-	—	-	—	3,455,000	—	* Borrowing powers transferred to the "London and North western" Company.
20,000 20,000	3½ 4½	3½ 4½	167,000	—	-	46,915 34,910	1¾ 3	78,825	246,525	3,750	
—	-	-	161,520	3,500 31,191 16,100 3,208	3½ 4 4½ 4½	—	-	53,999	215,519	—	
—	-	-	580,000	112,869 56,194	4 4½	—	-	169,063	699,063	202,050	
456,000	4½	4½	2,876,300	—	-	—	-	—	2,876,300	40,876	
100,000	5	Nil	325,000	—	-	40,000 207,000	5 5	247,000	572,000	—	* Preferred Stock. † Deferred Stock.

No. 1.—AMOUNT of CAPITAL, &c., upon the

| NAME OF COMPANY. | AUTHORISED CAPITAL. | | | PAID-UP STOCK AND | | | | |
| | By Shares and Stock. | By Loans and Debenture Stock. | Total. | Ordinary. | | Guaranteed. | | |
				Amount.	Rate of Dividend paid.	Amount.	Guaranteed Rate of Dividend.	Rate of Dividend paid.
	£	£	£	£	Per cent.	£	Per cent.	Per cent.
London and North-western—*cont.*								
Leased to or worked by the London and North-western—*cont.* { Shropshire Union Railways and Canal.	1,077,607	357,500	1,435,107	1,077,607	3½	—	—	—
Watford and Rickmansworth -	70,000	23,000	93,000	31,730	Nil	—	—	—
Wolverhampton and Walsall -	265,000	85,000	350,000	118,000	Nil	—	—	—
See also "Birkenhead," "Ludlow and Clee Hill," "Manchester, South Junction, and Altrincham," "North and South Western Junction," "North Union," "Oldham, Ashton-under-Lyne, and Guide Bridge Junction," "Preston and Wyre," "Shrewsbury and Hereford," "Tenbury," "Vale of Towy," and "West London."								
London and South-western - - -	13,934,809	5,295,830	19,230,639	7,974,529	5½	14,400 / 352,250 / 5,309 / 8,026	4 / 4 / 4½ / 5	4 / 4 / 4½ / 5
Leased to or worked by the London and South-western { Bishop's Waltham - -.	No Return.	—	—	—	—	—	—	—
Exeter and Crediton - -	105,000	34,999	139,999	70,000	5½	—	—	—
Lymington - - - -	34,000	7,000	41,000	22,140	Nil	—	—	—
Mid-Hants - - - -	175,000	225,000	400,000	62,681	Nil	—	—	—
Ringwood, Christchurch, and Bournemouth.	75,000	25,000	100,000	74,215	5½	—	—	—
Salisbury and Dorset Junction · -	196,000	65,300	261,300	147,493	Nil	—	—	—
Salisbury and Yeovil -	700,000	232,733	932,733	326,715	8¼	—	—	—
Salisbury Railway and Market House	17,000	4,600	21,600	12,000	4	—	—	—
Seaton and Beer - - -	48,000	16,000	64,000	36,000	Nil	—	—	—
Staines, Wokingham, and Woking -	340,000	103,000	443,000	255,100	4	—	—	—
Stokes Bay Railway and Pier	40,000	13,000	53,000	17,250	Nil	—	—	—
See also "Weymouth and Portland."								
London, Brighton, and South Coast -	15,185.000	5,061,667	20,246,667	6,839,943	3¼	—	—	—
Leased to or worked by the London, Brighton, and South Coast. { East London -	1,800,000	566,600	2,366,600	1,313,492	Nil	—	—	—
Hayling Railways	66,000	21,900	87,900	38,594	Nil	—	—	—
London Central - - - - -	1,500,000	500,000	2,000,000	—	—	—	—	—
London, Chatham, and Dover - -	13,151,225	5,955,082	19,106,307	8,294,417	Nil	150,637	4½	4½
Leased to or worked by the London, Chatham, and Dover. { Crystal Palace and South London Junction.	750,000	376,333	1,126,333	283,120	Nil	75,000	6	6
Mid-Kent (Bromley to St. Mary Cray).	70,000	23,000	93,000	61,550	4	—	—	—
Sevenoaks, Maidstone, and Tonbridge.	595,000	98,000	693,000	118,539	Nil	* 158,685	4½	—

31st December 1878.—ENGLAND AND WALES—*continued.*

Share Capital				Capital raised by Loans and Debenture Stock					Total Capital paid up and raised Loans and Debenture Stock.	Subscriptions to other Companies.	Remarks.
Preferential.			Total Paid-up Stock and Share Capital.	Loans.		Debenture Stock.		Total raised by Loans and Debenture Stock.			
Amount.	Preferential Rate of Dividend.	Rate of Dividend paid.		Amount.	Rate of Interest.	Amount.	Rate of Interest.				
£	Per cent.	Per cent.	£	£	Per cent.	£	Per cent.	£	£	£	
—	—	—	1,077,607	*—	—	*—	—	*—	1,077,607	—	The shares of the "Shropshire Union Railways" Company are in course of conversion into "London and Northwestern" Company's shares. *Loan Capital included in that of the "London and Northwestern."
3,200	5	Nil	34,930	13,500	5	—	—	13,500	48,430	—	
120,674	6	Nil	238,674	26,400	4½	—	—	76,700	315,374	—	
				50,300	5						
4,400	4	4	18,333,481	14,718	3½	1,000,000	4	5,094,734	18,428,215	836,888	
353,816	4½	4½		762,077	4	1,629,407	4				
500,000	4½	4½		145,318	4½	692,088	4½				
1,450,000	4½	4½		97,800	4½	753,831	4½				
1,000,000	4½	4½									
1,500,000	5	5									
171,251	7	7									
—	—	—	—	—	—	—	—	—	—	—	There are neither Directors nor Officers to make the Return.
20,000	5	5	90,000	2,750	4½	—	—	18,100	108,100	—	
				15,350	4½						
11,860	5½	5½	34,000	2,500	4½	4,500	5	7,000	41,000	—	
25,000	5	Nil	87,681	—	—	205,915	4	205,915	293,596	—	
—	—	—	74,215	25,000	4½	—	—	25,000	99,215	—	
15,000	5	Nil	162,493	50,384	5	—	—	58,300	220,793	—	* Rentcharge Stock.
				*7,916	5						
268,114	5	5	594,829	500	4	120,000	4½	212,000	806,829	—	
				60,000	4½						
				31,500	4½						
1,000	6	6	13,000	1,000	4½	—	—	3,500	16,500	—	
				2,500	5						
12,000	5	Nil	48,000	11,200	5	—	—	16,000	64,000	—	* Rentcharge Stock.
				4,000	5						
				*800	5						
50,000	5	5	305,100	5,800	4	—	—	89,485	394,585	—	
				21,285	4½						
				59,400	4½						
				3,000	5						
15,325	5	Nil	32,575	13,000	5	—	—	13,000	45,575	---	
470,580	4	4	14,091,073	59,490	4	1,306,239	4	4,740,613	18,831,686	—	
2,441,822	4½	4½		103,998	4½	2,833,999	4½				
3,707,600	5	5		346,117	4½						
411,178	6	6		17,000	4½						
220,000	7	7		73,770	5						
400,000	5	Nil	1,713,492	106,050	6	423,950	6	566,600	2,280,092	—	
				36,600	8						
16,000	5	5	54,594	16,600	5	—	—	21,900	76,494	—	
				5,300	6						
—	—	—	—	—	—	—	—	—	—	—	The Company is authorised by the Arbitration, Second and Final Award, to raise a further capital of 350,000*l.* by the issue of Shares or Loans as may be determined by the Proprietors.
4,694,183	4½	1 11/12	13,139,237	—	—	5,886,256	4½	5,886,256	19,025,493	—	
333,075	6	Nil	691,195	7,400	5	345,182	4½	367,582	1,058,777	—	
				15,000	6						
—	—	—	61,550	23,000	4½	—	—	23,000	84,550	—	
132,000	5	Nil	404,174	46,400	5	—	—	93,500	497,674	—	* Capital raised for the Maidstone Extension not entitled to dividend until the completion of the line.
				47,100	6						

No. 1.—AMOUNT of. CAPITAL, &c., upon the

NAME OF COMPANY.	AUTHORISED CAPITAL.			PAID-UP STOCK AND				
				Ordinary.		Guaranteed.		
	By Shares and Stock.	By Loans and Debenture Stock.	Total.	Amount.	Rate of Dividend paid.	Amount.	Guaranteed Rate of Dividend.	Rate of Dividend paid.
	£	£	£	£	Per cent.	£	Per cent.	Per cent.
Londonderry (Seaham to Sunderland) -	—	—	—	—	—	—	—	—
London, Tilbury, and Southend - - -	662,000	190,000	852,000	650,650	*6	—	—	—
Longton, Adderley Green, and Bucknall -	50,000	16,000	66,000	12,610	Nil	—	—	—
Lostwithiel and Fowey - - - -	30,000	10,000	40,000	15,102	Nil	—	—	—
Louth and East Coast - - - -	96,000	32,000	128,000	—	—	—	—	—
Louth and Lincoln - - - -	250,000	83,000	333,000	250,000	Nil	—	—	—
Lowestoft Railway and Harbour - -	Leased to the Great Eastern.							
Ludlow and Clee Hill - - -	30,000	10,000	40,000	30,000	Nil	—	—	—
Lymington - - - - -	Worked by the London and South-western.							
Lyme Regis - - - - -	65,000	21,600	86,600	—	—	—	—	—
Lynn and Hunstanton - - - -	Worked by the Great Eastern.							
Macclesfield Committee - - -	*—	*—	*—	—	—	—	--	—
Macclesfield, Knutsford, and Warrington -	400,000	133,000	533,000	—	—	—	—	—
Maidstone and Ashford - - - -	350,000	116,000	466,000	6,495	Nil	—	—	—
Malmesbury - - - - -	60,000	20,000	80,000	915	Nil	—	—	—
Manchester and Milford - - -	570,300	190,100	760,400	323,050	Nil	—	—	—
Manchester, Sheffield, and Lincolnshire -	13,435,998	4,485,699	17,921,697	5,492,553	2¼	366,698 225,000 559,506 687,768 1,131,120	3¼ 4¼ 4¼ 5 6	3¼ 4¼ 4¼ 5 6
South Yorkshire and River Dun - - See also the "Cheshire Lines Committee," "Macclesfield Committee," "Manchester, South Junction, and Altrincham," and "Oldham, Ashton-under-Lyne, and Guide Bridge Junction."	2,440,000	1,315,937	3,755,937	741,020	*7	448,980 500,000	4 5	4 5
Manchester South District - - -	350,000	118,000	468,000	2,585	Nil	—	—	—
Manchester, South Junction, and Altrincham Committee.	*—	216,666	216,666	—	—	—	—	—
Marlborough - - - - -	Worked by the Great Western.							
Maryport and Carlisle - - - -	592,000	190,000	782,000	* 601,530	13	2,000	4 minimum.	13
Mawddwy - - - - -	21,000	7,000	28,000	21,000	Nil	—	—	—

31st December 1873.—ENGLAND AND WALES—*continued.*

SHARE CAPITAL.				CAPITAL RAISED BY LOANS AND DEBENTURE STOCK.					TOTAL CAPITAL paid up and raised by Loans and Debenture Stock.	SUBSCRIP-TIONS TO OTHER COM-PANIES.	REMARKS.
Preferential.			Total Paid-up Stock and Share Capital.	Loans.		Debenture Stock.		Total raised by Loans and Debenture Stock.			
Amount.	Preferential Rate of Dividend.	Rate of Dividend paid.		Amount.	Rate of Interest.	Amount.	Rate of Interest.				
£	Per cent.	Per cent.	£	£	Per cent.	£	Per cent.	£	£	£	
—	—	—	—	—	—	—	—	—	—	—	Private property.
—	—	—	650,650	60,650 / 14,300 / 29,150	4½ / 4½ / 5	*45,900	4½	150,000	800,650	—	* Dividend guaranteed until July 1875 under lease of the line to Messrs. Peto, Brassey, and Betts.
—	—	—	12,610	—	—	—	—	—	12,610	—	Line in course of construction.
11,395	5	Nil	26,497	6,200 / 3,800	5 / 6	—	—	10,000	36,497	—	
—	—	—	—	—	—	—	—	—	—	—	
—	—	—	250,000	67,791	5	—	—	67,791	317,791	—	
—	—	—	30,000	10,000	5	—	—	10,000	40,000	—	This line is leased to the Great Western and London and North-western Companies jointly.
—	—	—	—	26,650	4½	—	—	26,650	26,650	—	* The Capital powers are trans-ferred to the "North Staf-ordshire" and "Manchester, Sheffield, and Lincolnshire" Railway Companies equally. The existing loans will be paid off as they fall due.
—	—	—	—	—	—	—	—	—	—	—	Line in course of construction. Capital provided by the "Manchester, Sheffield, and Lincolnshire" Company, and is included in that Com-pany's return.
—	—	—	6,495	—	—	—	—	—	6,495	—	
—	—	—	915	—	—	—	—	—	915	—	
190,200	5	Nil	513,250	170,898	5	—	—	170,898	684,148	—	
2,531,706	5	5	10,994,353	1,000 / 21,129 / 907,734 / 366,898 / 900	8½ / 4 / 4½ / 4½ / 5	79,577 / 2,358,908 / 300,000	4 / 4½ / 5	4,036,146	15,030,499	3,629,145	
260,000 / 220,000 / 270,000	5 / 5 / 5	5 / 5 / 5	2,440,000	200 / 8,500 / 116,335 / 77,185 / 58,990 / 8,000	3½ / 3½ / 4 / 4½ / 4½ / 4½	934,647	4½	1,203,757	†3,643,757	95,000	* Guaranteed by the "Man-chester, Sheffield, and Lin-colnshire" Railway Com-pany. † This includes all the Capital of the Company, both railway and navigation.
—	—	—	2,585	—	—	—	—	—	2,585	—	
—	—	—	—	105,295 / 95,537	4 / 4½	—	—	200,832	200,832	—	*This line is the property of "London and North-western" and "Manchester, Sheffield, and Lincolnshire" Railway Companies; the share capital being subscribed by the two companies jointly, and in-cluded in their Returns.
—	—	—	603,530	77,503 / 5,650 / 1,550 / †1,200	4 / 4½ / 4½ / 5	78,500	4	159,403	762,933	—	* Additional Share Capital is being created under 8 Vict. c. 16. for the redemption of the Loans as they fall due. † Rentcharge Stock.
—	—	—	21,000	7,000	5	—	—	7,000	28,000	—	

C 3

No. 1.—AMOUNT of CAPITAL, &c., upon the

NAME OF COMPANY.	AUTHORISED CAPITAL.			PAID-UP STOCK AND			
				Ordinary.		Guaranteed.	
	By Shares and Stock.	By Loans and Debenture Stock.	Total.	Amount.	Rate of Dividend paid.	Amount.	Guaranteed Rate of Dividend.	Rate of Dividend paid.
	£	£	£	£	Per cent.	£	Per cent.	Per cent.
Mellis and Eye - - - -	Worked by the Great Eastern.							
Merionethshire - - - -	90,000	26,600	106,600	5,322	Nil	—	—	—
Merrybent and Darlington - -	60,000	20,000	80,000	54,541	Nil	—	—	—
Mersey - - - - -	650,000	216,600	866,600	39,860	Nil	—	—	—
Methley Railway Joint Committee -	—	—	—	—		—	—	—
Metropolitan* - - -	6,450,000	2,115,666	8,565,666	4,008,370	2¼	—	—	—
Metropolitan and St. John's Wood See also Hammersmith and City.	850,000	282,000	1,132,000	300,000	Nil	—	—	—
Metropolitan and St. John's Wood - -	Worked by the Metropolitan.							
Metropolitan and South-western Junction -	240,000	80,000	320,000	—	—	—	—	—
Metropolitan District - -	3,750,000	1,750,000	5,500,000	2,220,380	Nil	—	—	—
Mid-Hants - - - - -	Worked by the London and South-western.							
Mid-Kent (Bromley to St. Mary's Cray) -	Leased to the London, Chatham, and Dover.							
Midland - - - -	38,286,901	11,495,210	49,782,111	978,533 17,992,061	5⅞ 6⅞	1,800,000 1,949,903 140,000	4 6 8	4 6 8
Barnoldswick - - -	40,000	13,300	53,300	20,162	Nil	—	—	—
Bedford and Northampton - -	400,000	133,000	533,000	200,000	5	—	—	—
Evesham and Redditch - -	149,000	49,600	198,600	147,770	1½	—	—	—
Keighley and Worth Valley -	90,000	30,000	120,000	35,075	Nil	—	—	—
Kettering, Thrapstone, and Huntingdon	230,000	75,600	305,600	100,000	3⅞	—	—	—
Midland and South-western Junction.	90,000	30,000	120,000	90,000	5	—	—	—
North-western - - -	1,412,609	346,691	1,759,300	—	—	314,224 471,336	3¼ 5	3¼ 5
Peterborough, Wisbeach, and Sutton	285,000	94,999	379,999	135,000	Nil	—	—	—
Redditch - - - -	50,000	16,500	66,500	34,820	4	—	—	—
Stonehouse and Nailsworth - -	75,940	29,000	104,940	65,940	Nil	—	—	—
Tewkesbury and Malvern - - See also the "Cheshire Lines Committee," "Midland and Eastern," "North and South-western Junction," and "Norwich and Spalding."	265,000	88,000	353,000	235,600	Nil	—	—	—
Midland and Eastern - - -	213,000	71,000	284,000	212,717	2½	—	—	—
Midland and South-western Junction -	Worked by the Midland.							

Leased to or worked by the Midland. (left margin note)

31st December 1873.—England and Wales—*continued.*

Share Capital. Preferential. Amount.	Preferential Rate of Dividend.	Rate of Dividend paid.	Total Paid-up Stock and Share Capital.	Capital raised by Loans and Debenture Stock. Loans. Amount.	Rate of Interest.	Debenture Stock. Amount.	Rate of Interest.	Total raised by Loans and Debenture Stock.	Total Capital paid up and raised by Loans and Debenture Stock.	Subscriptions to other Companies.	Remarks.
£	Per cent.	Per cent.	£	£	Per cent.	£	Per cent.	£	£	£	
—	-	-	5,322	—	-	—	-	—	5,322	—	
—	-	-	54,541	3,500	4½	—	-	3,500	58,041	—	
—	-	-	39,860	—	-	—	-	—	39,860	—	
—	-	-	—	—	-	—	-	—	—	—	Joint property of the "Great Northern," "Lancashire and Yorkshire," and "North-eastern" Railway Companies—the capital is included in the returns of those Companies.
1,841,630	5	5	5,850,000	40,150 410,952 950,856 8,500	4 4¼ 4½ 4¾	125,000 52,745 358,263	4 4¼ 4½	1,946,466	7,796,466	100,000	
183,170	5	1¾	483,170	136,490 2,500	5 5½	—	-	138,990	622,160	—	
—	-	-	—	—	-	—	-	—	—	—	
1,499,967	5	½	3,720,347	35,770 228,444 3,000	4½ 5 6	700 1,191,541	5 6	1,459,455	5,179,802	—	
675,000 1,853,087 2,612,052 7,013,875 170,000 *493,232	4 4½ 5 5 †6 4	4 4½ 5 5 6½ 4	35,677,743	2,370 12,043 2,091,352 500 31,220	3½ 3¾ 4 4¼ 4½	6,564,543 1,525,006 244,073	4 4¼ 4½	10,471,107	46,148,850	3,110,890	* Calls paid in advance. † Minimum.
—	-	-	20,162	—	-	—	-	—	20,162	—	
200,000	5	5	400,000	130,086 2,914	4 5	—	-	133,000	533,000	—	The interest on the ordinary stock is guaranteed by the contractors for 5 years from the opening of the line.
—	-	-	147,770	29,600 20,000	4½ 5	—	-	49,600	197,370	—	
34,300	6	3	69,375	22,772	5	—	-	22,772	92,147	—	
130,000	5	5	230,000	20,400 1,100 23,900	4½ 4¾ 5	30,000	4½	75,400	305,400	—	
—	-	-	90,000	30,000	4½	—	-	30,000	120,000	—	
—	-	-	785,560	288,152 58,132	4 4½	—	-	346,284	1,131,844	—	
150,000	5	2½	285,000	20,320 5,242	4½ 5	71,670	4½	97,232	382,232	—	
—	-	-	34,820	11,500	4	—	-	11,500	46,320	—	
10,000	5	Nil	75,940	28,000	5	—	-	28,000	103,940	—	
—	-	-	235,600	*88,500	5	—	-	88,500	324,100	—	* The sum of 500*l.* has been borrowed in excess of the Company's powers. The present Secretary can give no explanation, as the money was raised previous to his appointment.
—	-	-	212,717	43,746 2,750	4½ 5	26,004	4½	72,500	285,217	—	This line is worked jointly by the Midland and Great Northern Railway Companies.

No. 1.—Amount of Capital, &c., upon the

| | AUTHORISED CAPITAL. | | | PAID-UP STOCK AND | | | | |
| NAME OF COMPANY. | | | | Ordinary. | | Guaranteed. | | |
	By Shares and Stock.	By Loans and Debenture Stock.	Total.	Amount.	Rate of Dividend paid.	Amount.	Guaranteed Rate of Dividend.	Rate of Dividend paid.
	£	£	£	£	Per cent.	£	Per cent.	Per cent.
Mid-Wales - - - -	812,600	284,267	*1,096,867	403,390	Nil	—	—	—
Milford - - -	Worked by the Great Western.							
Milford Haven Dock and Railway - -	140,000	46,000	186,000	74,230	Nil	—	—	—
Minehead - - - -	65,000	—	65,000	100	Nil	—	—	—
Mistley, Thorpe, and Walton - -	51,000	17,000	68,000	20,126	Nil	—	—	—
Mitcheldean Road and Forest of Dean -	30,000	10,000	40,000	1,500	Nil	—	—	—
Mold and Denbigh Junction -	Worked by the London and North-western.							
Monmouthshire Railway and Canal -	1,165,000	386,450	1,551,450	829,805	6¼	—	—	—
Much Wenlock and Severn Junction - -	Worked by the Great Western.							
Muswell Hill Estate - - -	Worked by the Great Northern.							
Nantwich and Market Drayton - - -	Worked by the Great Western.							
Neath and Brecon - - -	379,030	1,104,870	1,483,900	256,230	Nil	—	—	—
Newent - - - -	160,000	53,300	213,300	—	—	—	—	—
Newport Pagnell - - - -	332,350	110,000	442,350	27,350	Nil	—	—	—
Newquay and Cornwall Junction - -	30,000	9,000	39,000	16,897	Nil	—	—	—
Northampton and Banbury Junction -	1,385,000	300,000	1,635,000	109,960	Nil	—	—	—
North and South-western Junction -	105,000	33,600	138,600	*128,600	7	—	—	—
North-eastern - - - - -	37,603,753	*12,357,287	*49,961,040	62,090 / 17,100,170	2½ / 9½	3,621,420 / 37,125 / 4,035,433 / 483,540 / 1,356,565 / 440,570	4 / 4 / 4½ / 5 / 6 / 8	4 / 12½¼½ / 4½ / 5 / 6 / 9½
Leased to or worked by the North-eastern. { Great North of England, Clarence, and Hartlepool Junction.	74,900	*—	74,900	41,875	3	16,918	4½	4½
Tees Valley - - -	62,000	20,600	82,600	49,486	Nil	—	—	—
Northern and Eastern - - -	Leased to the Great Eastern.							
North London - - - - See also North and South-western Junction.	2,925,000	970,866	3,895,866	1,975,000	5½	—	—	—

31st December 1873.—ENGLAND AND WALES—*continued.*

SHARE CAPITAL.				CAPITAL RAISED BY LOANS AND DEBENTURE STOCK.					TOTAL CAPITAL paid up and raised by Loans and Debenture Stock.	SUBSCRIPTIONS TO OTHER COMPANIES.	REMARKS.
Preferential.			Total Paid-up Stock and Share Capital.	Loans.		Debenture Stock.		Total raised by Loans and Debenture Stock.			
Amount.	Preferential Rate of Dividend.	Rate of Dividend paid.		Amount.	Rate of Interest.	Amount.	Rate of Interest.				
£ 402,600	Per cent. 5	Per cent. Nil	£ 805,990	£ 64,200	Per cent. 4	£ 32,267 102,600 65,200	Per cent. 4 4½ 5	£ 264,267	£ 1,070,257	£ —	*The Company is authorised to raise additional capital, sufficient to meet the existing debts of the Company, and to complete and open for traffic the 2nd section of the undertaking—the amount required not yet ascertained.
—	—	—	74,230	—	—	45,481	5	45,481	119,711	—	Line not open for traffic.
31,000	4½	Nil	31,100	—	—	—	—	—	31,100	—	Line in course of construction.
—	—	—	20,126	12,000	5	—	—	12,000	32,126	—	
—	—	—	1,500	—	—	—	—	—	1,500	—	
315,000	5	5	1,144,805	19,000 53,656 84,022 27	4 4½ 4½ 5	12,538 211,739	4 4½	380,982	1,525,787	60,000	
122,800	5	Nil	379,030	—	—	150,945 826,041	6 5*	976,986	1,356,016	—	*Payable only out of the profits of each year.
—	—	—	—	—	—	—	—	—	—	—	
58,358	5	Nil	85,708	—	—	60,072	5*	60,072	145,780	—	*Interest not paid.
993	6	Nil	17,890	1,250 4,100	5 6	—	—	5,350	23,240	—	Line worked by the Cornwall Minerals Railway Company
219,770	5	Nil	329,730	—	—	115,930 164,528	5 5	280,458	610,188	—	
—	—	—	128,600	—	—	—	—	—	128,600	—	Leased by "London and North-western," "Midland," and "North London" Railway Companies. *Under 8 Vict. cap. 16. the Company raised additional Share Capital and paid off the Debenture Debt.
1,869,000 5,268,371 535,000	4½ 5 5½	4½ 5 5½	34,809,274	89,049 2,743,359 862,192 27,675	3½ 4 4½ 4½	6,614,104 1,138,119	4 4½	11,474,498	46,283,772	223,437	*Including Loans of the Great North of England, Clarence, and Hartlepool Junction Railway Company.
13,725	5	5	72,518	—	—	—	—	—	72,518	—	*Borrowing powers exercised by the North-eastern Railway Company.
—	—	—	49,486	3,665 12,510	4½ 5	—	—	16,175	65,661	—	
170,130 700,000	4½ *	4½ 4½	2,845,130	1,250	4½	6,500 883,116	4 4½	890,866	3,735,996	—	*Minimum, 4½; Maximum, 5.

No. 1.—Amount of Capital, &c., upon the

Name of Company.	Authorised Capital.			Paid-up Stock and					
	By Shares and Stock.	By Loans and Debenture Stock.	Total.	Ordinary.		Guaranteed.			
				Amount.	Rate of Dividend paid.	Amount.	Guaranteed Rate of Dividend.	Rate of Dividend paid.
	£	£	£	£	Per cent.	£	Per cent.	Per cent.
North Staffordshire *See also* Macclesfield Committee.	5,701,000	1,893,233	7,594,233	3,200,000	2⅝	1,170,000	5	5
North Union	739,202	380,050	1,119,252	739,202	$8\frac{15}{16}$	—	—	—
North Wales (narrow gauge):								
General Undertaking	150,000	50,000	200,000	—	—	—	—	—
Moel Tryfan Undertaking	66,000	22,000	88,000	65,562	*6	—	—	—
North-western	*Leased to the Midland.*							
Norwich and Spalding	170,000	56,000	226,000	170,000	2⅜	—	—	—
Nottingham and Grantham Railway and Canal	*Leased to the Great Northern.*							
Oldham, Ashton-under-Lyne, and Guide Bridge Junction.	140,000	46,600	186,600	100,000	Nil	40,000	4¾	4¾
Pembroke and Tenby	421,000	131,200	552,200	79,876	Nil	23,335	4	4
Penarth Harbour, Dock, and Railway	*Worked by the Taff Vale.*							
Peterborough, Wisbeach, and Sutton	*Worked by the Midland.*							
Pontypool, Caerleon, and Newport	100,000	33,300	133,300	66,700	Nil	—	—	—
Poole and Bournemouth	60,000	20,000	80,000	60,000	Nil	—	—	—
Potteries, Shrewsbury, and North Wales	858,200*	537,901	1,396,101	487,555 171,060† 99,585‡	Nil Nil Nil	—	—	—
Preston and Wyre	677,380	134,343	811,723	638,000 30,000	$7\frac{103}{128}$ $12\frac{103}{128}$	—	—	—
Ravenglass and Eskdale	24,000	8,000	32,000	4,960	Nil	—	—	—
Redditch	*Worked by the Midland.*							
Redruth and Chasewater	49,500	7,500	57,000	49,500	Nil	—	—	—
Redruth and Falmouth Junction	80,000	26,600	106,600	—	—	—	—	—
Rhondda Valley and Hirwain Junction	135,000	45,000	180,000	9,394	Nil	—	—	—
Rhymney	1,012,000	337,300	1,349,300	237,480 1,146*	1¾ Nil	90,000	5	5
Ringwood, Christchurch, and Bournemouth	*Worked by the London and South-western.*							
Ross and Ledbury	180,000	60,000	240,000	—	—	—	—	—
Ross and Monmouth	*Worked by the Great Western.*							
Royston and Hitchin	*Leased to the Great Northern.*							
Ryde and Newport	65,000	21,600	86,600	33,500	Nil	—	—	—
Ryde Pier	95,500	35,000	130,500	92,542	7	—	—	—
Rye and Dungeness Railway and Pier	130,000	43,333	173,333	—	—	—	—	—

31st December 1873.—ENGLAND AND WALES—*continued.*

SHARE CAPITAL.				CAPITAL RAISED BY LOANS AND DEBENTURE STOCK.					TOTAL CAPITAL paid up and raised by Loans and Debenture Stock.	SUBSCRIPTIONS TO OTHER COMPANIES.	REMARKS.
Preferential.			Total Paid-up Stock and Share Capital.	Loans.		Debenture Stock.		Total raised by Loans and Debenture Stock.			
Amount.	Preferential Rate of Dividend.	Rate of Dividend paid.		Amount.	Rate of Interest.	Amount.	Rate of Interest.				
£	Per cent.	Per cent.	£	£	Per cent.	£	Per cent.	£	£	£	
137,620 971,000	4½ 5	4½ 5	5,478,620	445,627 737,663 5,000 54,016 88,800	4 4½ 4½ 4½ 4½	472,522 24,560	4½ 4½	1,778,188	7,256,808	182,454	
—	—	—	739,202	353,202 2,500 22,000	4 4½ 4½	—	—	377,702	1,116,904	—	This line is leased to the London and North-western and the Lancashire and Yorkshire Railway Companies.
—	—	—	—	—	—	—	—	—	—	—	
—	—	—	65,562	—	—	—	—	—	65,562	—	*A minimum dividend of 6 per cent. is guaranteed by contractor during construction, and by lessee for 21 years.
—	—	—	170,000	28,000 10,550	4½ 5	17,450	4½	56,000	226,000	—	This line is worked jointly by the Midland and Great Northern Railway Companies.
—	—	—	140,000	40,767 5,340	4½ 4½	—	—	46,107	186,107	—	The line is vested jointly in the "London and North-western" and "Manchester, Sheffield, and Lincolnshire" Railway Companies, each subscribing 50,000l. of the ordinary capital.
215,310	5	1½	318,521	3,000 85,915	4½ 5	19,780	5	108,695	427,216	—	
—	—	—	66,700	33,300	5	—	—	33,300	100,000	—	Line not open for traffic.
—	—	—	60,000	—	—	18,000	8	18,000	78,000	—	
100,000	5	Nil	858,200	—	—	529,876	5	529,876	1,388,076	—	*And an amount equal to the aggregate amount of certain debts and money claims against the Company, which amount has not yet been ascertained. †Deferred. ‡Preferred.
9,380	5	5	677,380	119,293 15,000	4 4	—	—	134,293	811,673	—	Line leased to the Lancashire and Yorkshire and London and North-western Railway Companies.
—	—	—	4,960	—	—	—	—	—	4,960	—	
—	—	—	49,500	7,500	5	—	—	7,500	57,000	—	
—	—	—	—	—	—	—	—	—	—	—	
—	—	—	9,394	—	—	—	—	—	9,394	—	
74,000 42,000 24,890 86,131 40,000 213,000	5 5 5 5½ 6 6	5 5 5 5½ 6 6	808,647	90,547 163,240 1,500 8,010	4½ 4½ 4½ 5	—	—	263,297	1,071,944	—	*Forfeited shares.
—	—	—	—	—	—	—	—	—	—	—	
—	—	—	33,500	—	—	—	—	—	33,500	—	Line in course of construction.
—	—	—	92,542	20,000	5	—	—	20,000	112,542	—	
—	—	—	—	—	—	—	—	—	—	—	

No. 1.—Amount of Capital, &c., upon the

Name of Company.	Authorised Capital.			Paid-up Stock and				
	By Shares and Stock.	By Loans and Debenture Stock.	Total.	Ordinary.		Guaranteed.		
				Amount.	Rate of Dividend paid.	Amount.	Guaranteed Rate of Dividend.	Rate of Dividend paid.
	£	£	£	£	Per cent.	£	Per cent.	Per cent.
Saffron Walden - - - - -	*Worked by the Great Eastern.*							
Salisbury and Dorset Junction - - -	*Worked by the London and South-western.*							
Salisbury and Yeovil - - - -	*Leased to the London and South-western.*							
Salisbury Railway and Market House -	*Worked by the London and South-western.*							
Sandbach and Winsford - - - -	114,000	38,000	152,000	—	—	—	—	—
Saundersfoot Railway and Harbour - -	*Line sold to the Bonvilles Court Coal and Iron Company (Limited).*					—		•
Scarborough and Whitby - - -	170,000	56,000	226,000	20,302	Nil	—	—	—
Scotswood, Newburn, and Wylam Railway and Dock.	85,000	28,300	113,300	54,076	Nil	—	—	—
Seaton and Beer - - - -	*Worked by the London and South-western.*							
Sevenoaks, Maidstone, and Tunbridge - -	*Worked by the London, Chatham, and Dover.*							
Severn and Wye Railway and Canal - -	263,561	87,853	351,414	99,561	3½	30,000	4½	4½
Severn Bridge - - - -	225,000	75,000	300,000	5,235	Nil	—	—	—
Severn Bridge and Forest of Dean Central -	42,000	14,000	56,000	—	—	—	—	—
Sheffield and Midland Committee - -	*Line owned by the Manchester, Sheffield, and Lincolnshire, and Midland Railway Companies.*							
Shrewsbury and Hereford - - - Great Western and London and North-western Companies in respect of the.	675,000	79,700	754,700	—	—	50,000 625,000	4½ 6	4½ 6
Shropshire Union Railways and Canal -	*Leased to the London and North-western.*							
Sidmouth - - - - -	66,000	22,000	88,000	36,276	Nil	—	—	—
Sirhowy - - - - - -	170,000	56,633	226,633	105,000	7½	—	—	—
Snailbeach District - - - -	20,000	6,600	26,600	—	—	—	—	—
Somerset and Dorset - - - -	1,597,000	993,920	2,590,920	306,234	Nil	—	—	—
South Devon - - - - -	2,988,894	950,553	3,939,447	1,534,305	3½	—	—	—
Leased to or worked by the South Devon. { Buckfastleigh, Totnes, and South Devon.	96,000	32,000	128,000	65,874	Nil	—	—	—
Launceston and South Devon.	155,200	90,000	245,200	149,187	2¹⁄₁₆	—	—	—
South-eastern - - - - -	15,236,230	5,078,744	20,314,974	8,798,649 1,991,160† 1,991,160‡	5 6 4	984,300 800,000	4½ 5¼	4½ 5¼
London and Greenwich - - -	760,000	233,333	993,333	550,000	2¹¹⁄₁₂	—	—	—

31st December 1873.—ENGLAND AND WALES—continued.

SHARE CAPITAL.				CAPITAL RAISED BY LOANS AND DEBENTURE STOCK.						TOTAL CAPITAL paid up and raised by Loans and Debenture Stock.	SUBSCRIPTIONS TO OTHER COMPANIES.	REMARKS.
Preferential.			Total Paid-up Stock and Share Capital.	Loans.		Debenture Stock.		Total raised by Loans and Debenture Stock.				
Amount.	Preferential Rate of Dividend.	Rate of Dividend paid.		Amount.	Rate of Interest.	Amount.	Rate of Interest.					
£	Per cent.	Per cent.	£	£	Per cent.	£	Per cent.	£	£	£		
—	—	—	—	—	—	—	—	—	—	—		
—	—	—	—	—	—	—	—	—	—	—		The line is only a small Tramroad for the conveyance of coal and culm from the collieries to the shipping port.
—	—	—	20,302	—	—	—	—	—	20,302	—		
—	—	—	54,076	—	—	—	—	—	54,076	—		Line in course of construction.
81,599	5	5	231,160	47,366	4½	—	—	67,853	299,013	—		As at 30th September 1873.
20,000	5½	5½		20,487	5							
—	—	—	5,235	—	—	—	—	—	5,235	—		
—	—	—	—	—	—	—	—	—	—	—		
The Capital is included in their Returns.												
—	—	—	675,000	79,200	4	—	—	79,700	754,700	5,000		
				500	4½							
—	—	—	36,276	—	—	22,000	5	22,000	58,276	—		
61,000	5	5	166,000	16,333	4½	—	—	48,300	214,300	—		
				31,967	5							
—	—	—	—	—	—	—	—	—	—	—		
35,655	4½	Nil	877,769	—	—	872,553*	—*	872,553	1,750,322	12,000		* Interest at the rate of 5 per cent. was paid on 256,341*l.* of this amount.
85,000	5	Nil										
90,880	5	Nil										
360,000	5	Nil										
264,745	4½	4½	2,579,607	68,250	4	70,460	4	883,431	3,463,038	123,750		
780,557	5	5		161,918	4½	448,433	5					
				106,135	4½							
				29,235	5							
30,000	5	Nil	95,874	7,777	4½	—	—	31,967	127,841	—		
				24,190	5							
3,840	5	5	153,027	29,670	4	—	—	83,940	236,967	—		
				22,790	4½							
				14,090	4½							
				17,390	5							
1,888,660*	4½	4½	13,782,650	464,340	4	67,980	4	4,912,898	18,695,548	65,000		* On 442,020*l.* now included in this Stock a dividend at the rate of 5 per cent. per annum was paid up to the date of its conversion, October to December 1873.
190	4½	Nil		18,100	4½	1,500	4½					† Preferred.
149,480	5	5		38,700	4½	4,281,578	5					‡ Deferred.
2,178,826	5	5		10,100	4½							
225	5	Nil		30,600	5							
210,000	5	5	760,000	202,300	4	—	—	227,300	987,300	—		
				25,000	4½							

No. 1.—AMOUNT of CAPITAL, &c., upon the

| NAME OF COMPANY. | AUTHORISED CAPITAL. | | | PAID-UP STOCK AND | | | | |
| | By Shares and Stock. | By Loans and Debenture Stock. | Total. | Ordinary. | | Guaranteed. | | |
				Amount.	Rate of Dividend paid.	Amount.	Guaranteed Rate of Dividend.	Rate of Dividend paid.
	£	£	£	£	Per cent.	£	Per cent.	Per cent.
South Kensington - - - -	60,000	20,000	80,000	—	—	—	—	—
South Wales Mineral - - -	145,000	48,000	193,000	55,610	Nil	—	—	—
South Yorkshire and River Dun - -	*Leased to the Manchester, Sheffield, and Lincolnshire.*							
Spilsby and Firsby - - -	*Worked by the Great Northern.*							
Stafford and Uttoxeter - - -	180,000	59,900	239,900	134,260	Nil	—	—	—
Staines and West Drayton - -	48,000	16,000	64,000	—	—	—	—	—
Staines, Wokingham, and Woking -	*Leased to the London and South-western.*							
Stamford and Essendine - -	*Leased to the Great Northern.*							
Stokes Bay Railway and Pier -	*Worked by the London and South-western.*							
Stonehouse and Nailsworth - -	*Worked by the Midland.*							
Stony Stratford - ∴- - -	7,500	2,500	10,000	—	—	—	—	—
Stratford-upon-Avon - - -	*Worked by the Great Western.*							
Swansea and Carmarthen - -	*Name changed to Central Wales and Carmarthen Junction by Act of 28th July 1873.*							
Swansea Vale - - -	335,000	111,600	446,600	189,685	7	—	—	—
Swindon, Marlborough, and Andover -	375,000	125,000	500,000	1,752	Nil	—	—	—
Taff Vale - - - - -	1,700,000	587,000	2,287,000	1,063,460	12	—	—	—
Aberdare - - -	50,000	16,600	66,600	—	—	50,000	10	10
Dare Valley - - -	56,000	18,500	74,500	45,500	5*	—	—	—
Llantrissant and Taff Vale Junction.	181,000	60,000	241,000	95,048	5*	—	—	—
Penarth Harbour, Dock, and Railway.	622,000	207,000	829,000	539,000	4	—	—	—
Talyllyn - - - -	15,000	5,000	20,000	15,000	Nil	—	—	—
Tees Valley - - - -	*Worked by the North-eastern.*							
Teign Valley - - - -	31,000	79,000	110,000	19,510	Nil	—	—	—
Tenbury Railway - - - Great Western and London and North-western Companies in respect of.	30,000	—	30,000	—	—	30,000	4½	4½
Tendring Hundred - - -	*Worked by the Great Eastern.*							
Tewkesbury and Malvern - -	*Worked by the Midland.*							

(Rows for Aberdare, Dare Valley, Llantrissant and Taff Vale Junction, and Penarth Harbour, Dock, and Railway are bracketed under: "Leased to or worked by the Taff Vale.")

31st December 1873.—ENGLAND AND WALES—*continued.*

SHARE CAPITAL.				CAPITAL RAISED BY LOANS AND DEBENTURE STOCK.					TOTAL CAPITAL paid up and raised by Loans and Debenture Stock.	SUBSCRIPTIONS TO OTHER COMPANIES.	REMARKS.
Preferential.			Total Paid-up Stock and Share Capital.	Loans.		Debenture Stock.		Total raised by Loans and Debenture Stock.			
Amount.	Preferential Rate of Dividend.	Rate of Dividend paid.		Amount.	Rate of Interest.	Amount.	Rate of Interest.				
£	Per cent.	Per cent.	£	£	Per cent.	£	Per cent.	£	£	£	
79,854	6	Nil	135,464	46,700 1,300	5 6	—	—	48,000	183,464	—	This Railway is leased to and worked by the Glyncorrwg Colliery Company (Limited).
79,838	5	Nil	214,098	18,600	5	72,015	5	90,615	304,713	—	
—	—	—	—	—	—	—	—	—	—	—	
—	—	—	—	—	—	—	—	—	—	—	
11,200 94,920 79,660	4 5 6	4 5 6	325,465	800 9,920 79,180	4 4½ 5	—	—	89,900	415,365	—	
—	—	—	1,752	—	—	—	—	—	1,752	—	Act passed in 1873.
58,225 66,775 165,000	4½ 5 5	4½ 5 12	1,353,460	1,700 937,941 92,863 3,000 1,000	3¾ 4 4½ 4½ 4½	99,917	4	435,921	1,789,381	5,000	
—	—	—	50,000	16,600	4	—	—	16,600	66,600	—	
—	—	—	45,500	8,100 3,400	4 4½	—	—	11,500	57,000	—	* Guaranteed by the Taff Vale Railway Company.
—	—	—	95,048	6,150 6,850	4 4½	—	—	13,000	108,048	—	* Guaranteed by the Taff Vale Railway Company.
—	—	—	539,000	160,045 22,805 24,150	4 4½ 4½	—	—	207,000	746,000	—	
—	—	—	15,000	—	—	—	—	—	15,000	—	As at 30th September 1873.
—	—	—	19,510	—	—	27,650	5	27,650	47,160	—	
—	—	—	30,000	—	—	—	—	—	30,000	—	

RAILWAY RETURNS.—1873.

NAME OF COMPANY.	AUTHORISED CAPITAL.			PAID-UP STOCK AND				
	By Shares and Stock.	By Loans and Debenture Stock.	Total.	Ordinary.		Guaranteed.		
				Amount.	Rate of Dividend paid.	Amount.	Guaranteed Rate of Dividend.	Rate of Dividend paid.
	£	£	£	£	Per cent.	£	Per cent.	Per cent.
Thetford and Watton - - -	61,000	20,300	81,300	45,000	Nil	—	—	—
Tivy Side - - - - - -	46,000	15,333	61,333	529	Nil	—	—	—
Torbay and Brixham - - -	18,000	6,000	24,000	18,000	Nil	—	—	—
Tottenham and Hampstead Junction - -	510,000	169,866	679,866	273,170	Nil	—	—	—
Trent, Ancholme, and Grimsby - -	180,000	60,000	240,000	120,000	3¾	60,000	4½	4½
Truro and Perran Mineral - - - -	100,000	33,300	133,300	—	—	—	—	—
Tonbridge Wells and Eastbourne - -	115,000	38,333	153,333	—	—	—	—	—
Upwell, Outwell, and Wisbeach - - -	40,000	13,300	53,300	—	—	—	—	—
Usk and Towy - - - - -	130,000	43,300	173,300	1,300	Nil	—	—	—
Vale of Llangollen - - - -	Worked by the Great Western.							
Vale of Towy - - -. - - -	60,000	18,000	78,000	55,000	5	—	—	—
Victoria Station and Pimlico - -	412,500	137,500	550,000	225,000	9⅛	—	—	—
Wainfleet and Firsby - - - -	Worked by the Great Northern.							
Watford and Rickmansworth - -	Worked by the London and North-western.							
Watlington and Princes Risborough - -	36,000	12,000	48,000	31,688	Nil	—	—	—
Watton and Swaffham - - -	60,000	20,000	80,000	4,169	Nil	—	—	—
Wellington and Drayton - - - -	Worked by the Great Western.							
Wellington and Severn Junction - -	Leased to the Great Western.							
Wenlock - - - -	Worked by the Great Western.							
West Cornwall Committee - - -	950,000	—	950,000	—	—	691,413 86,000	4½ 5	4½ 5
West Lancashire - - - -	272,000	90,666	362,666	7,755	Nil	—	—	—
West London - - - - - -	185,960	—	185,960	—	—	101,180 64,000 15,300	3 3½ 6	3 3½ 6
West London Extension - - -	555,000	185,000	740,000	555,000	Nil	—	—	—
West Norfolk Junction - - - -	Worked by the Great Eastern.							
West Riding and Grimsby Joint Committee -	Line owned by the Great Northern and Manchester, Sheffield, and Lincolnshire Companies.							
West Somerset - - - -	Leased to the Bristol and Exeter.							

31st December 1873.—ENGLAND AND WALES—*continued.*

SHARE CAPITAL.				CAPITAL RAISED BY LOANS AND DEBENTURE STOCK.						TOTAL CAPITAL paid up and raised by Loans and Debenture Stock.	SUBSCRIP- TIONS TO OTHER COM- PANIES.	REMARKS.
Preferential.			Total Paid-up Stock and Share Capital.	Loans.		DebentureStock.		Total raised by Loans and Debenture Stock.				
Amount.	Preferential Rate of Dividend.	Rate of Dividend paid.		Amount.	Rate of Interest.	Amount.	Rate of Interest.					
£	Per cent.	Per cent.	£	£	Per cent.	£	Per cent.	£		£	£	
—	–	–	45,000	1,000	4	11,000	4	13,400		58,400	—	
				1,400	5							
—	–	–	529	—	–	—	–	—		529	—	
—	–	–	18,000	6,000	5	—	–	6,000		24,000	—	
69,120	5	2½	379,120	103,183	5	—	–	103,183		482,303	—	Line worked by "Midland" and "Great Eastern" Railway Companies.
36,830	5	5										
—	–	–	180,000	5,150	4	—	–	57,340		237,340	—	
				13,100	4¼							
				39,090	4½							
—	–	–	—	—	–	—	–	—		—	—	
—	–	–	—	—	–	—	–	—		—	—	
—	–	–	1,200	—	–	—	–	—		1,200	—	
—	–	–	55,000	18,000	4½	—	–	18,000		73,000	—	This Railway is leased to the "London and North-western" and "Llanelly Railway and Dock" Companies.
180,000	4½	4½	355,000	—	–	132,322	4½	132,322		487,322	—	
—	–	–	31,688	12,000	5	—	–	12,000		43,688	—	
—	–	–	4,169	—	–	—	–	—		4,169	—	
—	–	–	777,413	—	–	—	–	—		777,413	120,582	
—	–	–	7,755	—	–	—	–	—		7,755	—	
—	–	–	180,380	—	–	—	–	—		180,380	—	
—	–	–	555,000	22,500	4	—	–	27,800		582,800	—	
				4,300	4¼							
				1,000	4½							

The Capital is included in their Returns.

No. 1.—Amount of Capital, &c., upon the

Name of Company.	Authorised Capital.			Paid-up Stock and				
	By Shares and Stock.	By Loans and Debenture Stock.	Total.	Ordinary.		Guaranteed.		
				Amount.	Rate of Dividend paid.	Amount.	Guaranteed Rate of Dividend.	Rate of Dividend paid.
	£	£	£	£	Per cent.	£	Per cent.	Per cent.
West Somerset Mineral - - -	75,000	30,000	105,000	42,500	5	—	—	—
Weymouth and Portland - - -	75,000	25,000	100,000	75,000	4½	—	—	—
Whitby, Redcar, and Middlesborough Union -	250,000	83,300	333,300	249,981	Nil	—	—	—
Whitehaven, Cleator, and Egremont - -	383,000	126,600	509,600	317,086	11¼	—	—	—
Whitland and Taff Vale - - - -	37,000	12,300	49,300	37,000	Nil	—	—	—
Widness - . - - -	60,000	20,000	80,000	—	—	—	—	—
Witney - - - - -	Worked by the Great Western.							
Wivenhoe and Brightlingsea - - -	Worked by the Great Eastern.							
Wolverhampton and Walsall - -	Worked by the London and North-western.							
Wolverhampton, Walsall, and Midland Junction	250,000	83,300	333,300	—	—	—	—	—
Worcester, Bromyard, and Leominster -	200,000	66,500	266,500	108,299	Nil	—	—	—
Wrexham, Mold, and Connah's Quay -	425,000	284,600	709,600	262,633	Nil	—	—	—
Buckley - - - - -	90,000	30,000	120,000	—	—	46,072	4¾	4¾
Wye Valley - - - -	230,000	76,600	306,600	—	—	—	—	—
Yarmouth and Ventnor Railway, Tramway, and Pier	180,000	60,000	240,000	—	—	—	—	—
Total England and Wales - £	410,843,169	148,223,144	559,066,313	205,801,711	—	58,340,391	—	—

31st December 1873.—ENGLAND AND WALES—*continued.*

SHARE CAPITAL.				CAPITAL RAISED BY LOANS AND DEBENTURE STOCK.					TOTAL CAPITAL paid up and raised by Loans and Debenture Stock.	SUBSCRIPTIONS TO OTHER COMPANIES.	REMARKS.
Preferential.			Total Paid-up Stock and Share Capital.	Loans.		Debenture Stock.		Total raised by Loans and Debenture Stock.			
Amount.	Preferential Rate of Dividend.	Rate of Dividend paid.		Amount.	Rate of Interest.	Amount.	Rate of Interest.				
£ 32,500	Per cent. 6	Per cent. 6	£ 75,000	£ 15,600	Per cent. 5	£ 14,400	Per cent. 5	£ 30,000	£ 105,000	£ 10,000	
—	–	–	75,000	14,250	4½	10,750	4½	25,000	100,000	—	Line worked by the "Great Western" and "London and South-western" Companies jointly.
—	–	–	249,981	66,185	5	—	–	66,185	316,166	—	Line not open for traffic.
48,000	5	5	365,086	99,050 11,850	4 4½	—	–	110,900	475,986	—	
—	–	–	37,000	3,000	5	—	–	3,000	40,000	—	
—	–	–	—	—	–	—	–	—	—	—	
—	–	–	—	—	–	—	–	—	—	—	
—	–	–	108,299	—	–	47,995	5	47,995	156,294	—	
75,000	5	Nil	337,633	54,561	5	61,989 72,371	4 5	188,921	526,554	—	
20,000	5	5	66,072	20,000	5	—	–	20,000	86,072	—	
—	–	–	—	—	–	—	–	—	—	—	
—	–	–	—	—	–	—	–	—	—	—	
95,709,393	–	–	359,851,495	39,422,137	–	90,745,362	–	130,167,499	490,018,994	15,356,382	TOTAL ENGLAND AND WALES.

No. 1.—AMOUNT of CAPITAL, &c., upon the

Name of Company.	Authorised Capital.			Paid-up Stock and				
	By Shares and Stock.	By Loans and Debenture Stock.	Total.	Ordinary.		Guaranteed.		
				Amount.	Rate of Dividend paid.	Amount.	Guaranteed Rate of Dividend.	Rate of Dividend paid.
	£	£	£	£	Per cent.	£	Per cent.	Per cent.
Aboyne and Bracmar	*Worked by the Great North of Scotland.*							
Alyth	*Leased to the Caledonian.*							
Arbroath and Forfar	*Leased to the Caledonian.*							
Ayr and Maybole	*Leased to the Glasgow and South-western.*							
Berwickshire	*Worked by the North British.*							
Blane Valley	*Worked by the North British.*							
Broxburn	*Sold to the North British.*							
Busby	*Worked by the Caledonian.*							
Caledonian	20,008,460	6,829,989	26,838,449*	7,203,284 21,276†	$3\frac{7}{8}$ 4	499,712 136,826 830,000 299,700 649,579 735,447 70,000 276,343 1,141,338 600,000 150,000 240,000 200,000	3 $3\frac{1}{2}$ 4 $4\frac{1}{4}$ $4\frac{1}{2}$ 5 $5\frac{1}{4}$ 6 $6\frac{1}{4}$ $6\frac{71}{120}$ 7 $7\frac{7}{8}$ $10\frac{11}{80}$	3 $3\frac{1}{2}$ 4 $4\frac{1}{4}$ $4\frac{1}{2}$ 5 $5\frac{1}{4}$ 6 $6\frac{1}{4}$ $6\frac{71}{120}$ 7 $7\frac{7}{8}$ $10\frac{11}{80}$
Leased to or worked by the Caledonian.								
Alyth	33,000	11,000	44,000	29,177	$3\frac{1}{4}$	—	—	—
Arbroath and Forfar	250,000	16,666	266,666	185,950	6	40,000	5	6
Busby	105,000	35,000	140,000	42,850	$\frac{3}{16}$	—		
Callander and Oban	243,900	81,300	325,200	242,787	Nil	—	—	—
Dundee and Newtyle	140,000	30,000	170,000	111,650*	$1\frac{7}{80}$	—	—	—
Glasgow, Garnkirk, and Coatbridge	156,355	—	156,355	156,355	8	—	—	—
Greenock and Wemyss Bay	150,000	50,000	200,000	96,710	Nil	—	—	—
Lesmahagow	105,700	—	105,700	—	—	45,700 60,000	5 6	$4\frac{223}{240}$* $5\frac{223}{240}$*
Montrose and Bervie	70,000	23,000	93,000	70,000	$\frac{1}{2}$	—	—	—
Portpatrick	552,000	184,000	736,000	435,282	3	—	—	—
Solway Junction	380,000	126,600	506,600	249,998	Nil	—	—	—

See also "Glasgow, Barrhead, and Neilston."

31st December 1873.—SCOTLAND.

Share Capital.				Capital raised by Loans and Debenture Stock.					Total Capital paid up and raised by Loans and Debenture Stock.	Subscriptions to other Companies.	Remarks.
Preferential.			Total Paid-up Stock and Share Capital.	Loans.		Debenture Stock.		Total raised by Loans and Debenture Stock.			
Amount.	Preferential Rate of Dividend.	Rate of Dividend paid.		Amount.	Rate of Interest.	Amount.	Rate of Interest.				
£	Per cent.	Per cent.	£	£	Per cent.	£	Per cent.	£	£	£	
168,514	4	4	18,084,476	27,534	3½	971,966	4	6,043,183	24,127,659‡	375,184	As at 31st January 1874. * In addition to the amount here stated the Company is authorised by Caledonian Railway (Additional Powers) Act, 1873, sec. 48, to raise by loans or Debenture Stock contingent on agreement with Alyth Railway Company, for extinction of that Company's Debentures 11,000*l.*; and by Dingwall and Skye Railway Act, 1865, to raise by shares 100,000*l.* † Amount paid in advance of calls. ‡ This total is exclusive of 30,997*l.* received on shares cancelled and abated, unappropriated.
159,369	4¼	4¼		123,038	3½						
2,331,640	4½	4½		4,920,645	4						
1,175,000	5	5									
89,231	6	6									
1,112,122	7	7									
2,950	5	5	32,127	11,000	4½	—	–	11,000	43,127	—	
—	–	–	225,950	4,000	4	—	–	4,000	229,950		
45,000	5	5	87,850	18,600	4½	—	–	33,773	121,623		As at 31st January 1874.
				15,173	4½						
—	–	–	242,787	4,160	4½	—	–	30,303	273,090	—	As at 31st January 1874.
				26,143	4½						
—	–	–	111,650	—	–	—	–	—	111,650	—	* Of this capital, 71,650*l.* was issued at 40 per cent. discount.
—	–	–	156,355	—	–	—	–	—	156,355	—	
30,000	5	Nil	126,710	35,177	4½	—	–	35,177	161,887	—	*
—	–	–	105,700	—	–	—	–	—	105,700	—	* 7*d.* per 100*l.* of stock being deducted to meet the expense of management.
—	–	–	70,000	18,500	5	—	–	18,500	88,500	—	
—	–	–	435,282	89,408	3½	—	–	110,618	545,900	—	
				21,210	4						
60,000	4	Nil	309,998	22,424	5	57,861	3½	80,285	390,283	—	

E 3

No. 1.—AMOUNT of CAPITAL, &c., upon the

NAME OF COMPANY.	AUTHORISED CAPITAL.			PAID-UP STOCK AND				
	By Shares and Stock.	By Loans and Debenture Stock.	Total.	Ordinary.		Guaranteed.		
				Amount.	Rate of Dividend paid.	Amount.	Guaranteed Rate of Dividend.	Rate of Dividend paid.
	£	£	£	£	Per cent.	£	Per cent.	Per cent.
Callander and Oban - : - -	Worked by the Caledonian.							
Carlisle and Silloth Bay - -	Leased to the North British.							
City of Glasgow Union - -	1,800,000	200,000	2,000,000	600,000	Nil	100,000	5	5
Deeside - - - -	Leased to the Great North of Scotland.							
Deeside Extension - - -								
Devon Valley - - -	Worked by the North British.							
Dingwall and Skye - - -	Worked by the Highland.							
Duke of Sutherland's Railway -	Worked by the Highland.							
Dundee and Newtyle - - -	Leased to the Caledonian.							
Dunfermline and Queensferry -	105,000	35,000	140,000	2,418	Nil	—	—	—
Edinburgh and Bathgate - -	Leased to the North British.							
Edinburgh, Loanhead, and Roslin -	84,000	28,000	112,000	39,496	Nil	—	—	—
Findhorn - - - -	9,000	3,000	12,000	8,962	Nil	—	—	—
Forth and Clyde Junction - -	Leased to the North British.							
Forth Bridge - - -	1,250,000	416,666	1,666,666	—	—	—	—	—
Girvan and Portpatrick Junction -	335,000	111,620	446,620	178,945	Nil	—	—	—
Glasgow and Milngavie Junction -	Amalgamated with the North British from 1st August, 1874.							
Glasgow and South-western - -	6,660,000	2,075,500	8,735,500	50,000 4,727,710	3½ 4⅞	156,250 342,110 321,000	5 5 5	5 5 5
Leased to or worked by the Glasgow and South-western. Ayr and Maybole -	34,500	*—	34,500	34,500	7	—	—	—
Kilmarnock and Troon -	40,000	—	40,000	40,000	9	—	—	—
See also " Glasgow, Barrhead, and Neilston." Glasgow, Barrhead, and Neilston Direct -	275,000	—	275,000	125,000 150,000	3¾ 4⅞	—	—	—
Glasgow, Garnkirk, and Coatbridge - -	Leased to the Caledonian.							
Glencairn - - - -	60,000	20,000	80,000	—	—	—	—	—
Great North of Scotland - -	2,554,443	864,919	3,419,362	860,968	½	102,822 13,810 27,450 46,010 193,733	3 min. 4½ 5 5 5	3 4½ 5 5 5
Leased to or worked by the Great North of Scotland. Aboyne and Braemar -	66,000	22,000	88,000	38,250	2¼	—	—	—
Deeside - - -	140,250	43,400	183,650	116,228	7¾	—	—	—
Deeside Extension -	80,000	26,600	106,600	79,644	4	—	—	—
Morayshire - - - -	139,700	46,433	186,133	57,887	Nil	—	—	—

31st December 1873.—SCOTLAND—*continued.*

Share Capital.				Capital raised by Loans and Debenture Stock.					Total Capital paid up and raised by Loans and Debenture Stock.	Subscriptions to other Companies.	Remarks.
Preferential.			Total Paid-up Stock and Share Capital.	Loans.		Debenture Stock.		Total raised by Loans and Debenture Stock.			
Amount.	Preferential Rate of Dividend.	Rate of Dividend paid.		Amount.	Rate of Interest.	Amount.	Rate of Interest.				
£	Per cent.	Per cent.	£	£	Per cent.	£	Per cent.	£	£	£	
600,000	5	5	1,300,000	460 35,230 85,010 74,650	3¾ 4 4¼ 4½	—	-	195,350	1,495,350	—	As at 31st January 1874.
—	-	-	2,418	—	-	—	-	—	2,418	—	
—	-	-	39,496	—	-	—	-	—	39,496	—	
—	-	-	8,962	1,750	4½	—	-	1,750	10,712	—	The revenue never paid the working expenses, and in consequence the working of the line was discontinued in 1869.
—	-	-	—	—	-	—	-	—	—	—	
—	-	-	178,945	30,075 2,000 1,000	4½ 4¾ 5	—	-	33,075	212,020	—	As at 28th February 1874.
25,000 150,000 12,200 36,000 69,905 250,000 105,675	4 4½ 5 5 5 5 5	4 4½ 5 5 5 5 *Nil	6,245,850	27,390 61,125 1,484,291 4,775 4,800	3½ 3¾ 4 4¼ 4½	371,155	4	1,953,536	8,199,386	500,000	As at 31st January 1874. * Dividend to accrue from 1st February 1876.
—	-	-	34,500	—	-	—	-	—	34,500	—	* Borrowing powers assumed by the Glasgow and South-western Railway Company.
—	-	-	40,000	—	-	—	-	—	40,000	—	
—	-	-	275,000	—	-	—	-	—	275,000	—	The line is leased to the "Caledonian" and "Glasgow and South-western" Railway Companies.
—	-	-	—	—	-	—	-	—	—	—	
218,080 40,765 482,050 291,090	3* 4 4½ 5 min.	1½ 4 4½ 5	2,276,723	4,960 401,689 303,799 86,462 1,000 13,500	3¾ 4 4¼ 4½ 4¾ 5	11,915 35,095	4 4¼	858,420	3,135,143	23,152	As at 31st January 1874. *To 31st July 1877.
—	-	-	38,250	8,465 7,240 6,295	4½ 4¾ 5	—	-	22,000	60,250	—	As at 31st January 1874.
23,825	4½	4½	140,053	43,400	4	—	-	43,400	183,453	15,000	
—	-	-	79,644	24,300	4	—	-	24,300	103,944	—	
55,840	5	Nil	113,227	200 600 5,550 31,780	4 4¼ 4½ 5	—	-	38,130	151,357	—	

| Name of Company. | Authorised Capital. | | | Paid-up Stock and | | | | |
| | By Shares and Stock. | By Loans and Debenture Stock. | Total. | Ordinary. | | Guaranteed. | | |
				Amount.	Rate of Dividend paid.	Amount.	Guaranteed Rate of Dividend.	Rate of Dividend paid.
	£	£	£	£	Per cent.	£	Per cent.	Per cent.
Greenock and Wemyss Bay	Worked by the Caledonian.							
Highland	2,379,000	700,880	3,079,880	1,270,270	4¼	76,000	6	6
Dingwall and Skye	238,500	79,500	318,000	228,546	Nil	—	—	—
Duke of Sutherland's	Private Property.							
Sutherland	180,000	60,000	240,000	126,920	Nil	—	—	—
Kelvin Valley	90,000	30,000	120,000	...	—	—	—	—
Kilmarnock and Troon	Leased to the Glasgow and South-western.							
Lesmahagow	Leased to the Caledonian.							
Leven and East of Fife	130,000	43,300	173,300	35,000 / 37,000	4¾ / 10½	—	—	—
Montrose and Bervie	Worked by the Caledonian.							
Morayshire	Worked by the Great North of Scotland.							
Newport	46,000	15,300	61,300	—	—	—	—	—
North British	19,580,661	7,937,813	27,518,474	2,777,652 / 98,360 / 1,327,266	Nil / Nil / Nil	—	—	—
Berwickshire	130,000	43,060	173,060	129,444	2	—	—	—
Blane Valley	75,000	25,000	100,000	32,991	Nil	—	—	—
Carlisle and Silloth Bay	240,000	25,000	265,000	163,139	Nil	—	—	—
Devon Valley	100,000	31,763	131,763	39,838	Nil	—	—	—
Edinburgh and Bathgate	250,000	83,000	333,000	233,384	5	—	—	—
Forth and Clyde Junction	192,000	64,000	256,000	106,373	3¾	64,000	5	5

Leased to or worked by the Highland.
Leased to or worked by the North British.

31st December 1873.—SCOTLAND—*continued.*

Share Capital.				Capital raised by Loans and Debenture Stock.							
Preferential.			Total Paid-up Stock and Share Capital.	Loans.		Debenture Stock.		Total raised by Loans and Debenture Stock.	Total Capital paid up and raised by Loans and Debenture Stock.	Subscriptions to other Companies.	Remarks.
Amount.	Preferential Rate of Dividend.	Rate of Dividend paid.		Amount.	Rate of Interest.	Amount.	Rate of Interest.				
£	Per cent.	Per cent.	£	£	Per cent.	£	Per cent.	£	£	£	
513,650 45,000 400,000 59,080	4½ 5 5 6	4½ 5 5 6	2,364,000	1,200 1,950 350,557 90,550	3½ 3¾ 4 4½	150 256,400	4 4¼	700,807	3,064,807	115,000	
—	-	-	228,546	78,915 500	4½ 5	—	-	79,415	307,961	—	
—	-	-	126,920	36,156 23,844	4 4½	—	-	60,000	186,920	—	
—	-	-	—	—	-	—	-	—	—	—	
54,790	4½	4½	126,790	34,750 1,400	4 4½	—	-	36,150	162,940	—	
—	-	-	—	—	-	—	-	—	—	—	
20,291 1,625 22,000 22,830 44,200 2,419,578 7,860,996 238,392 2,880 563,379 * 175,605 * 110,009 71,985	‡ 3 3½ 3¾ 3¾ 4½ 4 5 5 6 5¼ 4 †3	4/15 3 3½ 3¾ 3¾ 2⅞ 4 2½ 5 6 Nil Nil Nil	15,752,103	20,265 850 88,324 3,130,235 695,406 103,263	3 3½ 3¾ 4 4¼ 4½	45,000 903,047 510,114 788,375 1,099,024	3½ 4 4¼ 4½ 5	7,579,533	28,331,686	488,807	As at 31st January 1874. * Not yet earning revenue. † Second Preference. ‡ Contingent.
—	-	-	129,444	10,310 22,750	4 4¼	—	-	33,060	162,504	—	
30,210	4½	2¾	63,201	1,350 4,450 5,187	4¼ 4½ 5	—	-	10,987	74,188	—	
75,000	5	2⅛	238,189	19,629 5,370	4½ 5	—	-	24,999	263,188	—	
60,000	*4 minimum.	Nil	99,838	1,400 21,525 8,838	1½ 4½ 4¾	—	-	31,763	131,601	—	* Out of profits of each year.
—	-	-	233,384	16,844	4	—	-	16,844	250,228	—	
4,520 16,480	5 6	5 6	191,373	34,550 14,300 200 9,850 150 4,250 700	4 4¼ 4⅜ 4½ 4⅝ 4¾ 5	—	-	64,000	255,373	—	As at 31st January 1874.

No. 1.—AMOUNT of CAPITAL, &c., upon the

NAME OF COMPANY.	AUTHORISED CAPITAL.			PAID-UP STOCK AND				
	By Shares and Stock.	By Loans and Debenture Stock.	Total.	Ordinary.		Guaranteed.		
				Amount.	Rate of Dividend paid.	Amount.	Guaranteed Rate of Dividend.	Rate of Dividend paid.
	£	£	£	£	Per cent.	£	Per cent.	Per cent.
North British—*continued.*								
Peebles - - -	97,000	32,000	129,000	70,000	7	—	—	—
Penicuick - - - -	54,000	25,000	79,000	84,825	4½	—	—	—
Port Carlisle Dock and Railway -	70,600	73,538	144,138	70,600	1½	—	—	—
St. Andrews - - -	27,000	7,000	34,000	21,000	6¼	—	—	—
North British, Arbroath, and Montrose -	185,580	61,860	247,440	4,490	Nil	—	—	—
North Monkland - - - -	60,000	—	60,000	4,917	Nil	—	—	—
Peebles - - - - -	*Leased to the North British.*							
Penicuick - - - - -	*Worked by the North British.*							
Port Carlisle Dock and Railway -	*Leased to the North British.*							
Port Patrick - - -	*Worked by the Caledonian.*							
St. Andrews - - - -	*Worked by the North British.*							
Solway Junction - - -	*Leased to the Caledonian.*							
Sutherland - - - -	*Worked by the Highland.*							
Sutherland and Caithness - -	360,000	120,000	480,000	202,704	Nil	—	—	—
Wigtownshire - - -	96,000	32,000	128,000	17,697	Nil	—	—	—
TOTAL SCOTLAND - - £	60,408,649	20,770,707	81,179,356	32,987,738	—	7,417,825	—	—

(Left margin bracket label: "Leased to or worked by the North British.")

31st December 1873.—SCOTLAND—*continued.*

Share Capital.				Capital raised by Loans and Debenture Stock.					Total Capital paid up and raised by Loans and Debenture Stock.	Subscriptions to other Companies.	Remarks.
Preferential.			Total Paid-up Stock and Share Capital.	Loans.		Debenture Stock.		Total raised by Loans and Debenture Stock.			
Amount.	Preferential Rate of Dividend.	Rate of Dividend paid.		Amount.	Rate of Interest.	Amount.	Rate of Interest.				
£ 27,000	Per cent. 5	Per cent. 5	£ 97,000	£ 800 2,700 28,500	Per cent. 3½ 3¾ 4	£ —	Per cent. —	£ 32,000	£ 129,000	£ —	As at 31st January 1874.
—.	–	–	34,825	25,000	4½	—	–	25,000	59,825	—	
—	–	–	70,600	—	–	73,538	3	73,538	144,138	—	As at 31st January 1874.
—	–	–	21,000	5,300	4	—	–	5,300	26,300	—	
—	–	–	4,490	—	–	—	–	—	4,490	—	As at 31st January 1874.
—	–	–	4,917	—	–	—	–	—	4,917	—	
—	–	–	202,704.	47,300	4½	—	–	47,300	250,004	.—	
—	–	–	17,697	—	–	—	–	—	17,697	—	
20,363,361	–	–	50,768,924	13,238,256	–	5,119,240	–	18,357,496	69,126,420	1,517,143	Total Scotland.

No. 1.—AMOUNT OF CAPITAL, &c., upon the

NAME OF COMPANY.	AUTHORISED CAPITAL			PAID UP-STOCK AND				
	By Shares and Stock.	By Loans and Debenture Stock.	Total.	Ordinary.		Guaranteed.		
				Amount.	Rate of Dividend paid.	Amount.	Guaranteed Rate of Dividend.	Rate of Dividend paid.
	£	£	£	£	Per cent.	£	Per cent.	Per cent.
Athenry and Ennis Junction - - -	Leased to the Waterford and Limerick.							
Athenry and Tuam - - - - -	Leased to the Waterford and Limerick.							
Ballymena, Cushendall, and Redbay - -	90,000	30,000	120,000	26,260	Nil	—	—	—
Banbridge Junction - - - -	Leased to the Dublin and Belfast Junction.							
Banbridge, Lisburn, and Belfast - - -	Leased to the Ulster.							
Belfast and County Down - - -	515,000	166,666	681,666	235,950 *22,260	Nil —	—	—	—
Downpatrick, Dundrum, and Newcastle	60,000	20,000	80,000	51,860	Nil	—	—	—
Belfast and Northern Counties - -	1,045,000	368,882	1,413,882	557,828	7½	—	—	—
Carrickfergus and Larne - -	125,000	41,500	166,500	80,400 *2,359	2 Nil	—	—	—
Belfast Central - - - - - -	150,000	675,000	825,000	150,000	Nil	—	—	—
Belfast, Holywood, and Bangor - -	311,000	158,000	469,000	132,210 98*	Nil —	—	—	—
Carrickfergus and Larne - - - -	Worked by the Belfast and Northern Counties.							
Castleisland - - - - -	20,000	10,000	30,000	6,837	Nil	—	—	—
Central Ireland Railways Committee - -	See Waterford and Central Ireland and Kilkenny Junction and Central Ireland.							
Cork and Bandon - - -	338,000	88,000	426,000	240,000	1½	—	—	—
Cork and Kinsale Junction - - -	65,000	36,600	101,600	20,800	Nil	—	—	—
Cork and Kinsale Junction - -	Worked by the Cork and Bandon.							
Cork and Macroom Direct - - -	120,000	50,000	170,000	75,850	4½	—	—	—
Cork, Blackrock, and Passage - - -	132,000	43,330	175,330	118,340	3½	—	—	—

31st December 1873.—IRELAND.

Share Capital.			Total Paid-up Stock and Share Capital.	Capital raised by Loans and Debenture Stock.					Total Capital paid up and raised by Loans and Debenture Stock.	Subscriptions to other Companies.	Remarks.
Preferential.				Loans.		Debenture Stock.		Total raised by Loans and Debenture Stock.			
Amount.	Preferential Rate of Dividend.	Rate of Dividend paid.		Amount.	Rate of Interest.	Amount.	Rate of Interest.				
£	Per cent.	Per cent.	£	£	Per cent.	£	Per cent.	£	£	£	
—	-	-	26,260	—	-	—	-	—	26,260	—	Line in course of construction.
11,050 / 255,550	4½ / 5	3⅜ / 5¾	524,810	148,255 / 2,794 / 8,330 / 4,530 / 1,700	3½ / 4 / 4½ / 4½ / 4¾	—	-	165,609	†690,419	25,000	* Forfeited shares. † In addition to this amount 49,490l. was received from the "Belfast, Holywood, and Bangor" Railway Company on account of the purchase of the Holywood Branch.
—	-	-	51,860	1,742 / 14,451	4 / 4½	—	'-	16,193	68,053	—	
160,000 / 159,600 / 135,000	4 / 4½ / 4½	4 / 4½ / 4½	1,012,428	51,413 / 1,100 / 221,880 / 60,000 / 9,395	4 / 4½ / 4½ / 4½ / 4½	6,585	4	350,373	1,362,801	12,500	
—	-	-	82,759	1,000 / 3,481 / 32,015	4 / 4½ / 4½	—	-	36,496	119,255	—	*Amount received on forfeited shares.
—	-	-	150,000	100,000	5	—	-	100,000	250,000	—	
79,220	5	Nil	211,528	108,000	5	—	-	108,000	319,528	24,650	*Amount received on forfeited shares.
—	-	-	6,837		-		-	—	6,837	—	The railway is in course of construction.
80,000 / 48,000	4 / 5½	4 / 5½	318,000	25,910 / 9,300	4½ / 5	8,810 / 44,380	4 / 4½	87,900	405,900		
6,530	5	Nil	27,330	4,550 / 17,050	5/8	795	5	22,395	49,725	—	
44,150	5	5	120,000		-	19,960 / 28,750	4½ / 5	48,710	168,710	—	
600	5	5	118,940	17,900 / 21,450	4½ / 5	—	-	39,350	158,290	—	As at 31st October 1873.

No. 1.—Amount of Capital, &c., upon the

NAME OF COMPANY.	AUTHORISED CAPITAL.			PAID-UP STOCK AND				
	By Shares and Stock.	By Loans and Debenture Stock.	Total.	Ordinary.		Guaranteed.		
				Amount.	Rate of Dividend paid.	Amount.	Guaranteed Rate of Dividend.	Rate of Dividend paid.
	£	£	£	£	Per cent.	£	Per cent.	Per cent.
Cork Harbour and Curraghbinney - -	16,000	8,000	24,000	—	—	—	—	—
Downpatrick, Dundrum, and Newcastle -	*Worked by the Belfast and County Down.*							
Dublin and Antrim Junction - - -	*Worked by the Ulster.*							
Dublin and Belfast Junction - -	873,500	291,150	1,164,650	873,500	4½	—	—	—
Banbridge Junction - - - -	60,000	20,000	80,000	22,128	1	—	—	—
Dublin and Drogheda - - - -	953,000	317,333	1,270,333	700,000	6	100,000 120,000	4 4½	4 4½
Dublin and Kingstown - - - -	*Leased to the Dublin, Wicklow, and Wexford.*							
Dublin and Meath - - - -	*Worked by the Midland Great Western of Ireland.*							
Dublin, Rathmines, Rathgar, Roundtown, Rathfarnham, and Rathcoole.	450,000	149,000	599,000	6,160	Nil	-	—	—
Dublin, Wicklow, and Wexford - -	1,445,000	480,933	1,925,933	602,150	3¼	—	—	—
Dublin and Kingstown - - -	350,000	110,000	460,000	350,000	9	—	—	—
Dundalk, Newry, and Greenore - -	400,000	133,200	533,200	134,365	Nil	—	—	—
Dunmanway and Skibbereen - -	80,000	40,000	120,000	—	—	—	—	—
Ennis and West Clare - - -	150,000	49,997	199,997	80	Nil	1,575	4	Nil
Enniskillen, Bundoran, and Sligo - -	*Worked by the Irish North-western.*							
Fermoy and Lismore - - -	*Worked by the Great Southern and Western of Ireland.*							
Finn Valley - - - -	*Worked by the Irish North-western.*							
Galway, Oughterard, and Clifden -	200,000	66,000	266,000	—	—	—	—	—
Great Northern and Western of Ireland -	*Worked by the Midland Great Western of Ireland.*							
Great Southern and Western of Ireland -	5,949,940	743,965	6,693,905	4,450,157	5¾	—	—	—
Fermoy and Lismore - - -	100,000	33,000	133,000	100,000	Nil	—	—	—
Parsonstown and Portumna Bridge -	85,000	21,600	106,600	32,580	Nil	—	—	—
Irish North-western - - -	900,000	300,000	1,200,000	171,420	Nil	—	—	—
Leased to or worked by the Irish North-western. { Enniskillen, Bundoran, and Sligo.	300,000	99,900	399,900	45,728	Nil	—	—	—
Finn Valley	80,000	20,000	100,000	44,980	2	—	—	—
Londonderry and Enniskillen	455,000	150,000	605,000	129,200	5	43,150	5	5
Kilkenny Junction - - - -	*Worked by the Waterford and Central Ireland.*							
Killorglin - - - -	40,000	20,000	60,000	—	—	—	—	—
Kilrush and Kilkee, and Poulnasherry Reclamation.	60,000	20,000	80,000	9,104	Nil	—	—	—

31st December 1873.—IRELAND—*continued*.

SHARE CAPITAL.				CAPITAL RAISED BY LOANS AND DEBENTURE STOCK.					TOTAL CAPITAL paid up and raised by Loans and Debenture Stock.	SUBSCRIPTIONS TO OTHER COMPANIES.	REMARKS.
Preferential.			Total Paid-up Stock and Share Capital.	Loans.		Debenture Stock.		Total raised by Loans and Debenture Stock.			
Amount.	Preferential Rate of Dividend.	Rate of Dividend paid.		Amount.	Rate of Interest.	Amount.	Rate of Interest.				
£	Per cent.	Per cent.	£	£	Per cent.	£	Per cent.	£	£	£	
—	–	–	873,500	2,300 12,000 28,500	4 4½ 4½	3,100 209,329	4 4½	255,129	1,128,629	41,928	
17,800	5	5	39,928	5,000 8,500 8,850	4½ 4½ 5	—	–	17,350	57,278	—	
—	–	–	920,000	1,000 34,540 8,500	4 4½ 4½	82,008 164,725	4 4½	285,773	1,205,773	27,613	
—	–	–	6,160	—	–	—	–	—	6,160	. –	
600,000 200,000	5 6	5 6	1,402,150	132,048 35,215 250 3,300	4 4½ 4½ 5	181,905 94,430	4½ 4½	447,148	1,849,298	—	
—	–	–	350,000	70,000	4	—	–	70,000	420,000	—	
—	–	–	134,365	—	–	—	–	—	134,365	—	
—	–	–	—	—	–	—	–	—	—	—	
—	–	–	1,655	—	–	—	–	—	1,655	—	
—	–	–	—	—	–	—	–	—	—	—	
1,329,100	4	4	5,779,257	8,000	4½	608,665	4	616,665	6,395,922	32,800	
—	–	–	100,000	29,876	5	—	–	29,876	129,876	—	
19,480	5	Nil	52,060	20,366	5	—	–	20,366	72,426	—	
420,223 116,753*	5 –	1 2	708,396	43,853	4	253,084 †801	5 5	297,738	1,006,134	50,051	* Clones and Cavan Extension shares. † Rentcharge Stock.
100,000	5	Nil	145,728	75,000 3,258	4 5	6,742	5	85,000	230,728	—	
17,480	6	6	62,460	14,813	3½	5,200	5	20,013*	82,473	—	* The 13l. borrowed in excess of the Statutory Powers was an oversight.
279,587 3,063	5 5	5 5	455,000	—	–	2,100 60,011 87,889	4½ 4½ 5	150,000	605,000	—	
—	–	–	—	—	–	—	–	—	—	—	
—	–	–	9,104	—	–	—	–	—	9,104	—	

F 4

No. 1.—Amount of Capital, &c., upon the

Name of Company.	Authorised Capital.			Paid-up Stock and				
	By Shares and Stock.	By Loans and Debenture Stock.	Total.	Ordinary.		Guaranteed.		
				Amount.	Rate of Dividend paid.	Amount.	Guaranteed Rate of Dividend.	Rate of Dividend paid.
	£	£	£	£	Per cent.	£	Per cent.	Per cent.
Larne and Ballyclare - - -	54,000	18,000	72,000	—	—	—	—	—
Letterkenny - - - - -	150,000	100,000	250,000	56,177	Nil	—	—	—
Limerick and Castle-Connell - - -	Amalgamated with the Waterford and Limerick from 1st January 1873.							
Limerick and Ennis - - -	Worked by the Waterford and Limerick.							
Limerick and Foynes - - - -	Amalgamated with the Waterford and Limerick from 1st July 1873.							
Limerick and Kerry - - - -	260,000	130,000	390,000	—	—	—	—	—
Londonderry and Enniskillen - - -	Worked by the Irish North-western.							
Londonderry and Lough Swilly - -	105,000	26,200	131,200	34,490	Nil	—	—	—
Midland Counties and Shannon Junction -	115,000	38,300	153,300	60,219	Nil	—	—	—
Midland Great Western of Ireland - -	2,750,000	1,447,202	4,197,202	2,806,100	4½	—	—	—
Leased to or worked by the Midland Great Western of Ireland. Dublin and Meath -	341,000	150,000	491,000	133,155	Nil	—	—	—
Great Northern and Western of Ireland.	455,160	292,540	747,700	383,605	4½	—	—	—
Navan and Kingscourt -	152,000	50,600	202,600	70,959	Nil	—	—	—
Navan and Kingscourt - - - -	Worked by the Midland Great Western of Ireland.							
Newry and Armagh - - - -	240,000	150,000	390,000	235,520	Nil	—	—	—
Newry, Warrenpoint, and Rostrevor -	120,000	39,900	159,900	99,925	Nil	—	—	—
Parsonstown and Portumna Bridge - -	Worked by the Great Southern and Western.							
Portadown, Dungannon, and Omagh Junction -	Leased to the Ulster.							
Rathkeale and Newcastle Junction - -	Worked by the Waterford and Limerick.							
Sligo and Ballaghaderreen Junction - -	50,000	16,600	66,600	33,763	Nil	—	—	—
Southern - - - - -	291,000	97,000	388,000	56,144	Nil	—	—	—
Ulster - - - - - -	1,200,000	309,000	1,509,000	1,000,000	7½	—	—	—
Leased to or worked by the Ulster. Banbridge, Lisburn, and Belfast	150,000	49,000	199,000	78,735	Nil	—	—	—
Dublin and Antrim Junction -	120,000	80,000	200,000	51,670	Nil	—	—	—
Portadown, Dungannon, and Omagh Junction.	395,775	131,385	527,160	252,050	Nil	—	—	—

31st December 1873.—IRELAND—*continued*.

Share Capital.				Capital raised by Loans and Debenture Stock.					Total Capital paid up and raised by Loans and Debenture Stock.	Subscriptions to other Companies.	Remarks.
Preferential.			Total Paid-up Stock and Share Capital.	Loans.		Debenture Stock.		Total raised by Loans and Debenture Stock.			
Amount.	Preferential Rate of Dividend.	Rate of Dividend paid.		Amount.	Rate of Interest.	Amount.	Rate of Interest.				
£	Per cent.	Per cent.	£	£	Per cent.	£	Per cent.	£	£	£	
—	—	—	—	—	—	—	—	—	— —	—	Bill passed in 1873.
—	—	—	56,177	—	—	—	—	—	56,177	—	The works were suspended in 1865 and have not since been resumed. An Act was obtained in 1871 extending the time for completion of the line.
—	—	—	—	—	—	—	—	—	—	—	
—	—	—	34,490	19,600	5	—	—	19,600	54,090	—	As at 31st January 1874.
—	—	—	60,219	100	Nil	—	—	100	60,319	—	
300,000	5	5	2,606,100	*380,652 6,200 226,178 37,925 3,900	3½ 4 4½ 4½ 5	464,282 201,700	4½ 4¼	1,320,832	3,926,932	113,350	* Government loan.
128,250 72,710	5 6	1¾ Nil	334,115	—	—	35,000 101,494	4 4½	136,494	470,609	—	
50,440 17,020	5 6	5 6	451,065	82,585 42,220	4 4½	128,268	4¼	253,073	704,138	—	
7,000 33,000	4 5	Nil Nil	110,959	13,300 26,600	5 5½	—	—	39,900	150,859	—	
—	—	—	235,520	—	—	126,324 20,000	4 5	146,324	381,844	12,500	
7,100 12,900	5½ 6	Nil Nil	119,925	500 38,500	4 5	—	—	39,000	158,925	—	
—	—	—	33,763	10,000	5	—	—	10,000	43,763	—	Line in course of construction.
3,560	5	Nil	59,704	—	—	—	—	—	59,704	—	Line in course of construction.
167,817	4½	4½	1,167,817	131,755 63,515 2,100	4 4½ 4½	102,752	4	300,122	1,467,939	92,518	
25,000 10,926	4 5	Nil Nil	114,661	500 47,150 1,300	4½ 5 5½	—	—	48,950	163,611	—	
10,200	6	Nil	61,870	40,000	5	—	—	40,000	101,870	—	
45,300 66,775	4½ 5	4½ 5	364,125	14,500 11,737 64,291	3 4 4½	36,680	4½	127,208	491,333	—	

No. 1.—Amount of Capital, &c., upon the

Name of Company.	Authorised Capital.			Paid-up Stock and				
	By Shares and Stock.	By Loans and Debenture Stock.	Total.	Ordinary.		Guaranteed.		
				Amount.	Rate of Dividend paid.	Amount.	Guaranteed Rate of Dividend.	Rate of Dividend paid.
	£	£	£	£	Per cent.	£	Per cent.	Per cent.
Waterford and Central Ireland - - -	450,000	189,000	639,000	250,000	Nil	—	—	—
Leased to or worked by the Waterford and Central Ireland. — Central Ireland Railways -	60,000	20,000	80,000	—	—	—	—	—
Kilkenny Junction -	214,000	256,480	470,480	60,575	Nil	—	—	—
Central Ireland Railways -	60,000	20,000	80,000	—	—	—	—	—
Waterford and Limerick - - - -	1,255,530	463,600	1,719,130	597,550	2¾	164,600	5	5
Leased to or worked by the Waterford and Limerick. — Athenry and Ennis Junction -	195,000	91,600	286,600	95,570	Nil	—	—	—
Athenry and Tuam - - -	90,000	30,000	120,000	61,818	Nil	—	—	—
Limerick and Ennis - - -	98,000	100,000	198,000	83,250	3	—	—	—
Rathkeale and Newcastle Junction -	63,000	31,600	94,600	18,130	Nil	—	—	—
Waterford and Tramore - - - -	58,000	19,350	77,350	48,000	4¼	—	—	—
Waterford and Wexford - - -	330,000	110,000	440,000	45,090	Nil	—	—	—
Waterford, Dungarvan, and Lismore -	280,000	93,333	373,333	8,390	5*	—	—	—
Waterford, New Ross, and Wexford Junction	330,000	199,880	529,880	80,050	Nil	—	—	—
West Cork - - - - -	320,000	257,436	577,436	66,817	Nil	—	—	—
Total Ireland - - £	26,670,905	9,770,012	36,440,917	15,660,356	—	429,325	—	—

31st December 1873.—IRELAND—*continued.*

Share Capital.				Capital raised by Loans and Debenture Stock.				Total Capital raised by Loans and Debenture Stock.	Total Capital paid up and raised by Loans and Debenture Stock.	Subscriptions to other Companies.	Remarks.
Preferential.			Total Paid-up Stock and Share Capital.	Loans.		Debenture Stock.					
Amount.	Preferential Rate of Dividend.	Rate of Dividend paid.		Amount.	Rate of Interest.	Amount.	Rate of Interest.				
£ 196,885	Per cent. 6	Per cent. 4	£ 446,885	£ 34,952 900 8,880 17,896 5,040	Per cent. 3½ 4 4½ 5 6	£ 100 30 82,168	Per cent. 4½ 4½ 5	£ 149,966	£ 596,851	£ 8,750	As at 29th September, 1873.
—	–	–	—	—	–	—	–	—	—	—	As at 29th September, 1873.
40,880	6	Nil	101,455	300	5	219,468	5	219,768	321,223	—	As at 1st November, 1873.
—	–	–	—	—	–	—	–	—	—	—	As at 1st November, 1873.
156,800 234,300 28,400	4½ 5 5½	4½ 5 5½	1,181,650	58,338 500 50,350 30,025 30,745 500 1,200 35,400	3½ 4 4½ 4½ 5 5½ 5½ 6	500 15,000 10,000 206,367	4 4½ 4½ 4½	438,825	1,620,475	35,662	
86,590	5	Nil	182,160	89,200	5	—	–	89,200	271,360	—	
—	–	–	61,818	30,000	5	—	–	30,000	91,818	—	
12,325	5	5	95,575	15,207 19,170 37,700	3½ 5 6	24,600	4½	96,677	192,252	—	
10,050	5	Nil	28,180	16,750	5	—	–	16,750	44,930	—	
10,000	5	5	58,000	2,500 5,000 10,850	4½ 4½ 5	—	–	18,350	76,350	—	
—	–	–	45,090	—	–	—	–	—	45,090	—	Line in course of construction.
—	–	–	8,390	—	–	—	–	—	8,390	—	* This dividend is payable by presentment to be levied off the rateable property of the County of Waterford, and of the County of the City of Waterford, for five years granted for the construction of the railway, and for thirty-five years after its opening for traffic.
44,940	5	Nil	124,990	60,000	5	44,940 44,940*	5 5	149,880	274,870	—	* Rent-charge Stock.
54,420	6	Nil	121,237	—	–	257,336	4	257,336	378,573	—	
5,866,774	–	–	21,956,455	3,227,921	–	3,990,518	–	7,218,439	29,174,894	477,322	Total Ireland.

RAILWAY RETURNS.—1873.

No. 2.—T R A F F I C, &c.

RETURN showing the NUMBER of PASSENGERS and QUANTITY of GOODS conveyed and the RECEIPTS therefrom upon the RAILWAYS in ENGLAND and WALES, SCOTLAND, and IRELAND, during the Year 1873.

No. 2.—Traffic, &c., ENGLAND

NAME OF COMPANY.	LENGTH OF LINE IN MILES open on 31st December 1873.			PASSENGER TRAFFIC. NUMBER OF PASSENGERS CONVEYED (exclusive of Season and Periodical Tickets).				Holders of Season or Periodical Tickets.	GOODS TRAFFIC.		NUMBER OF MILES TRAVELLED BY TRAINS.		
	Double or more.	Single.	TOTAL.	1st Class.	2d Class.	3d Class (including Parliamentary).	TOTAL.		Minerals.	General Merchandise.	Passenger Trains.	Goods and Mineral Trains.	TOTAL.
									Tons.	Tons.			
Aberdare	Leased to the Taff Vale.												
Abingdon	Leased to the Great Western.												
Anglesey Central		18	18	2,855	9,599	122,281	134,245	1	14,295	13,126	Mixed.		42,103
Aylesbury and Buckingham		12	12	1,158	2,705	27,940	31,803	-	5,306	3,877	Mixed.		22,519
Bala and Dolgelly	Worked by the Great Western.												
Barnoldswick	Worked by the Midland.												
Bedford and Northampton	Leased to the Midland												
Berks and Hants Extension	Worked by the Great Western.												
Birkenhead	Vested jointly in the Great Western and London and North-Western.												
Bishop's Castle		10	10	1,383	2,342	27,850	31,525	-	6,497	4,153	Mixed.		21,146
Bishop's Waltham	Worked by the London and South-Western.												
Blyth and Tyne	30	13	43	38,258	85,381	1,399,504	1,523,143	834	2,440,412	168,517	192,565	542,927	755,492
Bodmin and Wadebridge		15	15	21	1,053	3,752	4,826	-	20,779	7,508	3,546	8,692	12,238
Bourton-on-the-Water	Worked by the Great Western.												
Brecon and Merthyr Tydfil Junction	6	55	61	4,911	18,587	383,629	407,077	21	769,933	114,701	138,867	232,960	371,827
Bridport	Leased to the Great Western.												
Bristol and Exeter (Including the "Devon and Somerset" and "West Somerset.")	77	118	195	189,440	1,412,369	506,685	2,110,494	595	331,589	461,080	1,025,146	542,383	1,567,531
Bristol and North Somerset	Worked by the Great Western.												
Bristol and Portishead Pier and Railway		9	9	17,176	89,916	146,063	253,155	64	No account kept.		Mixed.		45,371
Bristol Port Railway and Pier		6	6	8,940	13,569	100,438	122,947	-	-	6,586	34,114		34,114
Buckfastleigh, Totnes, and South Devon	Worked by the South Devon.												
Buckinghamshire	Leased to the London and North-Western.												
Buckley	Worked by the Wrexham, Mold, and Connor's Quay.												
Burry Port and Gwendreath Valley		18	18	-	-	-	-	-	†200,000	-	-	14,556	14,556
Calne	Worked by the Great Western.												
Cambrian	7	171	178	37,834	67,252	1,140,734	1,245,820	76	358,185	133,258	445,591	333,563	778,154
Cannock Chase and Wolverhampton		6	6						246,761	-	No account kept.		
Carmarthen and Cardigan		19	19	8,632	21,519	252,419	282,570	-	68,168	43,355	Mixed.		55,380
Central Wales and Carmarthen Junction (From 1st August to 31st December 1873; for the first seven months see Swansea and Carmarthen Junction.)		13	13	1,710	2,576	36,798	41,084	-	7,111	9,352			
Cheshire Lines Committee	75	16	91	93,232	112,873	1,222,417	1,428,531	424	-	998,506	447,478	458,437	905,915
Chester and Holyhead	Worked by the London and North-Western.												
Cockermouth, Keswick, and Penrith		32	32	13,132	68,412	95,540	177,084	34	213,329	61,562	73,531	131,081	204,612
Colchester, Stour Valley, Sudbury, and Halstead	Leased to the Great Eastern.												
Coleford, Monmouth, Usk, and Pontypool	Leased to the Great Western.												
Colne Valley and Halstead		19	19	5,590	10,011	60,652	76,253	-	18,471	20,330	Mixed.		40,263
Cornwall	4	62	66	38,278	250,951	405,630	694,859	114	185,925	129,233	245,995	157,446	403,441
Corris *		11	11						15,594	-			
Corwen and Bala	Leased to the Great Western.												
Cowbridge		6	6	1,040	3,441	42,607	47,507	-	16,250	8,330	Mixed.		13,720
Cowes and Newport		5	5	17,874	89,823	24,924	132,621	17	-	-	36,380	-	36,380
Crosser and Portmadoc		5	5	-	-	-	-	-	21,016	475	-	5,730	5,730
Cromford and High Peak	Leased to the London and North-Western.												
Crystal Palace and South London Junction	Worked by the London, Chatham, and Dover.												
Dare Valley	Leased to the Taff Vale.												

* The line is used for the carriage of slates only.   † Including merchandise.   ‡ Including receipts from minerals and live stock.

AND WALES, in 1873.

1st Class.	2d Class.	3d Class (including Parliamentary).	Holders of Season or Periodical Tickets.	Total from passengers.	Excess Luggage, Parcels, Carriages, Horses, Dogs, &c.	Mails.	Total Receipts from Passenger Traffic.	Merchandise.	Live Stock.	Minerals.	Total Receipts from Goods Traffic.	Miscellaneous Rents, Tolls, Navigation, Steamboats, &c.	Total Receipts from all Sources of Traffic.	NAME OF COMPANY.
£	£	£	£	£	£	£	£	£	£	£	£	£	£	
														Aberdare.
														Abingdon.
207	459	3,583	12	4,201		-	-	4,681	2,488	291	559	3,278	-	-	7,909	Anglesey Central.
120	180	963	-	1,233	430 402	6	1,641	770	59	-	-	829	-	-	2,470	Aylesbury and Buckingham.
														Bala and Dolgelly.
														Barnoldswick.
														Bedford and Northampton.
														Berks and Hants Extension.
														Birkenhead.
117	185	991	-	1,243	150	-	-	1,393	1,017	130	586	1,733	125	3,251	Bishop's Castle.
														Bishop's Waltham.
2,739	4,488	42,160	1,833	51,220	2,308	47	53,575	15,731	318	113,184	129,233	894	183,702	Blyth and Tyne.
1	30	91	-	122	5	-	127	240	-	-	2,016	2,256	81	2,464	Bodmin and Wadebridge.
														Bourton-on-the-Water.
719	1,227	13,632	62	15,640	757	-	-	16,397	16,209	732	43,022	59,963	3,260	79,620	Brecon and Merthyr Tydfil Junction.
														Bridport.
53,343	127,153	75,860	4,290	260,646	33,286	11,987	305,919	142,443	7,432	46,289	196,164	19,322	521,405	Bristol and Exeter.
														Bristol and North Somerset.
1,021	2,696	3,414	360	7,483	130	79	7,642	11,417	-	-	1,417	765	9,824	Bristol and Portishead Pier and Railway.
207	266	1,565	-	2,038	74	-	2,112	247	-	-	247	-	2,359	Bristol Port Railway and Pier.
														Buckfastleigh, Totnes, and South Devon.
														Buckinghamshire.
														Buckley.
-	-	-	-	-	-	-	-	-	-	§5,921	5,921	4,861	10,782	Burry Port and Gwendreath Valley.
														Calne.
8,465	8,921	56,501	509	74,416	7,032	3,412	84,860	52,320	7,994	33,107	93,421	8,834	187,115	Cambrian.
-	-	-	-	-	-	-	-	-	-	3,908	3,908	-	3,908	Cannock Chase and Wolverhampton.
584	905	7,217	-	8,704	844	295	9,843	‖10,080	524	-	10,554	376	20,773	Carmarthen and Cardigan.
214	263	1,128	-	1,605	138	-	-	1,743	1,131	147	557	1,835	299	3,877	Central Wales and Carmarthen Junction.
7,471	5,364	31,066	1,380	45,671	7,915	10	53,596	‖136,050	6,602	-	142,632	-	-	196,248	Cheshire Lines Committee.
														Chester and Holyhead.
1,965	4,444	5,397	96	11,892	841	230	12,963	12,794	478	23,155	36,427	363	49,758	Cockermouth, Keswick, and Penrith.
														Colchester, Stour Valley, Sudbury, and Halstead.
469	872	1,977	-	3,018	334	15	3,367	3,379	153	1,408	4,940	334	8,681	Coleford, Monmouth, Usk, and Pontypool.
9,480	24,066	30,359	472	64,817	10,967	7,550	83,334	29,679	1,075	18,513	49,267	1,092	133,693	Colne Valley and Halstead.
-	-	-	-	-	-	-	-	-	-	1,594	1,594	-	1,594	Cornwall.
														Corris.
														Corwen and Bala.
108	136	1,224	-	1,468	**	40	1,508	1,388	49	707	2,144	108	3,760	Cowbridge.
1,581	3,471	1,097	43	5,942	1,239	23	7,194	-	-	-	-	65	7,259	Cowes and Newport.
-	-	-	-	-	-	-	-	36	-	-	612	648	-	648	Croesor and Portmadoc.
														Cromford and High Peak.
														Crystal Palace and South London Junction.
														Dare Valley.

§ Including receipts from merchandise. ‖ Including receipts from minerals. ** Included in receipts from general merchandise.

NAME OF COMPANY.	LENGTH OF LINE IN MILES open on 31st December 1873.			PASSENGER TRAFFIC.					GOODS TRAFFIC.		NUMBER OF MILES TRAVELLED BY TRAINS.		
				NUMBER OF PASSENGERS CONVEYED (exclusive of Season and Periodical Tickets).				Holders of Season or Periodical Tickets.					
	Double or more.	Single.	TOTAL.	1st Class.	2d Class.	3d Class (including Parliamentary).	TOTAL.		Minerals.	General Merchandise.	Passenger Trains.	Goods and Mineral Trains.	TOTAL.
Denbigh, Ruthin, and Corwen	..	19	19	,080	9,472	146,868	162,420	-	*Tons.* 18,512	*Tons.* 14,666	Mixed.		65,585
Devon and Somerset	*Worked by the Bristol and Exeter.*												
Dowlais (Including the "Dowlais Extension.")	2	..	2	-	-	-	-	-	109,699	8,296	-	9,786	9,786
East Cornwall Mineral	..	7	7	-	-	-	-	-	25,710	11,963	-	12,787	12,787
East and West Junction*	3	30	33	1,701	8,529	38,840	49,070	-	3,907	15,181	Mixed.		80,719
East Gloucestershire	*Worked by the Great Western.*												
East Lincolnshire	*Leased to the Great Northern.*												
East London	*Worked by the London, Brighton, and South Coast.*												
East Somerset	*Worked by the Great Western.*												
Ely, Haddenham, and Sutton	*Worked by the Great Eastern.*												
Ely Valley	*Worked by the Great Western.*												
Evesham and Redditch	*Worked by the Midland.*												
Exeter and Crediton	*Leased to the London and South-Western.*												
Faringdon	*Worked by the Great Western.*												
Festiniog	..	14	14	4,405	8,562	120,577	128,634	-	124,830	18,845	53,202	53,932	106,134
Festiniog and Blaenau†	..	4	4	886	1,255	35,851	37,992	9,964	2,685	3,510	13,782	-	13,782
Forcett	..	5	5	-	-	-	-	-	158,650				
Forest of Dean Central	*Worked by the Great Western.*												
Furness	65	37	102	78,703	123,459	1,491,090	1,693,252	253	3,517,841	418,273	401,145	533,704	934,849
Garstang and Knot-End	*Line closed since March 1872.*												
Gloucester and Dean Forest	*Leased to the Great Western.*												
Great Eastern (Including the "Colchester, Stour Valley, Sudbury, and Halstead," "Ely, Haddenham, and Sutton," "London and Blackwall," "Lowestoft Harbour and Railway," "Lynn and Hunstanton," "Mellis and Eye," "Northern and Eastern," "Saffron Walden," "Tendring Hundred," "Tendring Hundred Extension," West Norfolk," and the "Wivenhoe and Brightlingsea.")	‡419	417	836	261,763	5,258,404	21,567,164	29,087,391	16,884	1,753,416	2,795,246	4,894,530	3,057,222	8,551,782
Great Marlow (Line opened for traffic on the 26th June 1873.)	..	3	3	4,718	6,255	32,908	43,881	5	3,188	2,322	Mixed.		10,490
Great Northern (Including the "East Lincolnshire," "Hatfield and St. Albans," "Holme and Ramsey," "Horncastle," "Muswell Hill Estate" (from 24th May to 31st July), "Nottingham and Grantham," "Royston and Hitchin," "Spilsby and Firsby," "Stamford and Essendine," "Wainfleet and Firsby," and "Skegness Extension" and part of the "Midland and Eastern," and "Norwich and Spalding.")	‡428	156	584	858,747	2,838,293	9,702,852	13,399,892	12,484	2,625,989	3,344,636	4,651,814	5,628,113	10,279,927
Great North of England, Clarence, and Hartlepool Junction.	*Leased to the North-Eastern.*												
Great Western§ (Including the "Abingdon," "Bala and Dolgelly," "Berks and Hants Extension," "Bourton-on-the-Water," "Bridport," "Bristol and North Somerset" (from 2nd September 1873), "Calne," "Caledor, Monmouth, Usk, and Pontypool," "Corwen and Bala," "East Gloucestershire," "East Somerset," "Ely Valley," "Faringdon," "Forest of Dean Central," "Gloucester and Dean Forest," "Leominster and Kington," "Llanelly Railway and Dock," "Llangollen and Corwen," "Llynvi and Ogmore" (from 1st July 1873), "Marlborough," "Milford," "Much Wenlock and Severn Junction," "Nantwich and Market Drayton," "Ross and Monmouth" (from 4th August 1873), "Stratford-upon-Avon," "Vale of Llangollen," "Wellington and Drayton," "Wellington and Severn Junction," "Wenlock," and "Wenlock Extensions," and "Witney," and the "Birkenhead," "Hammersmith and City," "Ludlow and Clee Hill," "Shrewsbury and Hereford," "Shrewsbury and Wellington," "Shrewsbury and Welshpool," "Tenbury," "Vale of Towy," "Victoria Station and Pimlico," "West London," "Weymouth and Portland," and "Wrexham and Minera Extension," jointly with other Companies.)	867	635	1,502	3,167,394	5,065,416	25,395,341	32,628,151	11,669	10,434,304	3,283,415	8,809,291	10,609,148	19,418,539
Hammersmith and City Junction	*Vested jointly in the Great Western and Metropolitan Railways Companies.*												
Hatfield and St. Albans	*Worked by the Great Northern.*												
Hayling Railways	*Worked by the London, Brighton, and South Coast*												
Hereford, Hay, and Brecon	..	26	26	5,596	11,683	156,388	173,666	1	151,931		64,686	64,688	129,376
Hexham and Allendale	..	12	12	301	890	31,695	32,886	-	6,423	13,473	13,496	8,572	27,067
Holme and Ramsey	*Worked by the Great Northern.*												
Horncastle	*Worked by the Great Northern.*												
Hoylake	..	5	5	7,446	64,499	35,711	107,856	338	-	40	28,953	-	28,593

* This Railway was opened throughout on the 5th August 1873.   † For the year ended 28th February 1874.   ‡ See also Table No. 2 A, p. 64.
§ For the year ended 31st January 1874.

RECEIPTS (GROSS) FROM PASSENGER TRAFFIC.								RECEIPTS (GROSS) FROM GOODS TRAFFIC.				Miscellaneous, Rents, Tolls, Navigation, Steamboats, &c.	Total Receipts from all Sources of Traffic.	NAME OF COMPANY.
Receipts from Passengers.					Excess Luggage, Parcels, Carriages, Horses, Dogs, &c.	Mails.	Total Receipts from Passenger Traffic.	Merchandise.	Live Stock.	Minerals.	Total Receipts from Goods Traffic.			
1st Class.	2d Class.	3d Class (including Parliamentary).	Holders of Season or Periodical Tickets.	Total from Passengers.										
£ 670	£ 615	£ 4,882	£ —	£ 6,167	£ 396	£ 9	£ 6,572	£ 3,121	£ 483	£ 1,550	£ 5,154	£ 221	£ 11,947	Denbigh, Ruthin, and Corwen.
.	.	.	.	.	.	.	.	.	.	.	.	.	.	Devon and Somerset.
.	.	.	.	.	.	.	.	635	.	.	635	.	635‖	Dowlais.
.	.	.	.	.	.	.	.	897	.	1,892	2,789	117	2,906	East Cornwall Mineral.
267	475	1,305	.	2,047	155	.	2,202	672	94	937	1,703	155	4,060	East and West Junction.
.	.	.	.	.	.	.	.	.	.	.	.	.	.	East Gloucestershire.
.	.	.	.	.	.	.	.	.	.	.	.	.	.	East Lincolnshire.
.	.	.	.	.	.	.	.	.	.	.	.	.	.	East London.
.	.	.	.	.	.	.	.	.	.	.	.	.	.	East Somerset.
.	.	.	.	.	.	.	.	.	.	.	.	.	.	Ely, Haddenham, and Sutton.
.	.	.	.	.	.	.	.	.	.	.	.	.	.	Ely Valley.
.	.	.	.	.	.	.	.	.	.	.	.	.	.	Evesham and Redditch.
.	.	.	.	.	.	.	.	.	.	.	.	.	.	Exeter and Crediton.
.	.	.	.	.	.	.	.	.	.	.	.	.	.	Faringdon.
390	244	3,558	.	4,192	.	.	4,192	3,560	.	16,172	19,732	583	24,507	Festiniog.
36	26	599	393	1,058	.	.	1,058	207	.	68	275	12	1,345	Festiniog and Blaenau.
.	.	.	.	.	.	.	.	126	.	5,580	5,706	14	5,720	Forest.
.	.	.	.	.	.	.	.	.	.	.	.	.	.	Forest of Dean Central.
8,700	9,587	58,915	1,467	78,669	8,454	2,060	89,183	95,235	3,079	280,789	379,103	4,356	472,582	Furness.
.	.	.	.	.	.	.	.	.	.	.	.	.	.	Garstang and Knot-End.
.	.	.	.	.	.	.	.	.	.	.	.	.	.	Gloucester and Dean Forest.
296,816	155,495	631,026	54,814	1,071,349	87,178	26,044	1,184,271	842,813	107,900	267,240	1,217,953	199,689	2,602,213	Great Eastern.
156	135	416	4	711	38	.	749	279	7	180	466	.	1,215	Great Marlow.
225,295	230,369	518,962	46,204	1,010,740	134,056	13,947	1,158,743	974,208	58,049	552,250	1,584,507	60,627	2,803,877	Great Northern.
.	.	.	.	.	.	.	.	.	.	.	.	.	.	Great North of England, Clarence, and Hartlepool Junction.
425,234	476,294	1,124,637	43,385	2,069,198	239,723	55,826	2,364,747	1,429,157	78,597	1,496,426	3,004,180	82,868	5,451,875	Great Western.
.	.	.	.	.	.	.	.	.	.	.	.	.	.	Hammersmith and City Junction.
.	.	.	.	.	.	.	.	.	.	.	.	.	.	Hatfield and St. Albans.
.	.	.	.	.	.	.	.	.	.	.	.	.	.	Hayling Railways.
841	1,157	6,388	20	8,406	814	.	9,220	¶ 14,709	788	.	15,497	199	24,916	Hereford, Hay, and Brecon.
41	67	1,232	.	1,390	84	50	1,524	1,732	84	470	2,286	23	3,833	Hexham and Allendale.
.	.	.	.	.	.	.	.	.	.	.	.	.	.	Holme and Ramsey.
.	.	.	.	.	.	.	.	.	.	.	.	.	.	Horncastle.
412	2,432	1,092	339	4,275	43	.	4,318	12	.	.	12	.	4,330	Hoylake.

‖ All traffic except that of General Merchandise is carried on by the Dowlais Iron Company as part of their works.
¶ Including receipts from minerals.

NAME OF COMPANY.	LENGTH OF LINE IN MILES open on 31st December 1873.			PASSENGER TRAFFIC.					GOODS TRAFFIC.		NUMBER OF MILES TRAVELLED BY TRAINS.		
	Double or more.	Single.	TOTAL.	NUMBER OF PASSENGERS CONVEYED (exclusive of Season and Periodical Tickets).				Holders of Season or Periodical Tickets.	Minerals.	General Merchandise.	Passenger Trains.	Goods and Mineral Trains.	TOTAL.
				1st Class.	2d Class.	3d Class (including Parliamentary).	TOTAL.						
Isle of Wight · · · · ·	· ·	12	12	86,124	306,825	47,347	440,196	195	*Tons.* 15,182	*Tons.* 18,401	98,818	23,943	121,261
Keighley and Worth Valley · · · ·	*Worked by the Midland.*												
Kendal and Windermere · · · ·	*Leased to the London and North-Western.*												
Kettering, Thrapstone, and Huntingdon · ·	*Worked by the Midland.*												
King's Lynn Dock* · · · · ·	· ·	· ·	· ·	· ·	· ·	· ·	· ·	· ·	· ·	· ·	· ·	· ·	· ·
Lancashire and Yorkshire · · · · (Including part of the "Preston and Wyre" and "Preston and Longridge" Joint Lines).	388	45	433	2,290,025	2,410,282	27,288,405	31,988,712	12,050	6,958,007	4,187,589	5,464,643	5,156,998	10,621,641
Lancashire Union · · · ·	*Worked by the London and North-Western.*												
Lancaster and Carlisle · · · ·	*Leased to the London and North-Western.*												
Launceston and South Devon · · ·	*Worked by the South Devon.*												
Leominster and Kington · · · ·	*Worked by the Great Western.*												
Liskeard and Caradon · · · · (Including the Liskeard and Looe Union Railway and Canal.)	· ·	17	17	· ·	· ·	· ·	· ·	· ·	47,467	3,738	· ·	16,775	16,775
Liskeard and Looe Union Railway and Canal ·	*Worked by the Liskeard and Caradon.*												
Llanelly Railway and Dock · · · ·	*Worked by the Great Western.*												
Llangollen and Corwen · · · ·	*Leased to the Great Western.*												
Llantrissant and Taff Vale Junction · ·	*Leased to the Taff Vale.*												
Llynvi and Ormore · · · · (For six months ended 30th June, from which date the line was worked by the "Great Western" Railway Company.)	· ·	30½	30½	840	3,348	105,465	109,673	· ·	370,223	45,513	Mixed.		74,037
London and Blackwall · · · ·	*Leased to the Great Eastern.*												
London and Greenwich · · · ·	*Leased to the South-Eastern.*												
London and North-Western · · · (Including the "Buckinghamshire," "Chester and Holyhead and Branches," "Cromford and High Peak," "Kendal and Windermere," "Lancashire Union," "Lancaster and Carlisle," "Mold and Denbigh Junction," "North Union," "Shropshire Union," "Watford and Rickmansworth," and "Wolverhampton and Walsall," and half of the "Ashby and Nuneaton," from 1st September 1872, "Birkenhead and Branches," "Ludlow and Clee Hill," "Preston and Longridge," "Shrewsbury and Hereford," "Shrewsbury and Wellington," "Shrewsbury and Welshpool," "Tenbury," and "Vale of Towy," and part of the "Preston and Wyre," "West London," and "West London Extension.")	1,246½	348	1,594	6,055,223	5,444,807	33,464,929	41,964,759	8,839	24,453,743		14,361,772	15,880,103	30,241,875
London and South-Western · · · (Including the "Bishop's Waltham," "Exeter and Crediton," "Lymington," "Mid-Hants," "Ringwood, Christchurch, and Bournemouth," "Salisbury and Dorset," "Salisbury and Yeovil," "Salisbury Railway and Market House," "Seaton and Beer," "Staines, Wokingham, and Woking," "Stokes Bay Railway and Pier," and half of the "Weymouth and Portland," and part of the "West London Extension.")	418½	230	648	2,874,459	4,713,140	10,424,713	18,012,318	$6,869	939,199	1,097,368	5,273,682	2,015,992	7,289,674
London, Brighton, and South Coast · · (Including the "East London" and "Hayling Railway," and part of the "Victoria Station and Pimlico" and "West London Extension.")	254½	91	345	2,209,968	2,890,874	18,170,190	23,280,032	10,070	967,377	656,791	4,374,154	935,724	5,309,878
London, Chatham, and Dover · · · (Including the "Crystal Palace and South London Junction," "Mid-Kent (Bromley to St. Mary's Cray)," "Sevenoaks, Maidstone, and Tunbridge," and part of the "Victoria Station and Pimlico.")	132½	9	141	1,760,795	2,246,813	14,384,250	18,391,858	21,099	880,695	418,844	2,322,098	390,596	2,712,694
Londonderry (Seaham to Sunderland) · · (Private Property.)	6	1	7	14,294	23,696	289,207	327,197	25	539,120	41,690	33,288	159,883	193,171
London, Tilbury, and Southend · · ·	3	41	44	295,203	1,125,080	623,789	2,043,972	599	40,692	35,146	248,080	62,900	310,980
Lostwithiel and Fowey · · · ·	· ·	4	4	· ·	· ·	· ·	· ·	· ·	29,055	· ·	No account kept.		
Lowestoft · · · · ·	*Leased to the Great Eastern.*												
Ludlow and Clee Hill · · · ·	*Worked by the London and North-Western and Great Western jointly.*												
Lymington · · · · ·	*Worked by the London and South-Western.*												
Lynn and Hunstanton · · · ·	*Worked by the Great Eastern.*												
Macclesfield Committee · · · ·	11	· ·	11	5,575	9,815	225,536	240,826	30	91,543	79,876	43,735	57,125	100,860
Manchester and Milford · · · ·	· ·	42	42	2,411	5,534	124,700	132,645	· ·	24,739	16,534	Mixed.		127,212
Manchester, Sheffield, and Lincolnshire · · (Including the South Yorkshire and River Dun.)	220	38	258½	359,653	598,991	8,951,070	9,909,714	2,644	5,980,339	3,858,706	1,732,050	3,173,235	4,905,285
Manchester, South Junction, and Altrincham	9	· ·	9	471,062	247,280	1,921,486	2,639,727	1,647	781,965	417,309	143,811	11,663	155,474

* The short tramway belonging to the Company is only used for the transit of goods to and from the Great Eastern Railway. No returns can be given.
† On the 30th June.   ‡ See also Table No. 2A, p. 64.   § Including 268 workmen's tickets.

RECEIPTS (GROSS) FROM PASSENGER TRAFFIC.								RECEIPTS (GROSS) FROM GOODS TRAFFIC.				Miscellaneous, Rents, Tolls, Navigation, Steamboats, &c.	TOTAL RECEIPTS FROM ALL SOURCES OF TRAFFIC.	NAME OF COMPANY.
1st Class	2d Class	3d Class (Including Parliamentary).	Holders of Season or Periodical Tickets.	TOTAL from Passengers.	Excess Luggage, Parcels, Carriages, Horses, Dogs, &c.	Mails.	TOTAL Receipts from Passenger Traffic.	Merchandise.	Live Stock.	Minerals.	TOTAL Receipts from Goods Traffic.			
£ 5,475	£ 12,918	£ 1,679	£ 205	£ 20,277	£ 827	£ 47	£ 21,151	£ 1,736	£ -	£ 1,210	£ 2,946	£ 745	£ 24,842	Isle of Wight.
														Keighley and Worth Valley.
														Kendal and Windermere.
														Kettering, Thrapstone, and Huntingdon.
														King's Lynn Dock.
165,107	107,537	783,398	71,247	1,127,289	95,308	6,908	1,229,505	1,404,928	42,118	545,004	1,992,050	107,741	3,329,296	Lancashire and Yorkshire.
														Lancashire Union.
														Lancaster and Carlisle.
														Launceston and South Devon.
														Leominster and Kington.
								653	-	10,348	11,001	-	11,001	Liskeard and Caradon.
														Liskeard and Looe Union Railway and Canal.
														Llanelly Railway and Dock.
														Llangollen and Corwen.
														Llantrissant and Taff Vale Junction.
55	141	2,464	-	2,660	-	-	2,660	5,562	-	18,373	23,935	1,761	28,356	Llynvi and Ogmore.
														London and Blackwall.
														London and Greenwich.
754,547	558,981	1,668,951	82,274	3,064,753	397,153	145,684	3,607,590	3,067,297	210,800	1,766,377	5,044,574	115,555	8,767,719	London and North-Western.
325,273	351,889	465,189	91,285	1,233,636	114,184	23,067	1,372,902 ¶	507,682	30,963	138,474	677,109	145,859	2,195,170	London and South-Western.
[283,841]	247,427	450,471	109,190	1,090,929	69,612	3,900	1,164,441	259,981	9,526	120,529	390,036	63,984	1,618,461	London, Brighton, and South Coast.
149,780	84,574	232,026	46,328	562,708	30,535	394	593,637	92,544	4,293	83,502	180,339	130,533	904,509	London, Chatham, and Dover.
465	546	5,239	133	6,383	246	70	6,699	3,181	-	17,327	20,458	5,763	32,920	Londonderry (Seaham to Sunderland).
12,484	31,599	7,137	2,468	53,688	2,393	188	56,269	10,040	3,948	2,586	21,576	715	78,560	London, Tilbury, and Southend.
-	-	-	-	-	-	-	-			1,287	1,287	-	1,287	Lostwithiel and Fowey.
														Lowestoft.
														Ludlow and Clee Hill.
														Lymington.
														Lynn and Hunstanton.
178	175	3,825	44	4,222	414	-	4,636	3,217	43	2,936	6,196	54	10,886	Macclesfield Committee.
485	1,045	6,488	-	7,963	688	250	8,906	4,577	497	2,835	7,909	301	17,116	Manchester and Milford.
40,213	40,196	259,443	10,913	350,765	58,350	2,702	411,817	680,360	16,466	315,888	1,012,714	224,587	1,648,618	Manchester, Sheffield, and Lincolnshire.
13,678	5,856	33,647	17,233	70,412	4,320	60	74,792	12,054	627	12,527	25,208	2,831	102,831	Manchester, South Junction, and Altrincham.

‖ In addition to the 258 miles above given, the Manchester, Sheffield, and Lincolnshire Company are half owners of 88 miles, and one-third owners of 104½ miles, the returns for which lines are given separately.

¶ Including 3,325*l.* from excess fares, &c. not classified.

NAME OF COMPANY.	LENGTH OF LINE IN MILES open on 31st December 1873.			PASSENGER TRAFFIC.				Holders of Season or Periodical Tickets.	GOODS TRAFFIC.		NUMBER OF MILES TRAVELLED BY TRAINS.		
				NUMBER OF PASSENGERS CONVEYED (exclusive of Season and Periodical Tickets).									
	Double or more.	Single.	TOTAL.	1st Class.	2d Class.	3d Class (including Parliamentary).	TOTAL.		Minerals.	General Merchandise.	Passenger Trains.	Goods and Mineral Trains.	TOTAL.
									Tons.	*Tons.*			
Marlborough - - - -	*Worked by the Great Western.*												
Maryport and Carlisle - - -	28	11	39	16,583	27,385	399,144	443,062	149	954,350	175,145	108,674	291,213	399,887
Mawddwy - - - -	- -	7	7	632	679	29,805	30,616	4	3,583	2,499	16,873	- -	16,873
Mellis and Eye - - -	*Worked by the Great Eastern.*												
Merrybent and Darlington - -	- -	6	6	- -	- -	- -	- -	- -	93,926	- -	- -	3,756	3,756
Methley Joint Railway - - -	6	-	6	3,284	7,541	267,316	278,141	28	156,463	92,710	- -	- -	- -
Metropolitan	11	2	13	3,505,238	7,296,967	28,814,822	39,617,047	27,516	863,677	197,709	837,217	- -	837,217
(Including the "Metropolitan and St. John's Wood," and half the "Hammersmith and City.")													
Metropolitan and St. John's Wood - -	*Worked by the Metropolitan.*												
Metropolitan District - - -	7	- -	7	2,237,158	3,227,688	14,094,502	19,559,318	6,213	- -	- -	696,426	- -	696,426
Mid-Hants - - - -	*Worked by the London and South-Western.*												
Mid-Kent (Bromley to St. Mary's Cray) -	*Leased to the London, Chatham, and Dover.*												
Midland	791*	265	1,056	1,173,187	2,566,042	19,258,174	22,997,403	15,743	10,044,735	7,862,656	6,819,474	12,765,386	19,584,860
(Including the "Barnoldswick," "Bedford and North- ampton," "Evesham and Redditch," "Keighley and Worth Valley," "Kettering, Thrapstone, and Hunt- ington," "Manchester, Buxton, Matlock, and Midland Junction," "Midland and South-Western Junction," "North-Western," "Peterborough, Wis- beach, and Sutton," "Redditch," "Stonehouse and Nailsworth," "Tewkesbury and Malvern," the "Furness and Midland," Joint Line, and half the "Ashby and Nuneaton" (from 1st September), "Great Western and Midland," from Malvern Wells to Malvern Link, "Manchester, Sheffield and Lincolnshire, and Midland," "Midland and Eastern," "Norwich and Spalding," and "Otley and Ilkley" Joint Lines.)													
Midland and Eastern - - -	*Worked by the Midland and Great Northern.*												
Midland and South-Western Junction -	*Worked by the Midland.*												
Mid-Wales - - - -	- -	48	48	8,330	18,757	261,107	288,194	20	118,996	81,190	135,563	95,078	230,641
Milford - - - -	*Worked by the Great Western.*												
Mold and Denbigh Junction - -	*Worked by the London and North-Western.*												
Monmouthshire Railway and Canal -	33	21	54	20,576	126,486	1,395,237	1,542,299	113	2,636,346	317,392	129,863	869,228	999,091
Much Wenlock and Severn Junction -	*Worked by the Great Western.*												
Nantwich and Market Drayton - -	*Worked by the Great Western.*												
Neath and Brecon - - -	- -	40	40	3,059	6,674	133,227	141,960	6	109,637	14,380	Mixed.		164,610
Newport Pagnell - - -	- -	4	4	3,030	5,350	72,650	81,030	† 6,754	7,496	8,064	19,968	2,496	22,464
Newquay and Cornwall Junction -	- -	3	3	- -	- -	- -	- -	- -	75,684	- -	No account kept.		
Northampton and Banbury Junction -	- -	15	15	2,259	9,205	51,191	62,715	- -	51,081	10,420	60,348	14,482	74,830
North and South Western Junction -	4	1	5	9,632	87,250	839	97,721	8	- -	- -	- -	- -	- -
North-Eastern	872	467	1,339	1,242,751	1,800,178	21,941,448	25,074,377	10,357	22,389,419	7,505,390	6,959,339	12,894,200	19,853,539
(Including the "Great North of England, Clarence, and Hartlepool," the "Tees Valley," and part of the "Otley and Ilkley" Joint Lines.)													
Northern and Eastern - - -	*Leased to the Great Eastern.*												
North London - - -	12*	- -	12	2,156,975	6,775,663	10,346,969	19,279,507	49,340	649,016	1,063,954	1,259,159	279,083	1,538,242
North Staffordshire - - -	138	45	183	133,620	253,193	3,428,487	3,815,300	523	2,240,216	706,506	751,384	849,119	1,600,503
North Union - - -	*Leased to the London and North-Western.*												
North-Western - - -	*Worked by the Midland.*												
Norwich and Spalding - - -	*Worked by the Midland and Great Northern.*												
Nottingham and Grantham Railway and Canal -	*Leased to the Great Northern.*												
Oldham, Ashton-under-Lyne, and Guide Bridge Junction.	6	—	6	28,520	47,755	676,753	753,028	118	60,751	71,021	85,106	29,756	114,862
Pembroke and Tenby - - -	- -	29	29	10,527	29,747	194,079	234,353	53	41,312	14,660	70,015	38,025	108,040
Penarth Harbour, Dock, and Railway -	*Leased to the Taff Vale.*												
Peterborough, Wisbeach, and Sutton -	*Worked by the Midland.*												
Potteries, Shrewsbury, and North Wales -	- -	28	28	2,341	3,226	67,728	73,295	1	95,977	4,742	43,434	33,099	76,533
Preston and Wyre - - -	*Leased to the Lancashire and Yorkshire, and London and North-Western.*												

* See also Table No. 2A, p. 64.   † Including 6,749 workmen's weekly tickets.

RECEIPTS (GROSS) FROM PASSENGER TRAFFIC.								RECEIPTS (GROSS) FROM GOODS TRAFFIC.				Miscellaneous, Rents, Tolls, Navigation, Steamboats, &c.	Total Receipts from all Sources of Traffic.	NAME OF COMPANY.
Receipts from Passengers.					Excess Luggage, Parcels, Carriages, Horses, Dogs, &c.	Mails.	Total Receipts from Passenger Traffic.	Merchandise.	Live Stock.	Minerals.	Total Receipts from Goods Traffic.			
1st Class.	2d Class.	3d Class (including Parliamentary).	Holders of Season or Periodical Tickets.	Total from Passengers.										
£	£	£	£	£	£	£	£	£	£	£	£	£	£	
														Marlborough.
2,486	2,420	18,141	440	23,489	2,040	968	26,497	24,283	1,182	86,207	111,672	2,237	140,396	Maryport and Carlisle.
34	24	533	12	603	60	. .	663	330	3	373	706	33	1,402	Mawddwy.
														Mellis and Eye.
								105	. .	. .	2,200	2,305	. .	2,305	Merrybent and Darlington.
53	95	1,872	24	2,044	55	. .	2,099	1,770	. .	2,546	4,316	158	6,273	Methley Joint Railway.
75,600	93,140	238,689	21,106	428,485	762	. .	429,247	6,768	212	11,191	18,166	30,922	478,335	Metropolitan. .
														Metropolitan and St. John's Wood.
38,396	37,951	117,556	11,682	206,087	. .	. .	206,087	. .	. .	. .	. .	9,247	215,334	Metropolitan District.
														Mid-Hants.
														Mid-Kent (Bromley to St. Mary's Cray).
210,983	189,486	983,356	46,738	1,430,512	180,786	48,050	1,659,348	2,480,790	75,257	1,466,608	4,004,745	76,245	5,740,338	Midland.
														Midland and Eastern.
														Midland and South-Western Junction.
1,054	1,149	10,520	77	12,800	806	768	14,374	9,754	361	12,230	22,345	236	37,455	Mid-Wales.
														Milford.
														Mold and Denbigh Junction.
1,268	3,948	27,897	518	33,621	1,937	168	35,726	66,035	397	84,441	150,973	3,360	190,459	Monmouthshire Railway and Canal.
														Much Wenlock and Severn Junction.
														Nantwich and Market Drayton.
452	552	4,564	26	5,594	363	300	6,257	3,483	295	7,909	11,777	21	18,055	Neath and Brecon.
126	142	962	‡ 438	1,668	392	13	2,073	1,208	143	368	1,709	80	3,862	Newport Pagnell.
. .	. .	. .	. .	. .	. .	. .	. .	. .	. .	2,463	2,463	. .	2,463	Newquay and Cornwall Junction.
339	712	1,942	. .	2,993	352	20	3,355	2,423	307	1,977	4,706	77	8,138	Northampton and Banbury Junction.
93	561	4	4	663	11	. .	673	. .	. .	. .	. .	. .	673§	North and South-Western Junction.
221,819	174,364	953,447	40,659	1,400,189	180,518	44,677	1,625,384	1,994,755	90,360	2,213,809	4,299,484	116,535	6,041,333	North-Eastern.
														Northern and Eastern.
36,095	66,478	109,289	24,347	236,209	798	. .	237,007	89,489	7,363	33,349	130,401	. .	367,408	North London.
13,387	16,372	103,088	2,899	135,836	11,228	1,500	148,564	145,002	5,726	200,141	346,869	124,026	619,459	North Staffordshire.
														North Union.
														North-Western.
														Norwich and Spalding.
														Nottingham and Grantham Railway and Canal.
766	815	9,854	244	11,679	243	20	11,942	4,905	28	2,067	7,000	151	19,093	Oldham, Ashton-under-Lyne, and Guide Bridge Junction.
1,396	2,833	6,667	92	10,392	1,089	322	11,803	4,970	324	5,756	11,050	543	23,396	Pembroke and Tenby.
														Penarth Harbour Dock, and Railway.
														Peterborough, Wisbeach, and Sutton.
183	160	1,834	8	2,185	90	. .	2,275	580	75	6,404	7,449	684	10,408	Potteries, Shrewsbury, and North Wales.
														Preston and Wyre.

‡ Including 415l. received for workmen's tickets. § Receipts from local traffic only. The line is also used by the leasing companies.

H 3

NAME OF COMPANY.	LENGTH OF LINE IN MILES open on 31st December 1873.			PASSENGER TRAFFIC.					GOODS TRAFFIC.		NUMBER OF MILES TRAVELLED BY TRAINS.		
				NUMBER OF PASSENGERS CONVEYED (exclusive of Season and Periodical Tickets).									
	Double or more.	Single.	TOTAL.	1st Class.	2d Class.	3d Class (including Parliamentary).	TOTAL.	Holders of Season or Periodical Tickets.	Minerals.	General Merchandise.	Passenger Trains.	Goods and Mineral Trains.	TOTAL.
									Tons.	Tons.			
Redditch	*Worked by the Midland.*												
Redruth and Chasewater	- -	10	10	-	-	-	-	-	43,971	3,396	-	14,280	14,280
Rhymney	11	25	36	7,543	25,272	448,389	480,804	14	1,684,383	163,333	81,463	671,608	753,071
Ringwood, Christchurch, and Bournemouth	*Worked by the London and South-Western.*												
Ross and Monmouth	*Worked by the Great Western.*												
Royston and Hitchin	*Leased to the Great Northern.*												
Ryde Pier	1	1	2	71,998	174,458	-	246,456	-	-	-	20,086	-	20,086
Saffron Walden	*Worked by the Great Eastern.*												
Salisbury and Dorset Junction	*Worked by the London and South-Western.*												
Salisbury and Yeovil	*Leased to the London and South-Western.*												
Salisbury Railway and Market House	*Worked by the London and South-Western.*												
Saundersfoot Railway and Harbour	- -	7	7	-	-	-	-	-	49,174	-	-	-	-
Seaton and Beer	*Worked by the London and South-Western.*												
Sevenoaks, Maidstone, and Tonbridge	*Worked by the London, Chatham, and Dover.*												
Severn and Wye Railway and Canal *	25	9	34	-	-	-	-	-	428,544	130,233	No account kept.		
Sheffield and Midland Committee	12	-	12	70,401	84,062	1,523,168	1,677,631	517	687,138	598,395	76,559	17,874	94,433
Shrewsbury and Hereford	*Leased to the Great Western and London and North-Western.*												
Shropshire Union Railways and Canal	*Leased to the London and North-Western.*												
Sirhowy	- -	16	16	2,453	14,455	253,878	270,786	4	716,789	111,331	66,169	112,847	179,016
Somerset and Dorset	66	-	66	23,709	192,819	116,017	332,545	41	106,559	97,261	Mixed.		414,429
South Devon (Including the "Buckfastleigh, Totnes, and South Devon," and "Launceston and South Devon.")	87	35	122	142,453	553,699	1,461,985	2,158,117	650	163,890	318,586	616,060	217,822	833,872
South-Eastern (Including the "London and Greenwich.")	315†	13	338	2,166,680	3,144,290	16,538,591	21,849,561	21,127	438,230	758,486	3,552,765	823,894	4,376,659
South Wales Mineral	- -	13	13	-	-	-	-	-	170,966	4,792	No account kept.		
South Yorkshire and River Dun	*Leased to the Manchester, Sheffield, and Lincolnshire.*												
Spilsby and Firsby	*Worked by the Great Northern.*												
Stafford and Uttoxeter	- -	13	13	4,285	6,970	52,393	63,648	4	-	2,051	46,500	-	46,500
Staines, Wokingham, and Woking	*Leased to the London and South-Western.*												
Stamford and Essendine	*Worked by the Great Northern.*												
Stokes Bay Railway and Pier	*Worked by the London and South-Western.*												
Stonehouse and Nailsworth	*Worked by the Midland.*												
Stratford-upon-Avon	*Worked by the Great Western.*												
Swansea and Carmarthen (From 1st January to 31st July 1873; after which time the Swansea Section, 16 miles in length, was sold to the "London and North-Western" Railway Company, and the name of the Company, changed to "Central Wales and Carmarthen Junction," which see.)	- -	37‡	37‡	4,799	10,670	123,134	138,603	8	187,369	47,603	-	-	-
Swansea Vale	- -	21	21	3,338	14,501	318,647	336,466	53	317,945	105,603	42,652	86,234	128,886
Taff Vale (Including the "Aberdare," "Dare Valley," "Llantrissant and Taff Vale Junction," and "Penarth Harbour, Dock, and Railway.")	54†	20	74	23,400	68,188	1,359,377	1,449,974	778	4,547,509	299,585	155,601	961,206	1,116,807
Talyllyn *	- -	7	7	86	284	17,470	17,840	-	6,628	-	Mixed.		10,519
Tees Valley	*Worked by the North-Eastern.*												
Tenbury	*Worked by the London and North-Western and Great Western.*												
Tendring Hundred } *Tendring Hundred Extension*	*Worked by the Great Eastern.*												
Tewkesbury and Malvern	*Worked by the Midland.*												
Thetford and Watton	- -	9	9	1,526	2,172	16,783	20,481	-	5,175	7,260	Mixed.		24,480
Torbay and Brixham	- -	2	2	1,666	23,120	50,162	73,948	1	4,006	1,335	Mixed.		11,300
Tottenham and Hampstead Junction	5	-	5	80,184	167,048	456,024	703,256	151	136,473	180,032	-	-	-
Trent, Ancholme, and Grimsby	13	-	13	4,011	4,612	103,097	111,720	25	692,987	48,104	24,836	101,446	126,282
Vale of Llangollen	*Leased to the Great Western.*												
Vale of Towy	*Leased to the Llanelly and London and North-Western.*												
Victoria Station and Pimlico	*Used by the London, Chatham, and Dover, Great Western, London and North-Western, and London, Brighton, and South Coast.*												

* For the year ended 30th September 1873. † *See also* Table No. 2A, p. 64. ‡ On 31st July 1873.

RECEIPTS (GROSS) FROM PASSENGER TRAFFIC.								RECEIPTS (GROSS) FROM GOODS TRAFFIC.						NAME OF COMPANY.
RECEIPTS FROM PASSENGERS.					Excess Luggage, Parcels, Carriages, Horses, Dogs, &c.	Mails.	Total Receipts from Passenger Traffic.	Merchandise.	Live Stock.	Minerals.	Total Receipts from Goods Traffic.	Miscellaneous, Rents, Tolls, Navigation, Steamboats, &c.	Total Receipts from all Sources of Traffic.	
1st Class.	2d Class.	3d Class (including Parliamentary).	Holders of Season or Periodical Tickets.	Total from Passengers.										
£	£	£	£	£	£	£	£	£	£	£	£	£	£	
														Redditch.
								312			4,586	4,698	415	5,113	*Redruth and Chasewater.*
687	1,612	9,986	80	12,065	954	68	13,063	20,567	64	73,437	94,068	1,721	108,851	*Rhymney.*
														Bingwood, Christchurch, and Bournemouth.
														Ross and Monmouth.
														Royston and Hitchin.
1,642	3,405			5,047	2,817	33	7,897	411			411	7,498	15,806	*Ryde Pier.*
														Saffron Walden.
														Salisbury and Dorset Junction.
														Salisbury and Yeovil.
														Salisbury Railway and Market House.
										546	546		546	*Saundersfoot Railway and Harbour.*
														Seaton and Beer.
														Sevenoaks, Maidstone, and Tunbridge.
								6,455		19,502	25,957	2,249	28,206	*Severn and Wye Railway and Canal.*
2,322	2,229	20,077	866	25,496	1,842	50	27,388	12,053	879	8,476	21,408	886	49,682	*Sheffield and Midland Committee.*
														Shrewsbury and Hereford.
														Shropshire Union Railways and Canal.
133	656	4,326	26	5,143	268	16	5,427	3,416	49	21,679	25,144	141	30,712	*Sirhowy.*
3,098	10,606	5,613	186	19,503	1,678	90	21,271	20,025	1,238	13,108	34,371	6,045	61,687	Somerset and Dorset.
30,167	55,037	90,096	2,939	178,241	21,786	10,365	210,392	70,180	1,925	18,473	90,578	3,450	304,420	South Devon.
325,766	226,479	495,976	112,016	1,163,237	86,308	28,279	1,277,824	317,870	11,614	63,233	392,717	148,821	1,819,362	South-Eastern.
								654			8,148	8,802		8,802	South Wales Mineral.
														South Yorkshire and River Dun.
														Spilsby and Firsby.
467	526	1,776	6	2,745	42		2,787	279	94		373		3,160	Stafford and Uttoxeter.
														Staines, Wokingham, and Woking.
														Stamford and Essendine.
														Stokes Bay Railway and Pier.
														Stonehouse and Nailsworth.
														Stratford-upon-Avon.
460	632	4,387	45	5,514	261		5,775	6,400	94	7,345	13,839	25	19,639	Swansea and Carmarthen.
232	572	6,514	138	7,456	293		7,749	10,228		29,978	40,206	146	48,101	Swansea Vale.
2,609	4,858	53,744	1,444	63,655	2,668	1,400	66,733	52,729	261	323,610	376,600	66,518	509,841	Taff Vale.
4	13	352		369	112	10	491				1,070	1,070	118	1,679	Talyllyn.
														Tees Valley.
														Tenbury.
														{ *Tendring Hundred.* / *Tendring Hundred Extension.*
														Tewkesbury and Malvern.
155	156	685		996	214		1,150	1,113	96	346	1,555	35	2,740	Thetford and Watton.
36	351	591	7	985	263	20	1,268	282½			282	18	1,568	Torbay and Brixham.
2,651	3,171	2,811	194	8,827	7		8,834	3,856		1,215	5,071	121	14,026	Tottenham & Hampstead Junction.
326	271	2,063	59	2,738	215		2,953	2,663	279	22,563	25,505	6	28,464	Trent, Ancholme, and Grimsby.
														Vale of Llangollen.
														Vale of Towy.
														Victoria Station and Pimlico.

§ Including receipts from minerals.

H 4

NAME OF COMPANY.	LENGTH OF LINE IN MILES open on 31st December 1873.			PASSENGER TRAFFIC.					GOODS TRAFFIC.		NUMBER OF MILES TRAVELLED BY TRAINS.		
	Double or more.	Single.	TOTAL.	NUMBER OF PASSENGERS CONVEYED (exclusive of Season and Periodical Tickets).				Holders of Season or Periodical Tickets.	Minerals.	General Merchandise.	Passenger Trains.	Goods and Mineral Trains.	TOTAL.
				1st Class.	2d Class.	3d Class (including Parliamentary).	TOTAL.						
									Tons.	Tons.			
Wainfleet and Firsby - - - -	Worked by the Great Northern.												
Watford and Rickmansworth - -	Worked by the London and North-Western.												
Watlington and Princes Risborough -	- -	8	8	1,304	2,538	14,995	18,837	-	4,188	4,185	Mixed.		18,866
Wellington and Drayton - - -	Worked by the Great Western.												
Wellington and Severn Junction - -	Leased to the Great Western.												
Wenlock - - - - -	Worked by the Great Western.												
West Cornwall Committee - -	- -	33	33	16,591	118,871	289,587	425,049	73	129,149	74,260	92,737	74,645	167,402
West London - - - -	Leased to the Great Western and London and North-Western.												
West London Extension - -	Line worked by the London and North-Western, Great Western, London and South-Western, and London, Brighton,												
West Norfolk Junction - -	Worked by the Great Eastern.												
West Riding and Grimsby - -	26	- -	26	42,610	136,295	303,337	482,242	91	74,029	541,139	160,030	199,829	359,859
West Somerset - - -	Leased to the Bristol and Exeter.												
West Somerset Mineral - -	- -	12	12	403	11,919	7,532	19,854	- -	35,294	5,682	15,400	25,400	40,800
Weymouth and Portland - -	Worked by the Great Western and London and South-Western.												
Whitehaven, Cleator, and Egremont (Including the Cleator and Furness Joint Line.)	5	22	27	10,961	10,761	289,976	311,698	234	1,564,951	25,637	75,504	183,486	258,990
Witney - - - - -	Worked by the Great Western.												
Wivenhoe and Brightlingsea - -	Worked by the Great Eastern.												
Wolverhampton and Walsall - -	Worked by the London and North-Western.												
Wrexham, Mold, and Connah's Quay (Including the Buckley.)	- -	16	16	3,174	11,013	170,929	185,116	- -	247,803	33,700	29,596	48,125	77,721
TOTAL ENGLAND AND WALES -	7,138	4,231	11,369	32,474,219	62,866,761	306,124,106	401,465,086	257,470	93,227,065	44,987,591 and 24,605,674 tons not classified.	75,724,510	83,592,176	*162,561,304

* Including 1,244,618 miles travelled by mixed trains.

TABLE No. 2A.

The following Companies have, in addition, given the Number of Miles of Single, Double, Treble, and Quadruple or more Lines of Rails belonging to or worked by them.

NAME OF COMPANY.	LENGTH OF LINE IN MILES OPEN ON 31ST DECEMBER 1873.				
	Single Lines.	Double Lines.	Three Lines.	Four Lines or more.	TOTAL.
GREAT EASTERN - - - - -	417	416	3	- — -	836
GREAT NORTHERN - - - -	156	411	12	5	584
LONDON AND NORTH-WESTERN - -	348	1,177	58	11	1,594
LONDON AND SOUTH-WESTERN - -	230	411	2	5	648
LONDON, BRIGHTON, AND SOUTH COAST -	91	236	8	10	345
LONDON, CHATHAM, AND DOVER -	9	126	2	4	141
MIDLAND - - - - -	265	761	11	19	1,056
NORTH LONDON - - - -	—	7	1	4	12
SOUTH-EASTERN - - - -	13	309	3	3	328
TAFF VALE - - - - -	20	43	11	—	74

														NAME OF COMPANY.
RECEIPTS (GROSS) FROM PASSENGER TRAFFIC.								**RECEIPTS (GROSS) FROM GOODS TRAFFIC.**						
RECEIPTS FROM PASSENGERS.					Excess Luggage, Parcels, Carriages, Horses, Dogs, &c.	Mails.	Total Receipts from Passenger Traffic.	Merchandise.	Live Stock.	Minerals.	Total Receipts from Goods Traffic.	Miscellaneous, Rents, Tolls, Navigation, Steamboats, &c.	Total Receipts from all Sources of Traffic.	
1st Class.	2d Class.	3d Class (including Parliamentary).	Holders of Season or Periodical Tickets.	Total from Passengers.										
£	£	£	£	£	£	£	£	£	£	£	£	£	£	
														Wainfleet and Firsby.
														Watford and Rickmansworth.
114	140	478	-	732	129	-	861	980†	-	-	-	980	-	1,841	Watlington and Princes Risborough.
														Wellington and Drayton.
														Wellington and Severn Junction.
														Wenlock.
2,303	7,383	10,712	263	20,661	4,124	1,750	26,535	12,705	229	10,338	23,222	359	50,176	West Cornwall Committee.
														West London.
and South Coast Railway Companies.														*West London Extension.*
														West Norfolk Junction.
3,901	8,836	20,263	498	28,463	2,666	187	31,336	42,698	3,369	3,367	49,434	53	80,823	West Riding and Grimsby.
														West Somerset.
9	229	99	-	337	29	-	366	716	-	5,232	5,946	-	6,314	West Somerset Mineral.
														Weymouth and Portland.
401	291	5,402	485	6,579	249	54	6,882	3,189	87	68,900	72,176	1,997	81,055	Whitehaven, Cleator, & Egremont.
														Witney.
														Wivenhoe and Brightlingsea.
														Wolverhampton and Walsall.
126	296	3,075	-	3,497	194	-	3,691	4,717	68	11,281	16,066	245	20,002	Wrexham, Mold, and Connah's Quay.
3,887,636	3,438,122	9,940,661	655,034	17,921,455	1,820,452	445,973	20,187,185‡	15,227,390	301,025	10,845,589	26,374,804	1,795,289	48,357,278	TOTAL ENGLAND AND WALES.

† Including receipts from minerals.   ‡ Including 2,335*l.* receipts from excess fares not classified.

No. 2.—Traffic, &c.,

NAME OF COMPANY.	LENGTH OF LINE IN MILES open on 31st January 1874.			PASSENGER TRAFFIC.					GOODS TRAFFIC.		NUMBER OF MILES TRAVELLED BY TRAINS.		
				NUMBER OF PASSENGERS CONVEYED (exclusive of Season and Periodical Tickets).									
	Double or more.	Single.	TOTAL.	1st Class.	2d Class.	3d Class (including Parliamentary).	TOTAL.	Holders of Season or Periodical Tickets.	Minerals.	General Merchandise.	Passenger Trains.	Goods and Mineral Trains.	TOTAL.
									Tons.	Tons.			
Aboyne and Braemar - - - -	Worked by the Great North of Scotland.												
Alyth - - - - -	Leased to the Caledonian.												
Arbroath and Forfar - - -	Leased to the Caledonian.												
Berwickshire - - - -	Worked by the North British.												
Blane Valley - - - -	Worked by the North British.												
Busby - - - - -	Worked by the Caledonian.												
Caledonian (Including the "Alyth," "Arbroath and Forfar," "Busby," "Callander and Oban," "Dundee and Newtyle," "Montrose and Bervie," "Portpatrick," "Solway Junction," "Greenock and Wemyss Bay," and half the "Glasgow and Kilmarnock," "Glasgow and Paisley," and "Glasgow, Barrhead, and Neilston" joint lines.)	438	382	820	1,261,543	1,525,316	10,790,035	13,576,894	12,024	8,914,640	2,583,699	4,538,340	6,328,443	10,866,783
Callander and Oban - - -	Worked by the Caledonian.												
Carlisle and Silloth Bay - -	Leased to the North British.												
City of Glasgow Union - -	3	..	3	284,039	345,944	1,281,277	1,911,260	2,025	131,248	59,376	..		
Deeside / Deeside Extension	Leased to the Great North of Scotland.												
Devon Valley - - - -	Worked by the North British.												
Dingwall and Skye - - -	Worked by the Highland.												
Dundee and Newtyle - -	Leased to the Caledonian.												
Edinburgh and Bathgate - -	Leased to the North British.												
Findhorn* - - - -	..	..	..	..	..	..	..	..	..	..	..	..	
Forth and Clyde Junction - -	Leased to the North British.												
Glasgow and Milngavie Junction -	Worked by the North British till 31st July, and then amalgamated with that Company.												
Glasgow and South-Western (Including the "Ayr and Maybole," "Kilmarnock and Troon," and half the "Glasgow, Barrhead, and Neilston," "Glasgow and Kilmarnock," and "Glasgow and Paisley" joint lines.)	216	99	315	535,988	681,172	4,562,818	5,779,978	2,382	3,363,811	655,196	1,496,467	2,385,382	3,881,849
Great North of Scotland (Including the "Aboyne and Braemar," "Deeside and Deeside Extension," and "Morayshire.")	7	279	286	224,985	..	1,486,883	1,711,868	8,537	226,900	334,067	499,670	459,584	959,254
Greenock and Wemyss Bay - -	Worked by the Caledonian.												
Highland † (Including the "Dingwall and Skye," "Duke of Sutherland's," and "Sutherland.")	7	328	335	159,724	42,209	899,924	1,101,857	1,296	116,801	212,825	Mixed.		1,100,652
Kilmarnock and Troon - -	Leased to the Glasgow and South-Western.												
Leven and East of Fife - -	..	20	20	13,506	22,670	141,466	177,642	262	56,143	63,062	49,186	29,496	78,682
Montrose and Bervie - -	Worked by the Caledonian.												
Morayshire - - - -	Worked by the Great North of Scotland.												
North British (Including the "Berwickshire," "Blane Valley," "Carlisle and Silloth Bar," "Devon Valley," "Edinburgh and Bathgate," "Forth and Clyde Junction," "Glasgow and Milngavie Junction," "Peebles," "Penicuik," "Port Carlisle Dock and Railway," and "St. Andrews.")	377	456	833	1,463,634	1,082,672	10,777,991	13,295,297	10,889	6,069,240	2,186,936	3,692,950	4,779,912	6,472,862
Peebles - - - -	Leased to the North British.												
Penicuik - - - -	Worked by the North British.												
Port Carlisle Dock and Railway - -	Leased to the North British.												
Port Patrick - - - -	Worked by the Caledonian.												
St. Andrews - - - -	Worked by the North British.												
Solway Junction - - -	Leased to the Caledonian.												
Sutherland - - - -	Worked by the Highland.												
Sutherland's (Duke of) - -	Worked by the Highland.												
TOTAL SCOTLAND - - -	1,048	1,564	2,612	3,963,419	3,499,983	30,060,394	37,513,796	37,707	18,878,783	6,097,161	10,276,615	13,933,817	25,310,082

* Line closed since 30th January 1866.   † For the year ended 28th February 1874.

Note.—The financial year of the Scotch Railway Companies.

‡ Including 1,100,652 miles travelled by mixed trains.

SCOTLAND, in 1873.

1st Class.	2d Class.	3d Class (including Parliamentary).	Holders of Season or Periodical Tickets.	Total from Passengers.	Excess Luggage, Parcels, Carriages, Horses, Dogs, &c.	Mails.	Total Receipts from Passenger Traffic.	Merchandise.	Live Stock.	Minerals.	Total Receipts from Goods Traffic.	Miscellaneous, Rents, Tolls, Navigation, Steamboats, &c.	Total Receipts from all Sources of Traffic.	NAME OF COMPANY.
£	£	£	£	£	£	£	£	£	£	£	£	£	£	
														Aboyne and Braemar.
														Alyth.
														Arbroath and Forfar.
														Berwickshire.
														Blane Valley.
														Busby.
159,805	105,864	454,205	32,181	750,055	78,402	54,616	883,074	894,384	60,189	833,405	1,788,068	131,284	2,802,416	Caledonian.
														Callander and Oban.
														Carlisle and Silloth Bay.
2,148	1,192	5,532	894	9,766	806	100	10,672	1,363	164	3,117	4,644	27,801	43,117	City of Glasgow Union.
														Deeside.
														Deeside Extension
														Devon Valley.
														Dingwall and Skye.
														Dundee and Newtyle.
														Edinburgh and Bathgate.
..	..	..	..	..	..	..	..	..	..	..	..	..	..	Findhorn.
														Forth and Clyde Junction.
														Glasgow and Milngavie Junction.
47,696	42,884	177,409	12,511	290,502	23,423	5,200	309,125	254,563	15,342	279,584	549,969	21,920	881,034	Glasgow and South-Western.
22,404	-	74,474	6,863	103,201	8,470	5,199	117,470	92,830	6,640	26,088	123,506	6,538	249,616	Great North of Scotland.
														Greenock and Wemyss Bay.
36,425	12,009	72,722	2,558	123,714	12,753	24,190	160,657	81,270	21,524	24,288	127,082	9,689	297,428	Highland.
														Kilmarnock and Troon.
1,233	1,290	4,590	158	7,301	1,217	163	8,681	7,906	445	4,406	12,779	1,082	22,542	Leven and East of Fife.
														Montrose and Bervie.
														Morayshire.
144,704	79,102	463,174	31,859	688,839	70,977	12,111	771,927	614,977	41,309	522,902	1,202,736§	36,969	2,011,635	North British.
														Peebles.
														Penicuik.
														Port Carlisle Dock and Railway.
														Port Patrick.
														St. Andrews.
														Solway Junction.
														Sutherland.
														Sutherland's (Duke of).
414,478	240,371	1,222,106	97,024	1,963,979	196,046	101,379	2,261,606	1,947,455	145,103	1,695,740	3,810,339§	235,353	6,307,788	TOTAL SCOTLAND.

except when otherwise stated, ends on 31st January 1874.

§ Including 29,351l. receipts from goods traffic not classified.

No. 2.—Traffic, &c.,

NAME OF COMPANY.	LENGTH OF LINE IN MILES open on 31st December 1873.			PASSENGER TRAFFIC.					GOODS TRAFFIC.		NUMBER OF MILES TRAVELLED BY TRAINS.		
				NUMBER OF PASSENGERS CONVEYED (exclusive of Season and Periodical Tickets).				Holders of Season or Periodical Tickets.					
	Double or more.	Single.	TOTAL.	1st Class.	2d Class.	3d Class (including Parliamentary).	TOTAL.		Minerals.	General Merchandise.	Passenger Trains.	Goods and Mineral Traffic.	TOTAL.
									Tons.	Tons.			
Athenry and Ennis Junction - -	Leased to the Waterford and Limerick.												
Athenry and Tuam - - -	Leased to the Waterford and Limerick.												
Banbridge Junction - - -	Leased to the Dublin and Belfast Junction.												
Banbridge, Lisburn, and Belfast - -	Leased to the Ulster.												
Belfast and County Down - - (Including the " Downpatrick, Dundrum, and New-castle.")	-	55	55	71,809	156,942	435,428	664,179	1,879	61,325	62,997	183,861	79,087	262,948
Belfast and Northern Counties - (Including the " Carrickfergus and Larne.")	12	139	151	139,629	236,982	1,196,381	1,572,992	2,199	133,328	246,632	491,470	239,241	730,711
Belfast, Holywood, and Bangor -	-	12	12	134,071	227,324	121,303	482,698	5,016	-	-	95,080	-	95,080
Carrickfergus and Larne - -	Worked by the Belfast and Northern Counties.												
Cork and Bandon - - - (Including the " Cork and Kinsale Junction.")	-	51	51	11,206	43,933	152,591	207,730	7	-	70,904	53,780	77,962	131,742
Cork and Kinsale Junction - -	Worked by the Cork and Bandon.												
Cork and Macroom Direct - -	-	25	25	10,383	18,136	122,788	151,306	90	-	31,383	Mixed.		34,749
Cork, Blackrock, and Passage* -	-	6	6	81,980	135,016	336,712	553,708	313	-	-	60,263	-	60,263
Downpatrick, Dundrum, and Newcastle -	Worked by the Belfast and County Down.												
Dublin and Antrim Junction - -	Worked by the Ulster.												
Dublin and Belfast Junction - (Including the " Banbridge Junction.")	56	7	63	67,053	85,583	282,237	434,873	6	14,751	136,736	229,683	118,161	347,844
Dublin and Drogheda - -	32	43	75	133,385	216,054	632,463	981,902	410	-	116,159	356,597	78,769	435,366
Dublin and Kingstown - -	Leased to the Dublin, Wicklow, and Wexford.												
Dublin and Meath - - -	Worked by the Midland Great Western of Ireland.												
Dublin, Wicklow, and Wexford† - (Including the " Dublin and Kingstown.")	18	104	122	424,987	1,762,063	1,967,470	4,154,540	8,656	78,553	95,794	694,330	174,100	868,430
Dundalk, Newry, and Greenore -	The accounts are a subject of dispute between the Working Companies. No correct information can be given.												
Enniskillen, Bundoran, and Sligo -	Worked by the Irish North-Western.												
Fermoy and Lismore - -	Worked by the Great Southern and Western of Ireland.												
Finn Valley - - -	Worked by the Irish North-Western.												
Great Northern and Western of Ireland -	Worked by the Midland Great Western of Ireland.												
Great Southern and Western of Ireland - (Including the " Fermoy and Lismore," and the " Parsonstown and Portumna Bridge.")	195	269	464	274,376	899,255	1,566,471	2,740,102	-	79,342	543,561	1,555,801	948,647	2,504,448
Irish North-Western - - (Including the " Clones and Cavan Extension," " Enniskillen, Bundoran, and Sligo " (for the year ended 30th September 1873), " Finn Valley," and " Londonderry and Enniskillen.")	-	195	195	37,157	73,269	487,701	598,127	131	277,490		Mixed.		641,670
Kilkenny Junction - - -	Worked by the Waterford and Central Ireland.												
Limerick and Ennis - - -	Worked by the Waterford and Limerick.												
Limerick and Foynes - -	Worked by the Waterford and Limerick till 30th June 1873, and amalgamated with that Company from that date.												
Londonderry and Enniskillen -	Worked by the Irish North-Western.												
Londonderry and Lough Swilly‡ -	-	12	12	10,891	22,344	82,796	116,031	23	-	9,870	33,240	-	33,240

* For the year ended 31st October 1873.   † Including traffic and receipts of 6½ miles of tramway.   ‡ For the year ended 31st January 1874.

IRELAND, in 1873.

RECEIPTS (GROSS) FROM PASSENGER TRAFFIC.								RECEIPTS (GROSS) FROM GOODS TRAFFIC.				Miscellaneous, Rents, Tolls, Navigation, Steamboats, &c.	Total Receipts from all Sources of Traffic.	NAME OF COMPANY.
Receipts from Passengers.					Horses, Luggage, Parcels, Carriages, Horses, Dogs, &c.	Mails.	Total Receipts from Passenger Traffic.	Merchandise.	Live Stock.	Minerals.	Total Receipts from Goods Traffic.			
1st Class.	2d Class.	3d Class (Including Parliamentary).	Holders of Season or Periodical Tickets.	Total from Passengers.										
£	£	£	£	£	£	£	£	£	£	£	£	£	£	
														Athenry and Ennis Junction.
														Athenry and Tuam.
														Banbridge Junction.
														Banbridge, Lisburn, and Belfast.
6,047	8,016	16,907	1,907	32,877	1,781	348	35,006	12,243	1,381	3,691	17,315	4,473	56,794	Belfast and County Down.
16,353	18,436	46,255	3,143	84,187	6,159	5,458	95,804	68,394	4,700	14,442	87,536	3,553	186,898	Belfast and Northern Counties.
4,584	5,507	2,148	3,670	15,909	964	100	16,973	-	-	-	-	170	17,143	Belfast, Holywood, and Bangor.
														Carrickfergus and Larne.
1,523	4,203	8,420	12	14,158	1,045	1,350	16,553	16,187	1,929	-	18,116	1,111	35,780	Cork and Bandon.
														Cork and Kinsale Junction.
1,154	1,207	6,305	117	8,783	274	30	9,087	6,384	1,358	-	8,392	49	17,428	Cork and Macroom Direct.
3,637	3,171	5,207	1,675	13,690	763	30	13,463	-	-	-	-	159	13,642	Cork, Blackrock, and Passage.
														Downpatrick, Dundrum, and Newcastle.
														Dublin and Antrim Junction.
19,415	14,482	19,347	19	53,261	3,915	9,389	66,565	27,983§	2,778	-	30,761	986	98,312	Dublin and Belfast Junction.
13,954	17,651	28,064	1,405	66,074	5,216	6,253	77,543	35,183	6,635	-	41,868	3,264	122,675	Dublin and Drogheda.
														Dublin and Kingstown.
														Dublin and Meath.
26,094	62,780	53,101	18,899	160,874	9,269	6,500	176,643	34,484	4,585	10,083	49,062	-	225,695	Dublin, Wicklow, and Wexford.
														Dundalk, Newry, and Greenore.
														Enniskillen, Bundoran, and Sligo.
														Fermoy and Lismore.
														Finn Valley.
														Great Northern and Western of Ireland.
86,691	86,532	140,128	-	313,351	34,127	31,569	379,047	250,967	56,889	16,514	324,370	3,042	706,459	Great Southern and Western of Ireland.
10,062	12,687	36,361	713	59,793	4,306	5,140	69,239	70,433‖	10,416	‖	80,849	1,700	151,788	Irish North-Western.
														Kilkenny Junction.
														Limerick and Ennis.
														Limerick and Foynes.
														Londonderry and Enniskillen.
512	733	2,047	155	3,446	162	10	3,620	2,061	142	-	2,223	104	5,947	Londonderry and Lough Swilly.

§ Including receipts from minerals. ‖ Receipts from minerals included with those from merchandise.

I 3

NAME OF COMPANY.	LENGTH OF LINE IN MILES open on 31st December 1873.			PASSENGER TRAFFIC.				Holders of Season or Periodical Tickets.	GOODS TRAFFIC.		NUMBER OF MILES TRAVELLED BY TRAINS.		
				NUMBER OF PASSENGERS CONVEYED (exclusive of Season and Periodical Tickets).									
	Double or more.	Single.	TOTAL.	1st Class.	2d Class.	3d Class (including Parliamentary).	TOTAL.		Minerals.	General Merchandise.	Passenger Trains.	Goods and Mineral Trains.	TOTAL.
									Tons.	*Tons.*			
Midland Great Western of Ireland - - (Including the "Dublin and Meath," "Great Northern and Western of Ireland," and the "Navan and Kingscourt.")	116	284	400	97,282	110,696	779,916	987,896	158	21,967	299,101	961,722	622,611	1,604,333
Naoan and Kingscourt - - -	Worked by the Midland Great Western of Ireland.												
Newry and Armagh - - - -		22	22	19,415	31,116	147,892	198,423	127	67,591		Mixed.		83,368
Newry, Warrenpoint, and Rostrevor -		6	6	29,361	27,412	129,966	186,739	163	10,006	22,694	36,144	4,846	40,992
Parsonstown and Portumna Bridge -	Worked by the Great Southern and Western.												
Portadown, Dungannon, and Omagh Junction	Leased to the Ulster.												
Rathkeale and Newcastle Junction - -	Worked by the Waterford and Limerick.												
Ulster - - - - (Including the "Banbridge, Lisburn, and Belfast," "Dublin and Antrim Junction," and "Portadown, Dungannon, and Omagh Junction.")	48	92	140	144,125	256,338	1,191,886	1,592,349	1,147	67,973	507,385	483,715	206,580	690,295
Waterford and Central Ireland for the year ended 29th September 1873. (Including the "Kilkenny Junction" for the year ended 1st November 1873.)		60	60	18,352	50,298	66,200	134,850	1,475	11,226	81,096	129,279	53,774	183,053
Waterford and Limerick* (Including the "Athenry and Ennis," "Athenry and Tuam," "Limerick and Ennis," "Limerick and Foynes," and "Rathkeale and Newcastle Junction.")	24	179	203	73,785	95,954	628,077	797,816	121	32,646	246,839	445,602	176,852	622,454
Waterford and Tramore - - -		7	7	101,133	-	103,925	205,058	230	800	2,900	42,915	-	42,915
Waterford, New Ross, and Wexford† - -		34	34	1,467	3,173	9,278	13,988	-	155	2,052	32,058	-	32,038
West Cork - - - - -		18	18	2,370	8,774	56,905	67,049	17	876	21,129	37,404	-	37,404
TOTAL IRELAND - -	501	1,600	2,101	1,884,116	3,960,684	10,497,506	16,342,306	19,402	512,850 and 345,061 tons not classified.	2,399,252	5,942,944	2,780,032	9,483,363‡

* The Limerick and Castle-Connell and Killaloe Extension from the 1st January 1873, and the Limerick and Foynes from the 1st July 1873, were amalgamated with the Waterford and Limerick.

† The railway was closed from the 30th September to the end of the year.   ‡ Including 759,787 miles travelled by mixed trains.

RECEIPTS (GROSS) FROM PASSENGER TRAFFIC.								RECEIPTS (GROSS) FROM GOODS TRAFFIC.						NAME OF COMPANY.
RECEIPTS FROM PASSENGERS.					Excess Luggage, Parcels, Carriages, Horses, Dogs, &c.	Mails.	TOTAL Receipts from Passenger Traffic.	Merchandise.	Live Stock.	Minerals.	TOTAL Receipts from Goods Traffic.	MISCELLANEOUS, RENTS, TOLLS, NAVIGATION, STEAMBOATS, &c.	TOTAL RECEIPTS FROM ALL SOURCES OF TRAFFIC.	
1st Class.	2d Class.	3d Class (including Parliamentary).	Holders of Season or Periodical Tickets.	TOTAL from Passengers.										
£	£	£	£	£	£	£	£	£	£	£	£	£	£	
37,824	28,243	116,431	756	183,254	17,428	17,362	218,044	172,774	68,414	4,487	245,675	10,828	474,547	Midland Great Western of Ireland.
														Navan and Kingscourt.
1,155	1,375	4,534	67	6,951	360	20	7,331	6,740‖	676	-	7,416	1,481	16,228	Newry and Armagh.
1,042	729	2,563	245	4,579	136	- -	4,715	1,555	180	524	2,259	198	7,172	Newry, Warrenpoint, and Rostrevor.
														Parsonstown and Portumna Bridge.
														Portadown, Dungannon, and Omagh Junction.
														Rathkeale and Newcastle Junction.
17,958	21,773	55,756	2,416	97,903	7,089	11,050	116,042	77,269	9,352	8,513	95,134	1,042	212,218	Ulster.
3,649	6,526	4,563	807	15,545	1,320	925	17,790	19,029	7,895	2,108	29,032	332	47,154	Waterford and Central Ireland.
11,879	11,026	34,519	561	57,985	8,332	4,155	70,452	65,091	19,310	5,460	89,861	3,050	163,363	Waterford and Limerick.
3,178	-	2,304	421	5,903	176	55	6,134	214	26	28	268	64	6,466	Waterford and Tramore.
211	300	456	-	967	148	- -	1,115	806	136	33	975	-	2,090	Waterford, New Ross, and Wexford.
253	768	2,565	30	3,621	244	50	3,915	4,114‖	780	-	4,894	331	9,140	West Cork.
271,133	306,215	587,321	36,919	1,202,113	103,214	99,774	1,405,101	872,431	197,632	65,833	1,135,896	35,987	2,576,984	TOTAL IRELAND.

‖ Including receipts from minerals.

I 4

RAILWAY RETURNS.—1873.

No. 3.—WORKING EXPENDITURE, NET RECEIPTS, AND ROLLING STOCK.

RETURN showing the AMOUNT of the WORKING EXPENDITURE, and of the .NET RECEIPTS, &c., and NUMBER of EACH KIND of ROLLING STOCK, for the several RAILWAY COMPANIES, in ENGLAND and WALES, SCOTLAND, and IRELAND, for the Year 1873.

K

No. 3.—Working Expenditure, Net Receipts, and

NAME OF COMPANY.	Length of Line in Miles open on 31st December 1873.	WORKING EXPENDITURE.									
		Maintenance of Way, Works, &c.	Locomotive Power (including Stationary Engines).	Repairs and Renewals of Carriages and Waggons.	Traffic Expenses (Coaching and Merchandise).	General Charges.	Rates and Taxes.	Government Duty.	Compensation for Personal Injury, &c.	Compensation for Damage and Loss of Goods.	Legal and Parliamentary Expenses.
	No.	£	£	£	£	£	£	£	£	£	£
Aberdare - - - - - -	Leased to the Taff Vale.										
Abingdon - - - - -	Leased to the Great Western.										
Anglesey Central - - - - -	18	2,939	1,543	517	1,211	638	194	50	-	-	4	4
Aylesbury and Buckingham - - -	12	794	1,238	-	-	294	462	30	17	-	2	-
Bala and Dolgelly - - - - -	Worked by the Great Western.										
Barnoldswick - - - - -	Worked by the Midland.										
Bedford and Northampton - - -	Leased to the Midland.										
Berks and Hants Extension - - -	Worked by the Great Western.										
Birkenhead - - - -	Vested jointly in the Great Western and the London and North-Western										
Bishop's Castle - - - -	10	281	535	26	468	400	22	43	-	-	-	131
Bishop's Waltham - - - -	Worked by the London and South-Western.										
Blyth and Tyne - - - -	43	20,220	55,800	13,799	18,205	2,197	3,876	441	-	-	178	133
Bodmin and Wadebridge - - -	15	517	666	524	324	263	37	6	-	-	-	-
Bourton-on-the-Water - - -	Worked by the Great Western.										
Brecon and Merthyr Tydfil Junction - -	61	14,608	20,567	6,369	11,292	3,208	1,224	124	16	312	1,661	
Bridport - - - -	Leased to the Great Western.										
Bristol and Exeter (Including the "Devon and Somerset" and "West Somerset.")	195	46,519	76,339	22,763	67,784	15,165	11,237	9,318	43	306	451	
Bristol and North Somerset - , -	Worked by the Great Western.										
Bristol and Portishead Pier and Railway -	9	1,030	2,155	747	2,683	597	123	193	-	16	-	-
Bristol Port Railway and Pier - -	6	429	692	45	462	511	66	90	-	-	-	56
Buckfastleigh, Totnes, and South Devon -	Worked by the South Devon.										
Buckinghamshire - - - -	Leased to the London and North-Western.										
Buckley - - - - .	Worked by the Wrexham, Mold, and Connah's Quay.										
Burry Port and Gwendreath Valley - -	18	1,095	1,948	280	892	716	127	-	-	17	-	91
Calne - - - - -	Worked by the Great Western.										
Cambrian - - - -	178	32,846	32,078	11,955	25,855	6,906	2,509	946	78	860	1,150	
Cannock Chase and Wolverhampton -	6	1,329	-	-	404	83	-	-	-	-	-	-
Carmarthen and Cardigan - -	19	3,260	2,905	1,670	2,645	477	153	350	200	134	1,340	
Central Wales and Carmarthen Junction (From 1st August to 31st December 1873; for the first seven months see "Swansea and Carmarthen Junction.")	13	608	-	-	490	288	24	25	-	2	-	
Cheshire Lines Committee -	91	39,054	56,563	2,065	56,870	6,616	3,292	662	53	1,689	2,257	
Chester and Holyhead - - -	Worked by the London and North-Western.										
Cockermouth, Keswick, and Penrith -	32	6,302	16,089		3,066	1,400	399	346	-	49	64	
Colchester, Stour Valley, Sudbury, and Halstead -	Leased to the Great Eastern.										
Coleford, Monmouth, Usk, and Pontypool -	Leased to the Great Western.										
Colne Valley and Halstead -	19	2,606	1,910	262	2,425	789	155	58	-	4	175	
Cornwall - - - -	66	27,543	22,792	4,412	15,925	3,347	714	1,696	62	1,146	121	
Corris - - - -	11	529	8*	107		111	30	-	-	-	-	-
Corwen and Bala - - - -	Leased to the Great Western.										
Cowbridge - - - -	6	576	1,663	113	533		41	63	-	1	-	-
Cowes and Newport - - -	5	707		1,965		252 263	52	211	-	-	-	68
Croesor and Portmadoc - -	5	92	290	-	-		26	-	-	-	-	-
Cromford and High Peak - -	Leased to the London and North-Western.										
Crystal Palace and South London Junction - .	Worked by the London, Chatham, and Dover.										

* Hire of Horses.

† The traffic is carried in the trains of the London and North-Western Railway Company.

Rolling Stock.—ENGLAND AND WALES, in 1873.

Steamboat, Canal, and Harbour Expenses. (£)	Miscellaneous Working Expenditure not included in the foregoing. (£)	Total Working Expenditure. (£)	Total Receipts, as given in the Traffic Return, No. 2. (£)	Net Receipts. (£)	Proportion per Cent. of Expenditure to Total Receipts.	Locomotives. (No.)	Carriages used for the Conveyance of Passengers only. (No.)	Other Vehicles attached to Passenger Trains. (No.)	Waggons of all kinds used for the Conveyance of Live Stock, Minerals, or General Merchandise. (No.)	Any other Carriage or Waggons used on the Railway not included in the preceding Column. (No.)	Total Number of Vehicles of all descriptions for Conveyance of Passengers, Live Stock, Ballast, &c. (No.)	NAME OF COMPANY.
												Aberdare.
												Abingdon.
·	·	·	7,100	7,909	809	90	·	Hired from the London and North-Western				Anglesey Central.
·	·	33	2,870	2,470	400 Deficiency.	116	·	·	·	·	·	Aylesbury and Buckingham.
												Bala and Dolgelly.
												Barnoldswick.
												Bedford and Northampton.
												Berks and Hants Extension
												Birkenhead.
·	·	1,206	3,414	3,251	163 Deficiency.	106	2	8	2	14	· ·	24	Bishop's Castle.
												Bishop's Waltham.
·	·	·	114,354	183,702	68,848	63	37	67	10	3,340	· ·	3,417	Blyth and Tyne.
·	·	45	2,382	2,464	82	97	1	4	2	100	· ·	106	Bodmin and Wadebridge.
												Bourton-on-the-Water.
·	·	475	59,856	79,620	19,764	75	27	36	6	520	18	580	Brecon and Merthyr Tydfil Junction.
												Bridport.
1,797	1,431	253,155	521,405	268,250	49	100	166	85	2,049	47	2,347	Bristol and Exeter
												Bristol and North Somerset.
74	·	·	7,618	9,824	2,206	78	Provided by the Bristol and Exeter Railway Company.					Bristol and Portishead Pier and Rail.way.
·	·	·	2,345	2,359	14	99	2	15	2	4	· ·	21	Bristol Port Railway and Pier.
												Buckfastleigh, Totnes, and South Devon.
												Buckinghamshire.
												Buckley.
1,471	·	·	6,575	10,782	4,207	61	3	·	·	104	· ·	104	Burry Port and Gwendreath Valley.
												Calne.
·	·	·	115,785	187,115	71,330		44	92	18	1,316	30	1,456	Cambrian.
·	·	·	1,315	3,908	2,093		·	·	·	510	· ·	510	Cannock Chase and Wolverhampton.
·	·	776	18,900	20,773	6,873		3	6	·	20	· ·	26	Carmarthen and Cardigan.
·	·	37	1,474	3,877	2,403		†·	·	†·	80	†·	80	Central Wales and Carmarthen Junction.
·	·	19,527	188,347	196,248	7,901	66	·	49	13	12	· ·	74	Cheshire Lines Committee.
												Chester and Holyhead.
·	·	32	26,269	49,758	21,489	57	Provided by the "London and North-Western" and "North-Eastern" Railway Companies.					Cockermouth, Keswick, and Penrith.
												Colchester, Stour Valley, Sudbury, and Halstead.
												Calstock, Monmouth, Usk, and Ponty-pool.
·	·	333	8,723	8,631	92 Deficiency.	101	3	10	3	28	1 ·	42	Colne Valley and Halstead.
·	·	2,781	80,440	133,693	53,253		‡-	·	48	31	279	· ·	358	Cornwall.
·	·	·	785	1,594	809		Haulage done by horses. The Company has only a few slate trucks.					Corris.
												Corwen and Bala.
·	·	·	3,241	3,760	519	86	2	3	·	·	· ·	3	Cowbridge.
·	·	3,646	5,917	7,259	1,342	82	§	· §	· §	· §	· §	· §	Cowes and Newport.
·	·	·	545	642	97	85	‖	·	·	·	· ‖	-	Crossor and Portmadoc.
												Cromford and High Peak.
												Crystal Palace and South London Junction.

‡ Hired from the "South Devon" Railway Company. § line worked under an agreement. Rolling Stock provided by contractor.
‖ The Company has no Rolling Stock. The haulage is done by horses, and waggons are provided by the persons using the Railway.

NAME OF COMPANY.	Length of Line in Miles open on 31st December 1873.	Maintenance of Way, Works, &c.	Locomotive Power (including Stationary Engines).	Repairs and Renewals of Carriages and Wagons.	Traffic Expenses (Coaching and Merchandise).	General Charges.	Rates and Taxes.	Government Duty.	Compensation for Personal Injury, &c.	Compensation for Damage and Loss of Goods.	Legal and Parliamentary Expenses.
	No.	£	£	£	£	£	£	£	£	£	£
Dare Valley	Leased to the Taff Vale.										
Denbigh, Ruthin, and Corwen	19	1,505	1,931	356	2,277	727	125	180	.	.	19
Devon and Somerset	Worked by the Bristol and Exeter.										
Dowlais (Including the Dowlais Extension.)	2	168	1,048	.		882	.	38	.	.	.
East Cornwall Mineral	7	412	647	56	715	673	42	.	.	23	11
East and West Junction*	33	3,201	3,332	2,072	2,081	1,964	42	37	2	7	531
East Gloucestershire	Worked by the Great Western.										
East Lincolnshire	Leased to the Great Northern.										
East London	Worked by the London, Brighton, and South Coast.										
East Somerset	Worked by the Great Western.										
Ely, Haddenham, and Sutton	Worked by the Great Eastern.										
Ely Valley	Worked by the Great Western.										
Evesham and Redditch	Worked by the Midland.										
Exeter and Crediton	Leased to the London and South-Western.										
Faringdon	Worked by the Great Western.										
Festiniog	14	2,517	3,189	1,270	3,697	1,394	970	207	.	125	1,317
Festiniog and Blaenau†	4	137	326	.	309	15	9	53	.	.	5
Forcett	5	725	1,360‡	.	.	264	21	.	.	1	107
Forest of Dean Central	Worked by the Great Western.										
Furness	102	69,309	77,728	17,903	44,961	11,525	7,049	1,166	1,245	166	1,547
Garstang and Knot End	Line closed since March 1872.										
Gloucester and Dean Forest	Leased to the Great Western.										
Great Eastern (Including the "Colchester, Stour Valley, Sudbury, and Halstead," "Ely, Haddenham, and Sutton," "London and Blackwall," "Lowestoft Harbour and Railway," "Lynn and Hunstanton," "Mellis and Eye," "Northern and Eastern," "Saffron Walden," "Tendring Hundred," "Tendring Hundred Extension," "West Norfolk," and the "Wivenhoe and Brightlingsea.")	836	244,060	426,555§	116,216§	406,362	44,540	46,847	32,878	28,471	6,930	13,631
Great Marlow (Line opened for traffic on the 26th June 1873.)	3	.	537	.	128	34	7	36	.	.	.
Great Northern (Including the "East Lincolnshire," "Hatfield and St. Albans," "Holme and Ramsey," "Horncastle," "Maxwell Hill Estate" (from 24th May to 31st July), "Nottingham and Grantham," "Royston and Hitchin," "Spilsby and Firsby," "Stamford and Essendine," "Wainfleet and Firsby," and "Skegness Extension," and part of the "Midland and Eastern," and "Norwich and Spalding.")	554	286,929	461,188	114,886	445,800	63,653	48,071	25,082	24,084	15,005	19,536
Great North of England, Clarence, and Hartlepool Junction	Leased to the North-Eastern.										
Great Western‖ (Including the "Abingdon," "Bala and Dolgelly," "Berks and Hants Extension," "Bourton-on-the-Water," "Bridport," "Bristol and North Somerset" (from 2nd September 1873), "Calne," "Coleford, Monmouth, Usk, and Pontypool," "Corwen and Bala," "East Gloucestershire," "East Somerset," "Ely Valley," "Faringdon," "Forest of Dean Central," "Gloucester and Dean Forest," "Leominster and Kington," "Llanelly Railway and Dock," "Llangollen and Corwen," "Llynvi and Ogmore" (from 1st July 1873), "Marlborough," "Milford," "Much Wenlock and Severn Junction," "Nantwich and Market Drayton," "Ross and Monmouth" (from 4th August 1873), "Stratford-upon-Avon," "Vale of Llangollen," "Wellington and Drayton," "Wellington and Severn Junction," "Wenlock," and "Wenlock Extensions," and "Witney," and the "Birkenhead," "Hammersmith and City," "Ludlow and Clee Hill," "Shrewsbury and Hereford," "Shrewsbury and Wellington," "Shrewsbury and Welshpool," "Tenbury," "Vale of Towy," "Victoria Station and Pimlico," "West London," "Weymouth and Portland," and "Wrexham and Minera Extension," jointly with other Companies.)	1,502	500,131	771,481	210,045	741,790	96,270	83,987	52,145	25,000	27,544	33,946
Hammersmith and City Junction	Vested jointly in the Great Western and Metropolitan Railway Companies.										
Hatfield and St. Albans	Worked by the Great Northern.										
Hayling Railways	Worked by the London, Brighton, and South Coast.										
Hereford, Hay, and Brecon	26	9,311	—	(combined)	2,554	1,171	342	87	.	35	.
Hexham and Allendale	12	540	1,236	.	743	170	90	45	.	4	.

* This line was opened throughout on the 5th August 1873.
† For the year ended 28th February 1874.
‡ Amount paid to the North-Eastern Railway Company for the hire of locomotive power and wagons.
§ Including cost of "Locomotive power" and "Repairs, &c." for the London, Tilbury, and Southend Line.
‖ For the year ended 31st January 1874.

Steamboat, Canal, and Harbour Expenses.	Miscellaneous Working Expenditure not included in the foregoing.	TOTAL WORKING EXPENDITURE.	TOTAL RECEIPTS, as given in the TRAFFIC RETURN, No. 2.	NET RECEIPTS.	Proportion per Cent. of Expenditure to Total Receipts.	ROLLING STOCK on 31st December 1873. CARRIAGES, WAGGONS, TRUCKS, &c.						NAME OF COMPANY.
£	£	£	£	£		Locomotives.	Carriages used for the Conveyance of Passengers only.	Other Vehicles attached to Passenger Trains.	Waggons of all kinds used for the Conveyance of Live Stock, Minerals, or General Merchandise.	Any other Carriages or Waggons used on the Railway, not included in the preceding Columns.	Total Number of Vehicles of all descriptions for Conveyance of Passengers, Live Stock, Ballast, &c.	
						No.	No.	No.	No.	No.	No.	
..	..	..	..	..	..							*Dare Valley.*
..	..	7,120	11,947	4,827	60	3	8	5	53	..	66	Denbigh, Ruthin, and Corwen.
..	..	..	..	..	..							*Devon and Somerset.*
..	..	2,136	7635	..	..	**2	..	..	..	..	..	Dowlais.
..	..	2,579	2,906	337	89	**2	..	..	.	149	..	149	East Cornwall Mineral.
..	284	13,505	4,060	9,445 Deficiency.	333	7	20	11	93	..	124	East and West Junction.
												East Gloucestershire.
												East Lincolnshire.
												East London.
												East Somerset.
												Ely, Haddenham, and Sutton.
												Ely Valley.
												Bosham and Redditch.
												Exeter and Crediton.
												Faringdon.
..	178	14,614	24,507	9,893	60	3	60	3	1,037	12	1,113	Festiniog.
..	35	890	1,345	456	66	2	4	1	7	19	31	Festiniog and Blaenau.
..	172	2,850	5,720	3,070	46	Hired from "North-Eastern" Company					-	Forcett.
												Forest of Dean Central
8,013	..	240,625	472,582	231,957	51	87	157	41	4,420	48	4,666	Furness.
												Garstang and Knot End.
												Gloucester and Dean Forest.
111,394	..	1,477,823	2,602,213	1,124,390	57	459	1,512	431	9,594	200	11,546	Great Eastern.
..	57	790	1,215	416	66	Supplied by the "Great Western" Railway Company						Great Marlow.
7,516	1,420	1,512,829	2,803,877	1,391,048	54	925	1,136	362	12,474	1,231	15,203	Great Northern.
												Great North of England, Clarence, and Hartlepool Junction.
70,369	66,414	2,677,010	5,451,575	2,774,565	49	1,082	2,002	1,130	24,516	1,009	28,637	Great Western.
												Hammersmith and City Junction.
												Hatfield and St. Albans.
												Hayling Railways.
..	..	13,300	24,916	11,616	53	..	Supplied by the Midland Company				-	Hereford, Hay, and Brecon.
..	..	2,828	3,833	1,005	74	Hired from the North-Eastern Company					-	Hexham and Allendale.

¶ Receipts from the carriage of "General Merchandise" only. No comparison can be made between the receipts and expenditure on this line, which is used chiefly for the conveyance of the Company's minerals.
** And one stationary engine.

K 3

NAME OF COMPANY.	Length of Line in Miles open on 31st December 1873.	Maintenance of Way, Works, &c.	Locomotive Power (including Stationary Engines).	Repairs and Renewals of Carriages and Waggons.	Traffic Expenses (Coaching and Merchandise).	General Charges.	Rates and Taxes.	Government Duty.	Compensation for Personal Injury, &c.	Compensation for Damage and Loss of Goods.	Legal and Parliamentary Expenses.
	No.	£	£	£	£	£	£	£	£	£	£
Holms and Ramsey	*Worked by the Great Northern.*										
Horncastle	*Worked by the Great Northern.*										
Hoylake	5	866	1,673	-	804	225	55	206	-	-	-
Isle of Wight	12	3,564	4,698	723	2,734	2,475	348	974	32	26	46
Keighley and Worth Valley	*Worked by the Midland.*										
Kendal and Windermere	*Leased to the London and North-Western.*										
Kettering, Thrapstone, and Huntingdon	*Worked by the Midland.*										
King's Lynn Dock*	-	-	-	-	-	-	-	-	-	-	-
Lancashire and Yorkshire (Including part of the "Preston and Longridge" and "Preston and Wyre" Joint Lines.)	433	266,338	402,772	150,068	694,733	39,863	53,155	20,620	38,119	4,668	25,252
Lancashire Union	*Worked by the London and North-Western.*										
Lancaster and Carlisle	*Leased to the London and North-Western.*										
Launceston and South Devon	*Worked by the South Devon.*										
Leominster and Kington	*Worked by the Great Western.*										
Liskeard and Caradon (Including the "Liskeard and Looe Union Railway and Canal.")	17	1,401	1,315	333	2,926	107	144	-	-	-	-
Liskeard and Looe Union Railway and Canal	*Worked by the Liskeard and Caradon.*										
Llanelly Railway and Dock	*Worked by the Great Western.*										
Llangollen and Corwen	*Leased to the Great Western.*										
Llantrissant and Taff Vale Junction	*Leased to the Taff Vale.*										
Llynvi and Ogmore (For six months ended 30th June, from which date the line was worked by the "Great Western" Railway Company.)	30†	2,257	4,555	1,302	3,167	1,115	1,421	99	-	68	39
London and Blackwall	*Leased to the Great Eastern.*										
London and Greenwich	*Leased to the South-Eastern.*										
London and North-Western (Including the "Buckinghamshire," "Chester and Holyhead and Branches," "Cromford and High Peak," "Kendal and Windermere," "Lancashire Union," "Lancaster and Carlisle," "Mold and Denbigh Junction," "North Union," "Shropshire Union," "Watford and Rickmansworth" and "Wolverhampton and Walsall," and half of the "Ashby and Nuneaton," from 1st September 1873, "Birkenhead and Branches," "Ludlow and Clee Hill," "Preston and Longridge," "Shrewsbury and Hereford," "Shrewsbury and Wellington," "Shrewsbury and Welshpool" "Tenbury," and "Vale of Towy," and part of the "Preston and Wyre," "West London," and "West London Extension.")	1,504	862,336	1,286,167	289,622	1,406,175	150,695	136,232	76,521	67,094	57,078	77,858
London and South-Western (Including the "Bishops Waltham," "Exeter and Crediton," "Lymington," "Mid-Hants," "Ringwood, Christchurch, and Bournemouth," "Salisbury and Dorset," "Salisbury and Yeovil," "Salisbury Railway and Market House," "Seaton and Beer," "Stalnes, Wokingham, and Woking," "Stokes Bay Railway and Pier," and half the "Weymouth and Portland " and part of the "West London Extension.")	648	220,008	297,555	77,346	366,544	45,196	53,443	37,594	5,274	5,925	7,519
London, Brighton, and South Coast (Including the "East London," Hayling Railways," and part of the "Victoria Station and Pimlico," and "West London Extension.")	345	127,165	285,259	51,530	208,895	30,997	49,545	33,905	3,079	3,440	9,921
London, Chatham, and Dover (Including the "Crystal Palace and South London Junction," "Mid-Kent (Bromley to St. Mary's Cray)," "Sevenoaks, Maidstone, and Tonbridge," and part of the "Victoria Station and Pimlico.")	141	66,850	141,587	26,808	132,597	27,136	23,808	15,270	1,680	2,304	3,600
Londonderry (Seaham to Sunderland) (Private property.)	7	8,620	7,243	242	673	380	522	319	-	-	-
London, Tilbury, and Southend	44	14,449	12,193†	5,980†	10,504	4,087	1,346	2,777	45	34	7
Lostwithiel and Fowey	6	341	195	156	196	185	21	-	-	-	-
Lowestoft	*Leased to the Great Eastern.*										
Ludlow and Clee Hill	*Worked by the London and North-Western and Great Western, jointly.*										
Lymington	*Worked by the London and South-Western.*										
Lynn and Hunstanton	*Worked by the Great Eastern.*										
Macclesfield Committee	11	5,336	6,728		3,696	805	255	30	-	-	-
Manchester and Milford	42	3,896	4,555	1,256	2,637	1,383	176	181	-	88	685

* The short tramway belonging to the Company is only used for the transit of goods to and from the Great Eastern Railway. No returns can be given.

Steamboat, Canal, and Harbour Expenses.	Miscellaneous Working Expenditure not included in the foregoing.	Total Working Expenditure.	Total Receipts, as given in the Traffic Return, No. 1.	Net Receipts.	Proportion per Cent. of Expenditure to Total Receipts.	ROLLING STOCK on 31st December 1873.						NAME OF COMPANY.
						Locomotives.	Carriages used for the Conveyance of Passengers only.	Other Vehicles attached to Passenger Trains.	Waggons of all kinds used for the Conveyance of Live Stock, Minerals, or General Merchandise.	Any other Carriages or Waggons used on the Railway not included in the preceding Columns.	Total Number of Vehicles of all descriptions for Conveyance of Passengers, Live Stock, Ballast, &c.	
£	£	£	£	£		No.	No.	No.	No.	No.	No.	
												Holme and Ramsey.
												Horncastle.
..	..	3,829	4,330	501	88	2	13	3	5	25	46	Hoylake.
..	185	15,544	24,842	9,298	63	5	25	13	90	..	128	Isle of Wight.
												Keighley and Worth Valley.
												Kendal and Windermere.
												Kettering, Thrapstone, and Huntingdon.
												King's Lynn Dock.
4,622	5,283	1,795,478	3,329,296	1,533,823	54	607	1,716	302	15,764	..	17,782	Lancashire and Yorkshire.
												Lancashire Union.
												Lancaster and Carlisle.
												Launceston and South Devon.
												Leominster and Kington.
..	26	6,252	11,001	4,749	57	3	..	..	45	..	48	Liskeard and Caradon.
												Liskeard and Looe Union Canal.
												Llanelly Railway and Dock.
												Llangollen and Corwen.
												Llantrissant and Taff Vale Junction.
1,452	..	15,075	28,356	13,281	53	..	..	..	..	..	..	Llynvi and Ogmore.
												London and Blackwall.
												London and Greenwich.
75,963	101,017	4,586,055	8,767,719	4,181,664	52	2,060	3,111	1,834	38,218	..	42,963	London and North-Western.
..	64,786	1,194,291	3,195,370	1,000,079	54	810	1,886	502	5,125	600	7,881	London and South-Western.
18,927	11,090	832,461	1,618,461	786,010	51	245	1,404	390	3,891	256	5,941	London, Brighton, and South Coast.
57,138	14,425	512,963	904,509	391,526	57	124	643	117	1,044	43	1,846	London, Chatham, and Dover.
..	2,960	20,959	32,920	11,961	64	11	17	3	4	..	24	Londonderry (Seaham to Sunderland).
..	..	51,722	78,560	26,838	66	Rolling Stock supplied by the " Great Eastern " Railway Company, who work the line under a contract.						London, Tilbury, and Southend.
..	35	1,129	1,287	158	88	Provided by the Cornwall Railway Company					-	Lostwithiel and Fowey.
												Lowestoft.
												Ludlow and Clee Hill.
												Lymington.
												Lynn and Hunstanton.
..	..	16,340	10,886	5,954 Deficiency.	155	Rolling Stock is provided by the " Manchester, Sheffield, and Lincolnshire " Railway Company.						Macclesfield Committee.
..	..	14,361	17 31(	2,255	87	3	13	4	112	1	130	Manchester and Milford.

† On the 30th June.   ‡ These sums are paid to the " Great Eastern " Railway Company for the hire of rolling stock.

NAME OF COMPANY.	Length of Line in Miles open on 31st December 1873.	WORKING EXPENDITURE.									
		Maintenance of Way, Works &c.	Locomotive Power (including Stationary Engines).	Repairs and Renewals of Carriages and Wagons.	Traffic Expenses (Coaching and Merchandise).	General Charges.	Rates and Taxes.	Government Duty.	Compensation for Personal Injury &c.	Compensation for Damage and Loss of Goods.	Legal and Parliamentary Expenses.
	No.	£	£	£	£	£	£	£	£	£	£
Manchester, Sheffield, and Lincolnshire (Including the "South Yorkshire and River Dun.")	258*	151,516	220,136	63,615	221,305	33,965	19,257	7,573	7,511	3,680	15,469
Manchester, South Junction, and Altrincham	9	11,093	9,040	2,873	12,944	2,692	1,951	1,915	-	-	79	1,127
Marlborough		*Worked by the Great Western.*									
Maryport and Carlisle	39	13,290	19,190	5,636	8,797	2,340	1,607	296	177	124	59
Mawddwy	7	695	754	2	170	105	32	23	-	14	-
Mellis and Eye		*Worked by the Great Eastern.*									
Merrybent and Darlington	6	265	3,600	-	-	-	118	14	-	-	-	9
Methley Joint Railway	6	2,650	-	-	-	1,137	258	92	16	-	-	-
Metropolitan (Including the "Metropolitan and St. John's Wood," and half the "Hammersmith and City.")	13	23,689	37,832	9,425	51,864	18,792	15,551	11,442	12,816	20	3,225
Metropolitan and St. John's Wood		*Worked by the Metropolitan.*									
Metropolitan District	7	10,066	37,141	3,987	28,458	9,818	4,095	7,567	9,147	-	4,146
Mid-Hants		*Worked by the London and South-Western.*									
Mid-Kent (Bromley to St. Mary's Cray)		*Leased to the London, Chatham, and Dover.*									
Midland (Including the "Barnoldswick," "Bedford and Northampton," "Evesham and Redditch," "Keighley and Worth Valley," "Kettering, Thrapstone, and Huntingdon," "Manchester, Buxton, Matlock, and Midland Junction," "Midland and South-Western Junction," "North-Western," "Peterborough, Wisbeach, and Sutton," "Redditch," "Stonehouse and Nailsworth," "Tewkesbury and Malvern," the "Furness and Midland" Joint Line, and half the "Ashby and Nuneaton " (from 1st September), the "Great Western and Midland," from Malvern Wells to Malvern Link, "Manchester, Sheffield, and Lincolnshire, and Midland," "Midland and Eastern," "Norwich and Spalding," and "Otley and Ilkley" Joint Lines.)	1,056	632,948	882,230	181,862	902,921	83,836	90,594	26,767	28,425	36,559	28,252
Midland and Eastern		*Worked by the Midland and Great Northern.*									
Midland and South-Western Junction		*Worked by the Midland.*									
Mid-Wales	46	4,998	9,463	2,389	4,651	3,432	290	126	-	-	96	145
Milford		*Worked by the Great Western.*									
Mold and Denbigh Junction		*Worked by the London and North-Western.*									
Monmouthshire Railway and Canal	54	24,327	26,304	5,005	26,290	5,448	6,962	359	216	252	1,361
Much Wenlock and Severn Junction		*Worked by the Great Western.*									
Nantwich and Market Drayton		*Worked by the Great Western.*									
Neath and Brecon	40	3,635	5,919	746	3,346	2,738	149	42	76	-	114
Newport Pagnell	4	300	950	100	1,390	575	40	35	-	20	206
Newquay and Cornwall Junction	3		1,984			279	9	-	-	-	-	-
Northampton and Banbury Junction	15	1,114	3,231	63	1,763	887	85	53	-	7	161
North and South Western Junction	5	2,537	219		1,993	752	388	33	1,601	-	54
North-Eastern (Including the "Great North of England, Clarence, and Hartlepool," and "Tees Valley," and part of the "Otley and Ilkley" Joint Line.)	1,389	600,963	1,151,631	368,543	710,905	79,796	121,429	24,699	37,288	18,761	26,196
Northern and Eastern		*Leased to the Great Eastern.*									
North London	12	20,075	73,174	18,769	58,418	8,120	10,824	6,335	1,476	28	1,155
North Staffordshire	183	66,292	98,723	31,009	67,543	12,576	4,763	1,997	45	2,963	2,530
North Union		*Leased to the London and North-Western.*									
North-Western		*Worked by the Midland.*									
Norwich and Spalding		*Worked by the Midland and Great Northern.*									
Nottingham and Grantham Railway and Canal		*Leased to the Great Northern.*									
Oldham, Ashton-under-Lyne, and Guide Bridge Junction	6	4,821	6,655	-	5,366	730	145	106	-	-	69	1

* In addition to the 258 miles given above, the Manchester, Sheffield, and Lincolnshire Company are half owners of 88 miles, and one-third owners of 164½ miles, the working expenditure of which lines are given in separate returns.

Steamboat, Canal, and Harbour Expenses.	Miscellaneous Working Expenditure not included in the foregoing.	TOTAL WORKING EXPENDITURE.	TOTAL RECEIPTS, as given in the TRAFFIC RETURN, No. 1.	NET RECEIPTS.	Proportion per Cent. of Expenditure to Total Receipts.	ROLLING STOCK on 31st December 1875.						NAME OF COMPANY.
						Locomotives.	Carriages used for the Conveyance of Passengers only.	Other Vehicles attached to Passenger Trains.	Waggons of all kinds used for the Conveyance of Live Stock, Minerals, or General Merchandise.	Any other Carriages or Waggons used on the Railway, not included in the preceding Columns.	Total Number of Vehicles of all descriptions for Conveyance of Passengers, Live Stock, Ballast, &c.	
£	£	£	£	£		No.	No.	No.	No.	No.	No.	
146,636	28,587	921,240	1,648,618	727,378	56	330	468	164	8,933	175	9,740	Manchester, Sheffield, and Lincolnshire.
.	1,556	45,270	102,331	57,061	44	.	83	13	60	2	158	Manchester, South Junction, and Altrincham. *Marlborough.*
.	815	52,833	140,396	87,563	38	24	30	14	1,429	9	1,482	Maryport and Carlisle.
.	.	1,795	1,402	393 Deficiency.	123	2	4	.	6	.	10	Mawddwy. *Mollis and Eye.*
.	.	3,997	2,305	1,692 Deficiency.	173	.	.	.	.	.	.	Merrybent and Darlington.
.	.	4,153	6,573	2,420	63	Rolling Stock supplied by the Companies working the traffic.						Methley Joint Railway.
.	.	185,056	478,335	293,279	39	46	180	.	15	.	195	Metropolitan.
												Metropolitan and St. John's Wood.
.	3,358	117,783	215,334	97,551	55	24	152	.	3	.	155	Metropolitan District. *Mid-Hants.* *Mid-Kent (Bromley to St. Mary's Cray).*
.	9,294	2,933,291	5,740,338	2,807,047	51	1,040	1,970	886	27,361	.	30,217	Midland.
												Midland and Eastern. *Midland and South-Western Junction.*
.	.	25,582	37,455	11,873	68	8	41	5	489	.	485	Mid-Wales. *Milford.* *Mold and Denbigh Junction.*
2,251	1,709	100,939	190,459	89,520	53	47	59	9	457	24	549	Monmouthshire Railway and Canal. *Much Wenlock and Severn Junction.*
												Nantwich and Market Drayton.
.	.	16,682	18,055	1,373	92	8	15	8	43	.	66	Neath and Brecon.
.	100	3,716	3,862	146	96	2	4	.	.	.	6	Newport Pagnell.
.	.	2,222	2,463	241	90	2	.	.	.	.	.	Newquay and Cornwall Junction.
.	616	7,950	8,138	188	98	5	10	2	1	.	13	Northampton and Banbury Junction.
.	.	7,877	673†	†	†	.	.	.	.	.	.	North and South-Western Junction.
.	75	3,140,077	6,041,333	2,901,256	52	1,103	1,522	629	66,562	.	70,713	North-Eastern.
												Northern and Eastern.
4,964	.	202,238‡	367,406	179,238	51	66	354	68	403	50	875	North London.
40,387	1,631	330,761	619,459	288,698	53	103	199	75	4,968	50	5,312	North Staffordshire.
												North Union. *North-Western.* *Norwich and Spalding.* *Nottingham and Grantham Railway and Canal.*
.	.	402	18,295	19,093	796	96	Provided by the "London and North-Western" and "Manchester, Sheffield, and Lincolnshire" Railway Companies.					Oldham, Ashton-under-Lyne, and Guide Bridge Junction.

† Receipts from local traffic only. No comparison can be made between the working expenditure and the receipts.
‡ Against this amount the Company have received 14,088l. for working other lines.

NAME OF COMPANY.	Length of Line in Miles open on 31st December 1873.	WORKING EXPENDITURE.									
		Maintenance of Way, Works, &c.	Locomotive Power (including Stationary Engines).	Repairs and Renewals of Carriages and Waggons.	Traffic Expenses (Coaching and Merchandise).	General Charges.	Rates and Taxes.	Government Duty.	Compensation for Personal Injury, &c.	Compensation for Damage and Loss of Goods.	Legal and Parliamentary Expenses.
	No.	£	£	£	£	£	£	£	£	£	£
Pembroke and Tenby	29	2,298	4,535	929	2,905	1,583	383	221	-	46	57
Penarth Harbour, Dock, and Railway	*Leased to the Taff Vale.*										
Peterborough, Wisbeach, and Sutton	*Worked by the Midland.*										
Potteries, Shrewsbury, and North Wales	28	1,866	3,451	1,223	2,071	1,558	145	18	10	13	-
Preston and Wyre	*Leased to the Lancashire and Yorkshire and London and North-Western.*										
Redditch	*Worked by the Midland.*										
Redruth and Chasewater	10	572	1,116	226	1,444	583	68	-	-	-	-
Rhymney	36	8,568	26,425	2,174	11,796	4,218	1,855	141	-	172	207
Ringwood, Christchurch, and Bournemouth	*Worked by the London and South-Western.*										
Ross and Monmouth	*Worked by the Great Western.*										
Royston and Hitchin	*Leased to the Great Northern.*										
Ryde Pier	2	1,783	-	-	-	4,298	461	714	167	16	122
Saffron Walden	*Worked by the Great Eastern.*										
Salisbury and Dorset Junction	*Worked by the London and South-Western.*										
Salisbury and Yeovil	*Leased to the London and South-Western.*										
Salisbury Railway and Market House	*Worked by the London and South-Western.*										
Saundersfoot Railway and Harbour	7	288	-	-	-	50	44	-	-	-	-
Seaton and Beer	*Worked by the London and South-Western.*										
Sevenoaks, Maidstone, and Tonbridge	*Worked by the London, Chatham, and Dover.*										
Severn and Wye Railway and Canal *	34	6,068	2,840	-	730	2,023	1,243	-	-	-	92
Sheffield and Midland Committee	12	22,237	13,772	-	-	3,804	1,258	259	323	1,089	-
Shrewsbury and Hereford	*Leased to the Great Western and London and North-Western.*										
Shropshire Union Railways and Canal	*Leased to the London and North-Western.*										
Sirhowy	16	4,786	6,775	1,052	3,265	1,745	1,518	31	-	-	90
Somerset and Dorset	66	8,779	18,217	4,473	14,995	4,045	628	708	171	43	102
South Devon (Including the "Buckfastleigh, Totnes, and South Devon," and "Launceston and South Devon.")	122	28,434	47,111	9,625	41,622	8,056	3,541	4,805	825	883	626
South-Eastern (Including the "London and Greenwich.")	336	128,935	205,741	61,696	226,299	58,563	62,851	46,940	4,243	3,389	11,005
South Wales Mineral	13	2,623	2,757	606	1,005	406	219	-	-	-	-
South Yorkshire and River Dun	*Leased to the Manchester, Sheffield, and Lincolnshire.*										
Spilsby and Firsby	*Worked by the Great Northern.*										
Stafford and Uttoxeter	13	1,285	1,207	152	376	459	40	8	-	-	-
Staines, Wokingham, and Woking	*Leased to the London and South-Western.*										
Stamford and Essendine	*Worked by the Great Northern.*										
Stokes Bay Railway and Pier	*Worked by the London and South-Western.*										
Stonehouse and Nailsworth	*Worked by the Midland.*										
Stratford-upon-Avon	*Worked by the Great Western.*										
Swansea and Carmarthen (From 1st January to 31st July 1873; after which time the Swansea Section, 16 miles in length, was sold to the "London and North-Western," and the name of the Company changed to the "Central Wales and Carmarthen Junction," which see.)	29†	3,692	-	145	1,463	390	296	58	-	-	-
Swansea Vale	21	6,194	8,449	1,472	4,574	1,611	1,072	62	480‡	45	64
Taff Vale (Including the "Aberdare," "Dare Valley," "Llantrisant and Taff Vale Junction," and "Penarth Harbour, Dock, and Railway.")	74	43,392	100,757	21,271	53,227	9,779	18,317	3,135	3	429	2,656
Talyllyn *	7	475	442	211	553	154	169	13	-	-	-
Tees Valley	*Worked by the North-Eastern.*										
Tenbury	*Worked by the London and North-Western and Great Western.*										
Tendring Hundred } *Tendring Hundred Extension*	*Worked by the Great Eastern.*										

* For the year ended 30th September 1873.   † On the 31st July 1873.   ‡ Chiefly small waggons used upon the Company's tramway.

Steamboat, Canal, and Harbour Expenses.	Miscellaneous Working Expenditure not included in the foregoing.	Total Working Expenditure.	Total Receipts, as given in the Traffic Return, No. 2.	Net Receipts.	Proportion per Cent. of Expenditure to Total Receipts.	ROLLING STOCK on 31st December 1878.						NAME OF COMPANY.
						Locomotives.	Carriages used for the Conveyance of Passengers only.	Other Vehicles attached to Passenger Trains.	Waggons of all kinds used for the Conveyance of Live Stock, Minerals, or General Merchandise.	Any other Carriages or Waggons used on the Railway, not included in the preceding Columns.	Total Number of Vehicles of all descriptions for Conveyance of Passengers, Live Stock, Ballast, &c.	
£	£	£	£	£		No.	No.	No.	No.	No.	No.	
.	231	13,418	23,396	9,978	57	6	20	3	195	5	223	Pembroke and Tenby.
												Penarth Harbour, Dock, and Railway.
												Peterborough, Wisbeach, and Sutton.
.	90	10,375	10,408	33	100	6	13	3	373	.	389	Potteries, Shrewsbury, and North Wales.
												Preston and Wyre.
												Redditch.
.	248	4,203	5,113	910	82	3	.	.	112	.	112	Redruth and Chacewater.
.	.	55,558	108,851	53,293	51	32	26	5	160	22	215	Rhymney.
												Ringwood, Christchurch and Bournemouth.
												Ross and Monmouth.
												Royston and Hitchin.
.	443	7,999	15,806	7,807	51	.	9	7	.	19	35	Ryde Pier.
												Saffron Walden.
												Salisbury and Dorset Junction.
												Salisbury and Yeovil.
												Salisbury Railway and Market House.
.	.	382	546	164	70	.	.	.	.	.	.	Saundersfoot Railway and Harbour.
												Seaton and Beer.
												Sevenoaks, Maidstone, and Tonbridge.
.	2,352	15,346	28,306	13,858	54	7	.	.	152½	.	152½	Severn and Wye Railway and Canal.
.	545	45,297	49,692	6,395	87	.	.	.	.	.	.	Sheffield and Midland Committee.
												Shrewsbury and Hereford.
												Shropshire Union Railways and Canal.
.	114	19,376	30,712	11,336	63	9	12	.	.	27	39	Sirhowy.
.	1,036	53,192	61,687	8,495	86	19	55	28	625	41	749	Somerset and Dorset.
.	3,587	149,165	304,420	155,255	49	79	132	70	610	82	894	South Devon.
40,587	12,823	865,472	1,819,362	953,890	48	243	1,374	428	3,550	292	5,653	South-Eastern.
.	.	7,616	8,802	1,186	87	4	.	.	280	.	280	South Wales Mineral.
												South Yorkshire and River Dun.
												Spilsby and Firsby.
.	1,100	4,627	3,160	1,467 Deficiency.	146	2	8	1	16	1	26	Stafford and Uttoxeter.
												Staines, Wokingham, and Woking.
												Stamford and Essendine.
												Stokes Bay Railway and Pier.
												Stonehouse and Nailsworth.
												Stratford-upon-Avon.
.	233	6,269	19,639	13,370	32	‖-	‖-	‖-	‖-	‖-	.	Swansea and Carmarthen.
.	.	23,966	46,101	24,135	50	12	16	1	295	.	312	Swansea Vale.
6,400	33,547	302,913	509,841	206,928	59	91	70	18	2,783	183	3,054	Taff Vale.
.	.	2,047	1,879	568 Deficiency.	122	2	4	1	114	.	119	Talyllyn.
												Tees Valley.
												Tenbury.
												{ *Tendring Hundred.*
												{ *Tendring Hundred Extension.*

‖ The traffic is carried in the trains of the London and North-Western Railway Company.

NAME OF COMPANY.	Length of Line in Miles open on 31st December 1873.	WORKING EXPENDITURE.									
		Maintenance of Way, Works, &c.	Locomotive Power (including Stationary Engines).	Repairs and Renewals of Carriages and Waggons.	Traffic Expenses (Coaching and Merchandise).	General Charges.	Rates and Taxes.	Government Duty.	Compensation for Personal Injury, &c.	Compensation for Damage and Loss of Goods.	Legal and Parliamentary Expenses.
	No.	£	£	£	£	£	£	£	£	£	£
Towkesbury and Malvern	*Worked by the Midland.*										
Thetford and Watton	9	436	858	-	610	117	29	82	-	-	-
Torbay and Brixham	2	277	881	-	874	72	26	40	-	-	-
Tottenham and Hampstead Junction	5	*	*	*	4,342	270	*	*	-	-	-
Trent, Ancholme, and Grimsby	13	3,811	10,.66		1,630	675	132	52	-	-	-
Vale of Llangollen	*Leased to the Great Western.*										
Vale of Towy	*Leased to the Llanelly and London and North-Western.*										
Victoria Station and Pimlico	*Used by the London, Chatham, and Dover, Great Western, London and North-Western, and London, Brighton, and South Coast.*										
Wainfleet and Firsby	*Worked by the Great Northern.*										
Watford and Rickmansworth	*Worked by the London and North-Western.*										
Watlington and Princes Risborough	8	447	1,162	-	326	234	42	31	-	-	9
Wellington and Drayton	*Worked by the Great Western.*										
Wellington and Severn Junction	*Leased to the Great Western.*										
Wenlock	*Worked by the Great Western.*										
West Cornwall Committee	33	7,512	10,629	4,758	9,408	1,396	890	497	-	511	-
West London	*Leased to the Great Western and London and North-Western.*										
West London Extension	*Line worked by the London and North-Western, Great Western, London and South-Western, and London, Brighton, and South Coast Railway Companies.*										
West Norfolk Junction	*Worked by the Great Eastern.*										
West Riding and Grimsby	26	21,428	18,240	-	3,449	1,140	965	589	-	3	499
West Somerset	*Leased to the Bristol and Exeter.*										
West Somerset Mineral	12	1,957	1,270	320	836‡	-	139	12	-	-	-
Weymouth and Portland	*Worked by the Great Western and London and South-Western.*										
Whitehaven, Cleator, and Egremont (Including the "Cleator and Furness" Joint Line.)	27	8,065	14,343	4,206	8,481	1,739	648	289	-	24	40
Witney	*Worked by the Great Western.*										
Wivenhoe and Brightlingsea	*Worked by the Great Eastern.*										
Wolverhampton and Walsall	*Worked by the London and North-Western.*										
Wrexham, Mold, and Connah's Quay (Including the "Buckley.")	16	1,458	4,116	285	3,874	1,498	265	30	-	104	227
TOTAL ENGLAND AND WALES	11,369	4,619,007	7,640,741	1,952,608	7,209,782	943,462	904,551	462,317	300,683	196,531	318,475
		and 38,894*l.* not classified.									

* These charges are paid by and included in the returns of the Midland and Great Eastern Railway Companies.
‡ Including establishment charges.

Steamboat, Canal, and Harbour Expenses.	Miscellaneous Working Expenditure not included in the foregoing.	TOTAL WORKING EXPENDITURE.	TOTAL RECEIPTS, as given in the TRAFFIC RETURN, No. 2.	NET RECEIPTS.	Proportion per Cent. of Expenditure to Total Receipts.	ROLLING STOCK. on 31st December 1873.						NAME OF COMPANY.
							CARRIAGES, WAGGONS, TRUCKS, &c.					
						Locomotives.	Carriages used for the Conveyance of Passengers only.	Other Vehicles attached to Passenger Train.	Waggons of all kinds used for the Conveyance of Live Stock, Minerals, or General Merchandise.	Any other Carriages or Waggons used on the Railway, not included in the preceding Columns.	Total Number of Vehicles of all descriptions for Conveyance of Passengers, Live Stock, Ballast, &c.	
£	£	£	£	£		No.	No.	No.	No.	No.	No.	
												Tewkesbury and Malvern.
-	84	2,216	2,740	524	81	2	4	-	6	-	10	Thetford and Watton.
-	-	1,679	1,568	111 Deficiency.	107	1	2	-	-	-	2	Torbay and Brixham.
-	-	4,612	14,026	9,414	-	-	-	-	-	-	-	Tottenham and Hampstead Junction.
-	-	16,466	28,464	11,998	58	Provided by the Manchester, Sheffield, and Lincolnshire Railway Company.						Trent, Ancholme, and Grimsby.
												Vale of Llangollen.
												Vale of Towy.
												Victoria Station and Pimlico.
												Wainfleet and Firsby.
												Watford and Rickmansworth.
-	372	2,633	1,841	792 Deficiency.	143	†-	-†	-	-	6	-	6	Watlington and Princes Risborough.
												Wellington and Drayton.
												Wellington and Severn Junction.
												Wenlock.
-	186	35,234	50,176	14,942	70	11	9	22	615	-	646	West Cornwall Committee.
												West London.
												West London Extension.
												West Norfolk Junction.
-	9,913	55,335	80,823	25,488	68	Rolling Stock provided by the Great Northern and Manchester, Sheffield, and Lincolnshire Railway Companies.						West Riding and Grimsby.
												West Somerset.
-	635	5,169	6,314	1,145	82	4	3	-	91	3	97	West Somerset Mineral.
												Weymouth and Portland.
-	-	37,785	81,055	43,270	47	16	20	4	1,266	10	1,300	Whitehaven, Cleator, and Egremont.
												Witney.
												Wivenhoe and Brightlingsea.
												Wolverhampton and Walsall.
109	2,616	14,277	20,002	5,425	73	6	8	2	112	6	128	Wrexham, Mold, and Connah's Quay.
601,740	454,369	25,813,877§	48,857,278	23,043,901	53	9,536	20,421	7,590	249,117	4,228	281,356	TOTAL ENGLAND AND WALES.

† The Great Western Company supply engines and carriages for working the line.
§ Less 14,068*l.* received by North London Company for working other lines.

No. 3.—Working Expenditure, Net Receipts,

NAME OF COMPANY.	Length of Line in Miles open on 31st January 1874.	WORKING EXPENDITURE.									
		Maintenance of Way, Works, &c.	Locomotive Power (including Stationary Engines).	Repairs and Renewals of Carriages and Waggons.	Traffic Expenses (Coaching and Merchandise).	General Charges.	Rates and Taxes.	Government Duty.	Compensation for Personal Injury, &c.	Compensation for Damage and Loss of Goods.	Legal and Parliamentary Expenses.
	No.	£	£	£	£	£	£	£	£	£	£
Aboyne and Braemar	*Worked by the Great North of Scotland.*										
Alyth	*Leased to the Caledonian.*										
Arbroath and Forfar	*Leased to the Caledonian.*										
Berwickshire	*Worked by the North British.*										
Blane Valley	*Worked by the North British.*										
Busby	*Worked by the Caledonian.*										
Caledonian (Including the "Alyth," "Arbroath and Forfar," "Busby," "Callander and Oban," "Dundee and Newtyle," "Greenock and Wemyss Bay," "Montrose and Bervie," "Port Patrick," "Solway Junction," and half the "Glasgow and Kilmarnock," "Glasgow and Paisley," and "Glasgow, Barrhead, and Neilston" Joint Lines.)	820	251,446	496,763	161,153	377,598	48,275	46,307	14,349	32,924	8,221	12,400
Callander and Oban	*Worked by the Caledonian.*										
Carlisle and Silloth Bay	*Leased to the North British.*										
City of Glasgow Union	3	1,948	-	-	-	9,000*	1,506	1,711	53	-	1	2,273
Deeside	*Leased to the Great North of Scotland.*										
Deeside Extension											
Devon Valley	*Worked by the North British.*										
Dingwall and Skye	*Worked by the Highland.*										
Dundee and Newtyle	*Leased to the Caledonian.*										
Edinburgh and Bathgate	*Leased to the North British.*										
Findhorn†	-	-	-	-	-	-	-	-	-	-	-
Forth and Clyde Junction	*Leased to the North British.*										
Glasgow and Milngavie Junction	*Worked by the North British until the 31st July, from which date it was amalgamated with that Company.*										
Glasgow and South-Western (Including the "Ayr and Maybole," "Kilmarnock and Troon," and half of the "Glasgow, Barrhead, and Neilston," "Glasgow and Kilmarnock," and "Glasgow and Paisley" Joint Lines.)	315	116,739	155,806	45,272	116,023	17,507	18,481	5,390	1,242	2,835	6,487
Great North of Scotland (Including the "Aboyne and Braemar," "Deeside," "Deeside Extension," and "Morayshire.")	296	22,696	32,920	12,961	31,961	5,491	6,473	2,406	50	333	784
Greenock and Wemyss Bay	*Worked by the Caledonian.*										
Highland‡ (Including the "Dingwall and Skye," the "Sutherland," and the "Duke of Sutherland's.")	335	32,905	40,963	9,071	37,709	8,028	8,579	3,763	525	128	382
Kilmarnock and Troon	*Leased to the Glasgow and South-Western.*										
Leven and East of Fife	20	4,550	3,534	983	3,181	536	271	331	-	52	-
Montrose and Bervie	*Worked by the Caledonian.*										
Morayshire	*Worked by the Great North of Scotland.*										
North British (Including the "Berwickshire," "Blane Valley," "Carlisle and Silloth Bay," "Devon Valley," "Edinburgh and Bathgate," "Forth and Clyde," "Glasgow and Milngavie Junction," "Peebles," "Penicuik," "Port Carlisle Dock and Railway," and "St. Andrews.")	833	252,962	305,675	107,560	321,562	38,406	25,224	17,246	21,826	12,851	46,656
Peebles	*Leased to the North British.*										
Penicuik	*Worked by the North British.*										
Port Carlisle Dock and Railway	*Leased to the North British.*										
Port Patrick	*Worked by the Caledonian.*										
St. Andrews	*Worked by the North British.*										
Solway Junction	*Leased to the Caledonian.*										
Sutherland	*Worked by the Highland.*										
Sutherland's, Duke of	*Worked by the Highland.*										
TOTAL SCOTLAND	2,612	683,048	1,032,961	336,061	897,384	120,071	108,844	44,138	56,567	24,409	68,993

Note.—The financial year of the Scotch Railway Companies,

* Towards this expenditure other Companies contributed 7,037*l.*   † Line closed since 30th January 1869.   ‡ For the year ended 25th February 1874.

and Rolling Stock, SCOTLAND, in 1873.

Steamboat, Canal, and Harbour Expenses.	Miscellaneous Working Expenditure not included in the foregoing.	Total Working Expenditure.	Total Receipts, as given in the Traffic Return, No. 2.	Net Receipts.	Proportion per Cent. of Expenditure to Total Receipts.	ROLLING STOCK on 31st January 1874.						NAME OF COMPANY.
						Locomotives.	CARRIAGES, WAGGONS, TRUCKS, &c.					
							Carriages used for the Conveyance of Passengers only.	Other Vehicles attached to Passenger Trains.	Waggons of all kinds used for the Conveyance of Live Stock, Minerals, or General Merchandise.	Any other Carriages or Waggons used on the Railway, not included in the preceding Columns.	Total Number of Vehicles of all descriptions for Conveyance of Passengers, Live Stock, Ballast, &c.	
£	£	£	£	£		No.	No.	No.	No.	No.	No.	
												Aboyne and Braemar.
												Alyth.
												Arbroath and Forfar.
												Berwickshire.
												Blane Valley.
												Busby.
34,337	25,383	1,511,615	2,802,416	1,290,801	54	896	1,076	383	30,714	546	32,719	Caledonian.
												Callander and Oban.
												Carlisle and Silloth Bay.
..	1,358	17,350*	48,117	32,304	..	This Company has no Rolling Stock.						City of Glasgow Union.
												{Deeside.
												{Deeside Extension.
												Devon Valley.
												Dingwall and Skye.
												Dundee and Newtyle.
												Edinburgh and Bathgate.
..	..	..	..	..	..	..	..	..	..	..	..	Findhorn.
												Forth and Clyde Junction.
												Glasgow and Milngavie Junction.
8,556	3,769	496,114	881,054	382,920	57	219	475	166	9,168	240	10,049	Glasgow and South-Western.
411	6,623	122,490	249,616	127,126	49	53	171	27	1,739	33	1,960	Great North of Scotland.
												Greenock and Wemyss Bay.
..	6,061	147,933	297,428	149,495	50	87	171	64	1,514	22	1,771	Highland.
												Kilmarnock and Troon.
..	541	13,131	22,542	9,411	58	4	9	3	213	..	225	Leven and East of Fife.
												Montrose and Bervie.
												Morayshire.
42,920	22,965	1,213,968	2,011,685	797,647	60	449	1,170	330	22,012	150	23,662	North British.
												Peebles.
												Penicuik.
												Port Carlisle Dock and Railway.
												Port Patrick.
												St. Andrews.
												Solway Junction.
												Sutherland.
												Sutherland's, Duke of.
86,224	66,459	3,515,864||	6,307,738	2,789,704	56	1,380	3,072	973	65,350	991	70,286	TOTAL SCOTLAND.

except when otherwise stated, ends on 31st January 1874.

§ From the 31st July the Glasgow and Milngavie Company was amalgamated with the North British.

|| Exclusive of 7,687l. expended by the City of Glasgow Union for other Companies.

No. 3.—Working Expenditure, Net Receipts,

NAME OF COMPANY.	Length of Line in Miles open on 31st December 1873.	Maintenance of Way, Works, &c.	Locomotive Power (including Stationary Engines)	Repairs and Renewals of Carriages and Wagons	Traffic Expenses (Coaching and Merchandise).	General Charges.	Rates and Taxes.	Government Duty.	Compensation for Personal Injury, &c.	Compensation for Damage and Loss of Goods.	Legal and Parliamentary Expenses.
	No.	£	£	£	£	£	£	£	£	£	£
Athenry and Ennis Junction - - - -	Leased to the Waterford and Limerick.										
Athenry and Tuam - - - -	Leased to the Waterford and Limerick.										
Banbridge Junction - - - -	Leased to the Dublin and Belfast Junction.										
Banbridge, Lisburn, and Belfast - -	Leased to the Ulster.										
Belfast and County Down - - - (Including the "Downpatrick, Dundrum, and Newcastle.")	55	8,480	14,393	3,295	8,145	2,244	649	-	304	197	103
Belfast and Northern Counties - - (Including the "Carrickfergus and Larne.")	151	35,391	53,471	8,254	34,763	6,497	3,721	-	556	801	147
Belfast, Holywood, and Bangor - -	12	1,652	4,509	347	2,642	1,060	239	-	-	3	39
Carrickfergus and Larne - - -	Worked by the Belfast and Northern Counties.										
Cork and Bandon - - - (Including the "Cork and Kinsale Junction.")	31	4,676	6,315	1,537	5,347	982	1,768	-	1,490	66	-
Cork and Kinsale Junction - -	Worked by the Cork and Bandon.										
Cork and Macroom Direct - -	25	2,430	2,509	414	2,104	472	247	-	82	-	-
Cork, Blackrock, and Passage* - -	6	1,271	2,175	353	1,534	690	630	-	15	13	31
Downpatrick, Dundrum, and Newcastle -	Worked by the Belfast and County Down.										
Dublin and Antrim Junction - -	Worked by the Ulster.										
Dublin and Belfast Junction - - (Including the "Banbridge Junction.")	63	12,824	17,167	2,796	8,682	3,733	3,158	-	38	102	70
Dublin and Drogheda - - - -	75	14,388	19,042	4,122	12,332	3,639	3,756	-	42	246	727
Dublin and Kingstown - - -	Leased to the Dublin, Wicklow, and Wexford.										
Dublin and Meath - - - -	Worked by the Midland Great Western of Ireland.										
Dublin, Wicklow, and Wexford† - - (Including the "Dublin and Kingstown.")	122	25,978	29,854	7,261	27,370	4,961	8,965	-	260	412	1,266
Dundalk, Newry, and Greenore - -	The accounts are a subject of dispute between the working companies. No correct information can be given.										
Enniskillen, Bundoran, and Sligo - -	Worked by the Irish North-Western.										
Fermoy and Lismore - - - -	Worked by the Great Southern and Western of Ireland.										
Finn Valley - - - - -	Worked by the Irish North-Western.										
Great Northern and Western of Ireland -	Worked by the Midland Great Western of Ireland.										
Great Southern and Western of Ireland (Including the "Fermoy and Lismore" and the "Parsonstown and Portumna Bridge.")	464	114,400	120,113	26,588	84,344	12,090	22,785	-	1,980	2,702	1,165
Irish North-Western - - - (Including "Clones and Cavan Extension," "Enniskillen, Bundoran, and Sligo," "Finn Valley," and "Londonderry and Enniskillen.")	195	25,475	33,669	5,646	19,395	4,239	2,394	-	1,696	1,003	1,673
Kilkenny Junction - - - -	Worked by the Waterford and Central Ireland.										
Limerick and Ennis - - -	Worked by the Waterford and Limerick.										
Limerick and Foynes - - -	Worked by the Waterford and Limerick till 30th June 1873, and amalgamated with that Company from that date.										
Londonderry and Enniskillen - -	Worked by the Irish North-Western.										
Londonderry and Lough Swilly‡ - -	12	650	1,514	136	1,047	305	4	-	26	26	24

* For the year ended 31st October 1873.   † Including the working expenses of 6½ miles of tramway.   ‡ For the year ended 31st January 1874.

and Rolling Stock, IRELAND, in 1873.

Steamboat, Canal, and Harbour Expenses. £	Miscellaneous Working Expenditure not included in the foregoing. £	Total Working Expenditure. £	Total Receipts, as given in the Return, No. 2. £	Net Receipts. £	Proportion per Cent. of Expenditure to Total Receipts.	ROLLING STOCK on 31st December 1873. CARRIAGES, WAGGONS, TRUCKS, &c. Locomotives. No.	Carriages used for the Conveyance of Passengers only. No.	Other Vehicles attached to Passenger Trains. No.	Waggons of all kinds used for the Conveyance of Live Stock, Minerals, or General Merchandise. No.	Any other Carriages or Waggons used on the Railway, not included in the preceding Columns. No.	Total Number of Vehicles of all descriptions for Conveyance of Passengers, Live Stock, Ballast, &c. No.	NAME OF COMPANY.
												Athenry and Ennis Junction.
												Athenry and Tuam.
												Banbridge Junction.
												Banbridge, Lisburn, and Belfast.
-	81	37,791	56,794	19,008	67	13	54	13	296	-	363	Belfast and County Down.
-	504	114,554	186,893	72,339	61	41	109	38	984	31	1,112	Belfast and Northern Counties.
-	276	10,767	17,143	6,376	63	5	46	4	13	-	63	Belfast, Holywood, and Bangor.
												Carrickfergus and Larne.
-	869	22,900	35,780	12,880	64	8	13	10	115	-	138	Cork and Bandon.
												Cork and Kinsale Junction.
-	1,887	10,094	17,428	7,334	58	3	9	3	63	-	75	Cork and Macroom Direct.
-	94	7,098	13,648	6,546	52	3	12	1	2	-	16	Cork, Blackrock, and Passage.
												Downpatrick, Dundrum, and Newcastle.
												Dublin and Antrim Junction.
-	145	46,655	96,312	49,647	50	22	54	27	281	-	348	Dublin and Belfast Junction.
-	507	58,801	122,675	63,874	48	22	66	40	275	28	409	Dublin and Drogheda.
												Dublin and Kingstown.
												Dublin and Meath.
-	1,654	107,991	225,695	117,704	48	47	141	23	532	19	764	Dublin, Wicklow, and Wexford.
												Dundalk, Newry, and Greenore.
												Enniskillen, Bundoran, and Sligo.
												Fermoy and Lismore.
												Finn Valley.
												Great Northern and Western of Ireland.
-	4,550	390,617	706,459	315,842	55	131	241	149	2,404	-	2,794	Great Southern and Western of Ireland.
-	83	94,479	151,788	57,309	62	35	51	48	614	2	709	Irish North-Western.
												Kilkenny Junction.
												Limerick and Ennis.
												Limerick and Foynes.
												Londonderry and Enniskillen.
-	949	4,722	5,947	1,225	79	2	6	1	20	-	27	Londonderry and Lough Swilly.

34569.   M

NAME OF COMPANY.	Length of Line in Miles open on 31st December 1873.	WORKING EXPENDITURE.									
		Maintenance of Way, Works, &c.	Locomotive Power (including Stationary Engines).	Repair and Renewals of Carriages and Waggons.	Traffic Expenses (Coaching and Merchandise).	General Charges.	Rates and Taxes.	Government Duty.	Compensation for Personal Injury, &c.	Compensation for Damage and Loss of Goods.	Legal and Parliamentary Expenses.
	No.	£	£	£	£	£	£	£	£	£	£
Midland Great Western of Ireland . . . (Including the "Dublin and Meath," "Great Northern and Western of Ireland," and "Navan and Kingscourt.")	400	72,575	73,303	23,243	68,539	9,760	8,680	.	532	3,003	2,851
Navan and Kingscourt . . .	Worked by the Midland Great Western of Ireland.										
Newry and Armagh	22	1,315	4,089	302	2,788	1,356	104	.	.	.	172
Newry, Warrenpoint, and Rostrevor . .	6	741	2,707	1,090	1,235	412	57	.	.	80	.
Parsonstown and Portumna Bridge . .	Worked by the Great Southern and Western of Ireland.										
Portadown, Dungannon, and Omagh Junction	Leased to the Ulster.										
Rathkeale and Newcastle Junction . .	Worked by the Waterford and Limerick.										
Ulster . . . (Including "Banbridge, Lisburn, and Belfast," "Dublin and Antrim Junction," and "Portadown, Dungannon, and Omagh Junction.")	140	22,531	29,770	5,516	23,744	6,144	5,465	.	278	1,438	388
Waterford and Central Ireland* . . (Including the "Kilkenny Junction.")	60	8,387	9,068	1,371	7,047	1,338	878	.	.	110	102
Waterford and Limerick† . . . (Including the "Athenry and Ennis Junction," "Athenry and Tuam," "Limerick and Ennis," "Limerick and Foynes,"† and "Rathkeale and Newcastle Junction.")	203	23,549	26,476	4,883	20,278	4,361	2,769	.	45	325	608
Waterford and Tramore . . .	7	680	1,229	163	492	415	66	.	.	.	.
Waterford, New Ross, and Wexford‡ . .	34	754	1,517	127	1,099	696	27	.	13	5	19
West Cork	18	1,776	3,966	108	1,235	477	73	.	.	15	.
TOTAL IRELAND . .	2,161	381,341	436,808	99,464	323,701	66,366	66,648	.	7,259	10,747	9,360

* For the year ended 29th September 1873.
† The Limerick and Castle-Connell and Killaloe Extension from the 1st January 1873, and the Limerick and Foynes from the 1st July 1873, were amalgamated with the Waterford and Limerick.
‡ The line was closed from 30th September to the end of the year.

Steamboat, Canal, and Harbour Expenses.	Miscellaneous Working Expenditure not included in the foregoing.	Total Working Expenditure.	Total Receipts, as given in the Traffic Return, No. 1.	Net Receipts.	Proportion per Cent. of Expenditure to Total Receipts.	ROLLING STOCK on 31st December 1873.						NAME OF COMPANY.
						Locomotives.	CARRIAGES, WAGGONS, TRUCKS, &c.					
							Carriages used for the Conveyance of Passengers only.	Other Vehicles attached to Passenger Trains.	Waggons of all kinds used for the Conveyance of Live Stock, Minerals, or General Merchandise.	Any other Carriages or Waggons used on the Railway, not included in the preceding Columns.	Total Number of Vehicles of all descriptions for Conveyance of Passengers, Live Stock, Ballast, &c.	
£	£	£	£	£		No.	No.	No.	No.	No.	No.	
4,763	-	265,591	474,547	206,956	56	92	146	108	1,701	-	1,955	Midland Great Western of Ireland.
												Navan and Kingscourt.
.	.	496	10,594	16,228	5,634	65	7	12	5	175	3	195	Newry and Armagh.
.	.	.	6,322	7,172	850	88	4	9	-	83	-	91	Newry, Warrenpoint, and Rostrevor,
												Parsonstown and Portumna Bridge.
												Portadown, Dungannon, and Omagh Junction.
												Rathkeale and Newcastle Junction.
.	.	.	100,544	212,218	111,674	47	37	82	42	819	20	943	Ulster.
.	.	1,224	29,525	47,154	17,629	63	11	26	12	178	-	216	Waterford and Central Ireland.
.	.	1,570	86,256	163,363	77,107	53	29	59	39	626	-	724	Waterford and Limerick.
.	.	.	3,062	6,466	3,414	47	4	13	2	6	-	23	Waterford and Tramore.
.	.	.	4,256	2,090	2,166 Deficiency.	204	1	‖ :	‖	14	‖	14	Waterford, New Ross, and Wexford.
.	.	.	6,770	9,140	2,870	74	§2	11	7	32	-	§50	West Cork.
4,763	14,840	1,421,387	2,576,934	1,155,547	55	519	1,141	565	9,234	103	11,043	TOTAL IRELAND.

§ All the rolling stock is hired from the Railway Rolling Stock Company.
‖ The Great Southern and Western Railway Company supply part of the rolling stock.

LONDON:

Printed by GEORGE EDWARD EYRE and WILLIAM SPOTTISWOODE,
Printers to the Queen's most Excellent Majesty.
For Her Majesty's Stationery Office.

GENERAL REPORT

BY

CAPTAIN TYLER

IN REGARD TO

THE SHARE AND LOAN CAPITAL, THE TRAFFIC IN PASSENGERS AND GOODS,

AND THE

WORKING EXPENDITURE AND NET PROFITS FROM RAILWAY WORKING

OF THE

RAILWAY COMPANIES

OF THE

UNITED KINGDOM,

For the Year 1872.

LONDON:

PRINTED BY GEORGE EDWARD EYRE AND WILLIAM SPOTTISWOODE,

PRINTERS TO THE QUEEN'S MOST EXCELLENT MAJESTY.

FOR HER MAJESTY'S STATIONERY OFFICE.

1874.

[C.—928.]   *Price 2½d.*

1, Whitehall,
17th November 1873.

To the Secretary, Railway Department, Board of Trade.

Sir,

In pursuance of the course which I adopted for the two previous years, and in compliance with your instructions, I have now the honour to lay before the Board of Trade a General Report in regard to the share and loan capital, the traffic in passengers and goods, the working expenditure, and the realized profits of the Railway Companies of the United Kingdom for 1872; with such observations as appear to be called for in reference to alterations which have taken place, as well as in reference to the present condition and future prospects of the railway system of this country.

The accompanying tables, from 1 to 10 inclusive, forming a summary of the information furnished by the Railway Companies, and published at length in the returns of the Board of Trade already presented to Parliament, which have been prepared for me under the superintendence of Mr. M'Kenzie, show at a glance the most interesting particulars of this description.

Railway Extension.

, The total length of railway open for passenger traffic on the 31st December 1872, was, as returned by the Railway Companies, 15,814 miles, distributed as follows: —In England, 11,136 miles: in Scotland, 2,587 miles: in Ireland, 2,091 miles. There was an increase between the 31st December 1871 and the 31st December 1872, according to the figures compiled in both years from the returns of the Railway Companies, from 15,376 miles to 15,814 miles,˙or at the rate of nearly 3 per cent. There was thus an apparent increase from 10,850 miles to 11,136 miles, or 2·6 per cent., in England; from 2,538 miles to 2,587 miles, or 1·9 per cent., in Scotland; and from 1,988 miles to 2,091 miles, or 5·2 per cent., in Ireland. But the actual increase, as calculated from the portions of railway inspected on behalf of the Board of Trade, and authorised to be opened during the year, was, in England 135 miles; in Scotland 22 miles; and in Ireland 46 miles; making a total of 203 miles for the year. The great difference between the above apparent increase of 438 miles, and the actual increase, thus computed, of 203 miles, is due almost entirely to the incomplete returns furnished by some of the railway companies for the year 1871. A large addition to the above mileage may be expected when the railways which have been authorised by Parliament during the last few years for improving through routes, forming connecting links, and providing branch lines, have been constructed and opened. The aggregate length of railways so authorised during the three years 1870, 1871, and 1872 alone amount to more than 1,100 miles.

Capital.

The total capital raised by shares, stocks, and loans amounted to 552,680,107*l.* on the 31st December 1871, and to 569,047,346*l.* on the 31st December 1872, showing an increase of 16,367,239*l.* during the latter year. The average expenditure per mile of railway open, which was 34,099*l.* at the end of 1858, increased to 34,106*l.* at the end of 1870, to 35,944*l.* at the end of 1871, and to 35,984*l.* at the end of 1872. The progressive increase of expenditure per mile of railway open during these years must be attributed mainly to the necessity of providing further accommodation in stations, lines, and sidings, and extra rolling stock, for a constantly increasing traffic on the older lines, and especially in connexion with the traffic on the through lines and in the manufacturing districts; and it may be observed that if on some of the railways a much larger expenditure had been incurred in providing siding and other accommodation for goods and mineral traffic, greater safety, convenience, and even economy in working would at the present time be experienced. The above total increase of capital has occurred in very different proportions in the various descriptions of stocks and loans.

A 2

Whilst the increase in ordinary shares for the year 1871 over the year 1870 was rather under a million, or only ·42 per cent., the increase in ordinary shares for the year 1872 over the year 1871 was nearly 9 millions, viz., from 230,250,152*l.* to 239,039,089*l.*, or nearly 3·8 per cent. The increase in guaranteed and preference stocks or shares was from 173,051,875*l.* at the end of 1871 to 177,764,674*l.* at the end of 1872, or 2·7 per cent.; and that in loans and debenture stocks was from 149,378,080*l.* to 152,205,728*l,* or 1·9 per cent. But the debenture stocks increased at the rate of 28 per cent.—from 67,282,535*l.* to 85,891,511*l.*; whilst the terminable loans decreased at the rate of 19 per cent.—from 82,095,545*l.* to 66,224,217*l.* No interest whatever was paid upon 9,207,357*l.* of preference stock, apparently from an absence of profit in working; or upon 59,200*l.* of loans or 594,578*l.* of debenture stock, mainly from these sums not having matured sufficiently long to receive interest. No interest was pa d upon 32,901,496*l.* of ordinary stock, either of companies with lines or portions of lines not yet brought into work, or of companies whose affairs were in a low condition. It would not now be easy to ascertain what proportion of the par value of these stocks and loans has been actually paid for them by the public; but it is certain that in consequence of the mode in which the money has been raised there is a great difference between the nominal value of many of them and the amounts actually received by the companies for them.

Proportions of Ordinary and Preferential to total Capital.

The percentage proportions of ordinary capital, preferential capital, and debenture stocks and loans, taken together, to the total capital, have not altered during the year 1872. But the percentage of loans has decreased from 15 per cent. in 1871 to 12 per cent. in 1872, whereas the percentage of debenture stocks has increased from 12 per cent. in 1871 to 15 per cent. in 1872; and their proportions are therefore exactly reversed. The ordinary capital remains at 42 per cent., the debenture and loan capital at 27 per cent., and the guaranteed and preference stock at 31 per cent. of the whole, their proportions being the same at the end of 1872 as at the end of 1871.

I may repeat here what I have previously said that :—" There appears to be no good " reason why the shareholders of a company should not do as they think proper, and " find it expedient to do, in these respects. It may be right that in the instance of " a projected railway the proportions between the ordinary capital and the loans should " be regulated and defined, as is done by law in every Railway Act; but even these " legal restrictions have in some cases been evaded or overridden; and financial " restrictions upon existing companies, with working railways, either as to the power " of raising money, or as to the interest to be paid for it, have frequently done harm on " the one hand by aggravating financial difficulties, while they have failed, on the other " hand, as regards the protection which they were expected to afford."

Rates of Interest.

The average rate of interest paid on ordinary capital was 5·14 per cent. for 1872, against 5·07 per cent. for 1871, showing an increase of ·07 per cent.; whilst on preferential and loan capital the average interest paid was 4·39 for 1872, against 4·42 for 1871, showing a decrease of ·03 per cent. The average interest on debenture loans decreased from 4·37 in 1870, to 4·25 in 1871, and 4·19 in 1872; and that on debenture stock from 4·47 in 1870, to 4·37 in 1871, and 4·34 in 1872. The 4·54 per cent. of interest paid on 158,692,084*l.* of guaranteed and preference stock for 1870, was changed for 1871 into 4·51 per cent. on 173,051,875*l.*, and, for 1872, into 4·49 per cent. on 177,764,674*l.*

The average interest paid on the *total* capital increased from 3·75 per cent. for 1858, to 4·19 per cent. for 1870, to 4·43 per cent. for 1871, and to 4·51 per cent. for 1872; whilst the average interest on preferential and loan capital taken together decreased from 4·63 per cent. for 1858, to 4·48 per cent. for 1870, to 4·42 per cent. for 1871, and to 4·39 per cent. for 1872. These are, perhaps, the most interesting facts connected with railway working in the four years. The interest on the total capital exceeded the interest on the loans, debenture stock, and preferential capital in the proportion of 4·75 to 4·39 for 1872; but the interest on ordinary capital, which (including the portion on which no dividend was paid) averaged 5·14 per cent. exceeded the fixed interest on stocks and loans preferred to it, which (including also those which received no cash payment) averaged only 4·39 per cent.,—by no less than ·75 per cent.

Proportions of Capital according to Rates of Interest paid.

Of the ordinary share capital, amounting to rather more than 239 millions, nearly 33 millions received no dividend at all.

Of the remaining 206 millions, in round numbers—

10½	millions received dividends of less than 1 per cent.							
8	„	„	„	„	from 1 to a fraction under 2 per cent.			
2½	„	„	„	„	2	„	3	„
18	„	„	„	„	3	„	4	„
23	„	„	„	„	4	„	5	„
23	„	„	„	„	5	„	6	„
27	„	„	„	„	6	„	7	„
55½	„	„	„	„	7	„	8	„
15	„	„	„	„	8	„	9	„
18	„	„	„	„	9 and 9½ per cent.			
2¼	„	„	„	„	10 „ 10½ „			
3½	„	„	„	„	from 12 to 12¾ per cent.			

The above include upwards of 12 millions of capital of Companies whose lines are under lease, or which receive in some manner a fixed rate of interest. Although this amount of 12 millions was subscribed, and has been returned as the ordinary capital of the Companies whose lines are thus leased, it might in one sense be more properly considered as guaranteed capital of the leasing Companies. The rates of interest on these 12 millions are not, however, generally high, excepting in one case in which nearly 2½ millions receive 12¼ per cent. of interest.

Of the 33 millions of ordinary share capital on which no dividend was paid, 26½ millions belonged to English companies, nearly 3 millions to Scotch companies, and 3½ millions to Irish companies. The total ordinary capital of English companies was nearly 202 millions, of Scotch companies 22 millions, and of Irish companies rather more than 15 millions.

The average dividend paid upon the 239 millions of ordinary share capital, computed from the rates returned as having been paid, amounts, as already stated, to 5·14 per cent.; whilst the average amount of dividend or interest, computed at the rates returned as having been paid on the whole of the share and loan capital, namely, 569,047,346*l.*, amounts to 4·75 per cent. This last per-centage may at first sight appear to clash with the per-centage of net receipts to total share and loan capital given in Table No. 2, column 7, and quoted under the last heading, as only 4·51. The difference arises, partly from a duplication of figures, in consequence of the subscriptions by certain Companies to the undertakings of other Companies being credited (to the extent of about 16 millions) to the capital of the Company subscribing as well as to the capital of the Company subscribed to; and partly in consequence of the exclusion from the calculations on which column 7 of Table 2 are based, of the receipts and expenditure on account of navigations, harbours, canals, steamboats, &c. These latter are, of course, included in Table No. 3, as regards both the capital outlay, and the proportionate rates of interest paid on the different descriptions of capital raised for railway as well as for other purposes.

Of the amount of capital returned as guaranteed, amounting to 63 millions—

Nearly	2½	millions received dividends of 2½ per cent.				
„	1½	„	„	„	from 3 to 3⅞ per cent.	
„	18	„	„	„	from 4 to 4¾	„
Upwards of	30	„	„	„	from 5 to 5½	„
„	9½	„	„	„	from 6 to 6⅜	„
Nearly	1½	„	„	„	of 7 to 12½	„

Of the amount of capital returned otherwise as bearing preferen al interest, amounting to 114 millions, rather more than 9 millions received no dividend at all—

About	5	millions received dividends from ½ to 1¾ per cent.				
„	1	million	„	„	„	2¼ to 3¾ „
„	15	millions	„	„	„	4 to 4¼ „
„	23	„	„	„	„	4½ to 4⅝ „
Nearly	55½	„	„	„	„	5 per cent.
„	¾	million	„	„	„	5½ „
About	2½	millions	„	„	„	6 to 6¼ per cent.
„	1½	„	„	„	„	7 per cent.
„	½	million	„	„	„	8 to 12½ per cent.

Of the loans, amounting to 66 millions—
Upwards of 1¼ millions received interest at rates under 4 per cent.
About 33   ,,   ,,   ,,   4 per cent.
 ,, 14 ,,   ,,   ,,   4¼ ,,
 ,, 11 ,,   ,,   ,,   4½ to 4¾ per cent.
Upwards of 6 millions ,,   ,,   ,,   5 per cent.
 ,,   ¼ million ,,   ,,   ,,   6 ,,

Of the debenture stocks, amounting to nearly 86 millions—
About ¼ million stood under 3¼ per cent.
 ,, 45 millions   ,,   4 and 4¼ per cent.
 ,, 21   ,,   ,,   4½ per cent.
 ,, 17   ,,   ,,   5 ,,
 ,,   2   ,,   ,,   6 ,,

Revenue.

Under this head are omitted on the one side the receipts from navigations, steamboats, tolls, rent, &c., and on the other side the expenses connected with steamboats, harbours, and canals, &c. It appears that the total receipts from railway working amounted to 51,304,114*l.* on 15,814 miles for 1872, against 47,107,558*l.* on the supposed 15,376 miles (which may more properly be stated as 15,611 miles) for 1871; whilst the total expenses of railway working were 25,652,383*l.* for 1872 against 22,632,046*l.* for 1871. The proportion of working expenses to gross receipts was, therefore, 50·0 per cent. for 1872 against 48·4 per cent. for 1871, and the per-centage of net receipts to total capital increased, as already explained, from 4·43 for 1871 to 4·51 for 1872.

The proportion per cent. of expenditure to receipts increased, as between 1870, 1871, and 1872, from 52 in 1870, to 53 in 1871 and 1872 in Ireland, from 50 in 1870 and 1871 to 51 in 1872 in Scotland, and from 48 in 1870 and 47 in 1871 to 49 in 1872 in England.

The total receipts from passenger trains increased from 20,622,880*l.* for 1871 to 22,287,555*l.* for 1872, whilst the total receipts from goods trains increased from 26,484,978*l.* for 1871 to 29,016,559*l.* for 1872.

The per-centage of receipts from passenger and goods traffic for the United Kingdom, which was in 1858 as 49 from passengers to 51 from goods, remained in 1872 the same as for 1870 and 1871, namely, as 44 from passengers to 56 from goods. But it was very different in the three kingdoms. In England the per-centage proportions of receipts from passengers and goods were nearly the same for the 4 years named as for the three kingdoms combined. In Scotland those proportions decreased from 41 in 1858 to 38 in 1870 for passengers, and increased from 59 in 1858 to 62 in 1870 for goods; and they remained in 1872 the same as for 1870 and 1871. In Ireland they decreased from 66 in 1858 to 57 in 1870 and 56 in 1871 from passengers; and increased from 34 in 1858 to 43 in 1870 and 44 in 1871 from goods; and the proportions remained the same for 1872 as for 1871.

Passenger Receipts.

In my General Reports for 1870 and 1871 it was shown that the most important feature in regard to the receipts from passenger trains was the increase of the receipts from third-class passengers. This is again found to be the case, but in a still greater ratio, and from a cause not then operating. For, whereas the receipts from first-class passengers increased from 3,948,812*l.* in 1870, to 4,148,108*l.* in 1871, and to 4,319,185*l.* in 1872; and whereas those for second-class passengers increased from 4,925,542*l.* in 1870 to 5,167,535*l.* in 1871, but decreased to 4,198,201*l.* for 1872; those from third-class passengers increased from 7,473,727*l.* in 1870 to 8,115,304*l.* in 1871, and to 10,318,761*l.* in 1872. The figures showing the numbers of passenger-journeys by passengers of different classes give also similar important results with reference to the decrease of second-class and the increase of third-class passengers. Whilst the first-class passenger-journeys increased from 31,839,091 in 1870, to 35,642,199 in 1871, and to 37,678,538 in 1872; and whilst the second-class passenger-journeys increased from 74,153,113 in 1870, to 81,021,940 in 1871, and decreased to 72,459,562 in 1872; the passenger-journeys of the third-class increased from 224,012,194 in 1870, to 258,556,615 in 1871, and to 312,736,722 in 1872.

The above results are confirmatory of the following remarks which I made in the General Report for 1870 :—

" The elasticity of third-class traffic has thus proved itself to be so great, and the
" receipts from it have acquired so much importance from their amount, as above shown,
" in proportion to the other classes, that it becomes an interesting question to consider
" whether, by what means, and in what proportions, the receipts from this description of
" traffic may be still further augmented. This traffic is carried on at present under great
" disadvantages—of inconvenient hours, of slow travelling, and of impossibility of making,
" in many cases, through journeys in the 24 hours, or of returning the same day ; and
" it is probable that the railway companies might, by affording extra facilities for it, even
" more than by reducing the fares, obtain a greater benefit to themselves, and do more
" real good to the country, than in any other way. But no rule on this subject can be
" considered to be of general application. Each company must study the condition and
" requirements, not only of its own general district, but also of the various sections of
" that district ; improvements must be effected judiciously and gradually ; and time must
" be allowed for their development and ultimate fruit. The excursion system indicates
" to some extent what may be done as regards both profit to the companies and facilities
" to third-class passengers. There are many objections to that system as at present
" carried on,—too frequently with extra or acting servants, inferior rolling stock, and
' inefficient arrangements. By extending and introducing greater regularity into that
" system,—by affording greater facilities in the shape of trains conveying working men
" to and from the spheres of their labour, morning and evening,—and by cheapening and
" improving the third-class communication generally throughout the country,—an
" impetus might be given to third-class traffic which would by its results throw the
" above figures, astonishing as they are, completely into the shade."

During a portion of the year 1872, the experiment of conveying third-class passengers in fast trains, happily initiated by the Midland Railway Company, and carried out by the other principal Railway Companies, who felt compelled more or less to adopt a similar course, has been more fully tried than could then have been expected. It is important to observe, now that the returns for the year 1872 are made up, the partial results of that experiment, as shown in the above figures, not only upon the third-class traffic but also upon the traffic of the other classes. It will also be important to ascertain, when the figures for 1873 are received, whether, and how far, any further decrease in the receipts from and in the numbers of second-class passengers are counterbalanced, as they probably will be, by still greater increases from third-class passengers.

It should here be noticed also that the numbers of season-ticket-holders have increased from 156,403 in 1870, to 188,392 in 1871, and to 272,342 in 1872 ; the receipts from that source having increased from 686,488*l.* in 1870, to 781,778*l.* in 1871, and to 892,384*l.* in 1872 ; and further that the receipts from luggage, parcels, carriages, horses, dogs, extra fares, and such miscellaneous sources of traffic by passenger trains, have increased in the same periods from 2,262,669*l.* in 1870, to 2,406,002*l.* in 1871, and to 2,553,595*l.* in 1872.

Goods Receipts.

Goods receipts, as distinguished from receipts from passenger traffic, are taken to include moneys received for the conveyance of minerals, general-merchandise, live-stock, and all traffic by goods trains. The total receipts from goods trains have increased, from 24,115,159*l.* in 1870, to 26,484,978*l.* in 1871, and to 29,016,559*l.* in 1872, or at the rate of 10 per cent. for each year over each previous year ; and of these, the receipts from the conveyance of minerals have increased from 9,392,513*l.* in 1870, to 10,029,253*l.* in 1871, and to 11,226,157*l.* in 1872 ; while those from the conveyance of general-merchandise have increased from 13,810,196*l.* in 1870, to 15,418,171*l.* in 1871, and to 16,687,830*l.* in 1872 ; and those from the conveyance of live-stock have increased from 912,450*l.* in 1870, to 1,037,554*l.* in 1871, and to 1,077,867*l.* in 1872. It is to be observed that for the year 1871 the general-merchandise receipts were almost exactly 15 times, and for the year 1872 more than 16 times, the live-stock receipts, while the mineral receipts were for each year nearly 10 times the live-stock receipts.

Receipts per open Mile.

The total receipts per mile of open railway increased from 2,786*l.* in 1870, and 3,064*l.* in 1871, to 3,244*l.* in 1872 ; owing to an increase from passenger traffic from 1,235*l.* in

1870, and 1,340*l.* in 1871, to 1,409*l.* in 1872; and from goods trains, from 1,551*l.* in 1870, and 1,724*l.* in 1871, to 1,835*l.* in 1872. The cost of working per mile of open railway has at the same time increased, from 1,357*l.* for 1870, to 1,471*l.* for 1871, and to 1,622*l.* for 1872.

The total receipts per open mile were, in 1872, 1,140*l.* in Ireland, 2,142*l.* in Scotland, and 3,895*l.* in England; against, for 1871, 1,118*l.* in Ireland, 1,986*l.* in Scotland, and 3,672*l.* in England, and for 1870, 1,049*l.* in Ireland, 1,847*l.* in Scotland, and 3,322*l.* in England, respectively. The receipts per open mile from mails were for the United Kingdom 47*l.* for 1858, 37*l.* for 1870, 38*l.* for 1871, and 39*l.* for 1872.

Expenditure per open Mile.

The total expenditure per open mile for the United Kingdom, which was 1,357*l.* in 1870 and 1,471*l.* in 1871, increased to 1,622*l.* in 1872. This increase, as between 1871 and 1872, was from 1,744*l.* to 1,931*l.* in England, from 900*l.* to 1,108*l.* in Scotland, and from 592*l.* to 612. in Ireland. Looking to the details, to ascertain in what departments the increase has principally occurred, the following are the results for the three years 1870, 1871, 1872 :—

	1870. £	1871. £	1872. £
Maintenance of way - - - -	260	289	308
Locomotive department (engines, &c.) -	361	386	452
Rolling stock (except engines, &c.) -	119	129	136
Traffic expenses - - - -	391	433	479
General charges - - - -	61	61	68
Rates and taxes - - -	59	62	64
Government duty - - -	36	34	32
Compensation for personal injuries - -	21	20	19
„ for damage to goods	8	9	12
Legal and parliamentary expenses - -	15	17	19
Miscellaneous - - - -	26	31	33
Total - - -	1,357	1,471	1,622

Train-Mileage Receipts and Expenses.

The total number of miles run by trains during the year 1872 was 190,720,719, showing an increase of 11,644,825 miles, or more than 6 per cent. over the year 1871. The receipts per train-mile, which were 61·63*d.* for 1870, and 63·13*d.* for 1871, increased to 64·56*d.* for 1872; whilst the working expenses, which were 30·02*d.* for 1870, and 30·33*d.* for 1871, increased to 32·27*d.* for 1872. It should be remembered, however, in regard to these and other figures, that any attempt to separate the passenger from the goods train-mileage receipts and expenses is to some extent inaccurate on account of the practice on certain railways of running mixed trains. Analysing the train-mileage receipts and expenses as shown above, as regards the three kingdoms, it would appear that the increase in train-mileage receipts as between 1870, 1871, and 1872 has been, in England, from 63·64*d.* and 64·93*d.* to 66·21*d.*; in Scotland, from 51·69*d.* and 52·58*d.* to 54·81*d.*; and in Ireland, from 60·36*d.* and 61·73*d.* to 62·02*d.*; whilst the increase in train-mileage expenses at the same time has been, in England, from 30·68*d.* and 30·81*d.* to 32·83*d.*; in Scotland, from 25·86*d.* and 26·22*d.* to 28·33; in Ireland, from 31·54*d.* and 32·66*d.* to 33·30*d.*

From the above figures it would appear that both the receipts and the expenses per train-mile have increased in England, Scotland, and Ireland, in 1871 over 1870, and in 1872 over 1871; but that the train-mileage receipts have not increased in the same proportion as the train-mileage expenses for the year 1872; and hence it may be inferred that the traffic has not been so economically worked in 1872 as it was in 1870 and 1871. This is apparent alike in England, Scotland, and Ireland; and it is, no doubt, mainly due to the increased cost of labour and materials in 1872.

Train-Mileage Expenses in detail.

The details of the expenses per train-mile for the United Kingdom for 1871 may be thus stated :—

	d.		d.		d.	
Way and works - -	6·13 for 1872, against	5·98 for 1871 and	5·89 for 1870.
Locomotive charges -	8·99	„	7·96	„	7·92	„
Rolling stock (other than locomotive) charges -	2·70	„	2·65	„	2·63	„
Traffic expenses - -	9·53	„	8·92	„	8·64	„
General charges - -	1·35	„	1·28	„	1·35	„
Rates and taxes - -	1·29	„	1·28	„	1·32	„
Government duty (England and Scotland only)	0·63	„	0·69	„	0·72	„
Compensation for personal injury - -	0·38	„	0·42	„	0·45	„
Compensation for damage to goods - - -	0·23	„	0·19	„	0·17	„
Legal and parliamentary expenses - -	0·38	„	0·33	„	0·35	„
Miscellaneous - -	0·66	„	0·63	„	0·58	„
Total -	32·27 for 1872, against	30·33 for 1871 and	30·02 for 1870.

The average is, then, 32·27d. for 1872, against 30·33d. for 1871 and 30·02d. for 1870. But these figures vary considerably on the lines of different companies, principally, no doubt, in consequence of the different conditions and circumstances under which they are worked ; but, nevertheless, to a much greater extent in some cases than might be expected. Thus, the total expenditure per train-mile varied in 1872 from 29·07d. for the Caledonian Railway to 36·36d. for the North Eastern Railway ; the charges for the maintenance of way and works varied from 4·55d. for the Lancashire and Yorkshire, to 9·28d. for the Great Southern and Western (of Ireland) Railway ; the total charges for locomotive and rolling stock varied from 10·24d. for the London and North Western, to 16·79d. for the North Eastern Railway ; the traffic expenses and general charges for 1872 varied from 8·43d. for the Dublin and Drogheda to 15·36d. for the Lancashire and Yorkshire Railway ; and the rates, taxes, and Government duty (for England and Scotland) varied from 1·37d. for the Caledonian to 3·84d. for the London, Brighton, and South Coast Railway.

Net Profit per Train-Mile.

Since the expenditure per train-mile has increased from 30·02d. in 1870 to 30·33d. in 1871, and to 32·27d. in 1872, and the receipts per train-mile have increased from 61·63d. in 1870 to 63·13d. in 1871 and 64·56d. in 1872, the net profit per train-mile on railway working, which increased from 31·61d. in 1870 to 32·8d. in 1871, has decreased to 32·29d. in 1872.

Compensations for Personal Injury and damage to Goods, &c.

The total amounts paid for personal injury were, in 1870, 322,500l., in 1871, 312,334l., and 1872, 299,389l. ; and there was paid for damage to goods, &c. in 1870, 123,931l., in 1871, 141,288l., and 1872, 186,619l. But these amounts do not fairly represent the exact cost of the accidents on the railways. They do not include the cost of repairs to the rolling stock or the permanent way and works arising from accidents on the one hand, nor are all the damages to goods, on account of which compensations are paid, the result of accidents on the other hand. Nor, again, is the deterrent influence which such accidents exercise on passenger traffic here taken into consideration. The compensations paid, however, on account of injury or damage, together amounted in 1872, for England to 402,808l. ; for Scotland to 65,679l. ; and for Ireland to 17,521l. ; making a total for the year of 486,008l. And such totals were, in 1858 123,071l. ; in 1870 446,431l. ; in 1871 453,622l. ; and in 1872 486,008l.

Rolling Stock.

On referring to Table No. 8, it would appear, that on the railways in the United Kingdom, the number of locomotive engines increased from 9,379 in 1870, and 10,490 in

1871, to 10,933 in 1872; and the number of vehicles, exclusive of locomotives, increased from 285,994 in 1870, and 311,427 in 1871, to 337,899 in 1872; giving an increase per open mile, from ·60 for 1870, to ·68 for 1871 and 1872, as regards locomotive engines; and an increase per open mile from 18·38 for 1870, and 20·25 for 1871, to 21·36 for 1872, as regards other vehicles. In the one year, from 1870 to 1871, the increase of locomotives per open mile was four times as great as that in the 12 years from 1858 to 1870; while there was no increase per open mile for the year 1872 over 1871; and also, whereas from 1858 to 1870 the number of vehicles, other than locomotives, per open mile showed a slight decrease, there was a comparatively large increase per open mile in the two years from 1870 to 1872. In 1872, the number of locomotive engines was more than double, and the number of vehicles was nearly double, the number of engines and vehicles respectively in 1858. As regards the rolling stock in use on railways which is the property of private owners or of Companies other than Railway Companies, no returns are received; but the number of such vehicles is known to be very considerable; and the question of their acquisition by the Railway Companies, or at all events of the Railway Companies becoming the owners of all the rolling stock employed on their lines, is an exceedingly important one, and one for which it will be necessary before long to seek for a solution.

Summary.

The leading features of the railway system of the United Kingdom at the end of 1872 may thus be summarized. A total sum of 569,047,346l. had been expended on 15,814 miles of railway, or at the rate of nearly 36,000l. a mile. There were 10,933 locomotive engines, or about one to every mile and a half; and 337,899 vehicles, or about 21½ per mile, besides the waggons of traders and Companies other than Railway Companies. By the running of trains for 190,720,719 miles, 51,304,114l. were received during the year, of which 25,652,383l. were expended in working and maintenance, and 25,651,731l. remained as net profit; so that as nearly as possible one half of the gross receipts were expended in earning them. There were 422,874,822 passenger-journeys, besides 272,342 season-ticket-holders; and 179,302,121 tons of goods and minerals were conveyed. The average rate of dividend on ordinary capital was 5·14 per cent., and upon the total capital 4·75 per cent., including 32,901,496l. of ordinary capital, part of 42,582,631l. of total capital, which received no interest or dividend. The average cost of working each train was 32·27 pence per mile, and the average receipt from each train was 64·56 pence per mile; so that the average net profit from each train was 32·29 pence per mile; while the total cost of working was 1,622l. per mile, and 3,244l. per mile were received.

The more prominent facts connected with traffic-working in 1872 as compared with 1871, were as follows:—There was an increase of gross receipts amounting to 4,196,556l., but also an increase of working expenses amounting to 3,020,337l. While there was an increase of about 170,000l. in the receipts from first-class, and of 2,203,457l. from third-class passengers, there was a decrease of 969,334l. from second-class passengers. And whilst there was an increase of 2,036,339 in the number of first-class, and of 54,180,107 in the number of third-class passenger journeys, there was a decrease of 8,562,378 in the number of second-class passenger journeys. There was an increase in the receipts from goods, minerals, &c. of 2,531,581l. In looking at the details above given of the expenses per train-mile, it will be observed that the increase is pretty general from 1870 and 1871 to 1872; the exceptions being in the items of rates and taxes, government duty, and compensation for personal injury. The increased cost of way and works was comparatively small, but that for locomotive charges was more than a penny per train-mile; and this extra charge, occasioned principally by the enhanced price of fuel, accounts for more than half of the total increase in the cost of working—from 30·03 pence in 1871 to 32·27 pence in 1872 per train-mile.

As far as can at present be foreseen, the results of working in 1873, will, when the figures can be ascertained, present somewhat similar results of further increased receipts and further increased expenses; but it is hardly probable that either the one or the other will continue to increase in 1874 in the same ratio. The traffic of the country must be considered to have been for the last two years in an inflated condition, and the price of wages, fuel, and materials to have attained a point considerably above the average. There will, no doubt, be fluctuations in these respects in the future as there have been in the past. But upon the whole, and comparing longer than annual periods, the progress of the country as shown by its railway traffic has been marvellous. The gross receipts of the railways have increased from 23,956,749l. in 1858 to 51,304,114l. in 1872; or have been more than doubled in 14 years. There seems no reason why they should not in another series of years continue to manifest equally important progress. The Companies will be able, as their credit improves and their ordinary dividends increase, to raise money at cheaper rates. The additional outlay required for further accommodation and improved apparatus, though large in total amount will be merely fractional as regards the total capital; and will be the means of inducing increased traffic, and of saving largely in compensation, and of effecting economy in working; so that it will, on the whole, be beneficial in a pecuniary sense to the Companies. The railway system generally, having to a great extent overcome the troubles connected with competition and extension from which at one time it suffered so severely, would appear to have before it, in years to come, the prospect of increasing soundness and approaching prosperity.

I have the honour to be,

Sir,

Your most obedient Servant,

H. W. TYLER.

C

No. 1.

LENGTH OF RAILWAYS open, 1871 and 1872.

—	At 31st December 1871.	At 31st December 1872.
	Miles.	*Miles.*
In ENGLAND - - - - - - -	10,850	11,136
In SCOTLAND - · - - - -	2,538	2,587
In IRELAND - - - - - -	1,988	2,091
In UNITED KINGDOM - - -	15,376 .	15,814

No. 2.

COMPARISON OF CAPITAL PAID UP, AVERAGE INTEREST thereon, GROSS RECEIPTS, and WORKING EXPENDITURE, 1858, 1870, 1871, and 1872.

Year.	1. Ordinary, Preference, and Guaranteed Capital paid up on the 31st December in each Year.			2. Loans and Debenture Stock.	3. Total Capital raised at 31st December.	
	Ordinary.	Preference and Guaranteed.	TOTAL.		Per Mile open.	Amount.
	£	£	£	£	£	£
1858 - -	181,837,781	61,854,547	243,692,328	Loans, 81,683,179	34,099	· 325,375,507
1870 - -	229,282,150	158,692,084	387,974,234	Loans, 90,713,779 Debenture Stock, 51,220,660	34,106	529,908,673
1871 - -	*230,250,152	*173,051,875	403,302,027	Loans, *82,095,545 Debenture Stock, *67,282,535	35,944	552,682,107
1872 - -	239,039,089	177,764,674	416,803,763	Loans, 66,224,217 Debenture Stock, 85,981,511	35,984	†569,047,346

Year.	4. Average Interest on						5. Gross Receipts from Railway Working.	6. Total (Railway) Working Expenditure.		7. Percentage of Net Receipts to Total Share and Loan Capital.
	Guaranteed and Preference Shares.		Loans and Debenture Stock.		Total.			Amount.	Proportion per Cent. to Gross Receipts.	
	Rate.	Amount.	Rate.	Amount.	Rate.	Amount.				
		£		£		£	£	£	£	
1858 -	4·84	2,993,760	4·48	Loans, 3,659,406	4·63	6,653,166	‡23,956,749	‡11,738,807	49·	3·75
1870 -	4·54	7,220,100	4·37 / 4·47	Loans, 3,968,100 Debenture Stock, 2,290,600	4·48	13,478,800	‡43,417,070	‡21,193,877	49·	4·19
1817 -	4·51	7,816,202	4·25 / 4·37	Loans, 3,502,302 Debenture Stock, 2,937,540	4·42	14,256.044	‡47,107,558	‡22,632,046	48·4	4·43
1872 -	4·49	7,988,610	4·19 / 4·34	Loans, 2,774,648 Debenture Stock, 3,734,049	4·39	14,497,807	‡51,304,114	‡25,652,383	50·0	4·51

* No interest whatever was paid in 1872 upon 32,901,496l. of ordinary capital, or upon 9,207,357l. of preference stock, or upon 59,200l. of loans, or 594,578l. of debenture stock. The rates of interest are calculated upon the entire amounts whether paying interest or not.
  † Including 37,855l. rentcharge.
  ‡ Exclusive of steamboat, canal, and harbour receipts and expenses.

No. 3

Proportion of Capital in relation to Rates of Interest paid.

Loans.		Debenture Stock.		Guaranteed Capital.		Preference Capital.		Ordinary Capital.			
Rates of Interest.	Amount at each Rate.	Rates of Interest.	Amount at each Rate.	Rates of Dividend.	Amount at each Rate.	Rates of Dividend.	Amount at each Rato.	Rates of Dividend.	Amount at each Rate.	Rates of Dividend.	Amount at each Rate.
	£		£		£		£		£		£
Nil.	59,200	Nil.	594,578	Nil.	1,455	Nil.	9,207,357	Nil.	32,901,496	5	7,242,751
1 1/2	1,400	1 3/4	46,915	2	101,180	1/2	14,640	1/4	8,588,043	5 1/8	1,233,903
3	42,515	2 3/16	122,818	2 1/2	2,424,224	4/5	122,250	11/16	1,327,266	5 3/16	171,356
3 1/2	885,035	3	311,363	3	713,825	1	333,170	7/16	127,700	5 1/4	254,000
3 3/4	768,369	3 3/16	89,052	3 1/4	866,698	1 1/5	60,000	1/2	339,827	5 1/3	70,000
4	32,721,385	3 1/2	86,000	3 1/3	160,576	1 1/2	166,872	3/4	64,431	5 1/2	7,966,530
4 1/8	203,600	4	39,870,402	4	8,607,756	1 4/5	4,694,188	1	220,148	5 3/4	5,091,022
4 1/4	13,710,389	4 1/4	5,046,165	3 7/8	299,700	1 3/4	202,410	1 1/16	2,758,932	5 7/8	978,533
4 3/8	75,200	4 3/8	10,000	4 1/2	9,260,709	2 1/4	45,300	1 1/5	70,600	6	18,812,272
4 2/5	150	4 1/2	20,824,212	4 3/4	40,000	2 1/2	315,400	1·233	111,650	6 1/4	6,679,020
4 1/2	10,125,174	5	17,079,788	5	28,038,350	3	118,340	1 3/8	149,184	6 1/2	773,018
4 11/16	191,148	6	1,882,218	5 1/3	800,000	3 11/16	11,050	1 1/2	4,226,480	6 3/4	1,134,787
4 3/4	464,786	8	18,000	5 23/100	260,050	3 1/2	183,830	1 13/32	98,360	7	163,100
5	6,501,457			5 1/2	914,884	3 3/4	96,010	1 4/5	74,998	7 1/8	6,695,866
5 1/4	4,400	£	85,981,511	6	7,667,311	3 23/24	255,550	1 13/16	36,000	7 1/4	16,115,774
5 1/2	41,033			6 1/4	1,297,583	4	14,276,139	2	886,168	7 1/2	626,828
6	392,376		Average rate of Interest on Debenture 4·34.	6 11 10	600,000	4 1/4	556,254	2 1/10	99,561	7 3/4	31,850,754
8	36,600			6 1/2	18,283	4 1/2	22,738,500	2 1/4	80,810	7 17 2	638,000
				7	230,654	4 3/5	45,000	2 3/8	170,000	8	156,355
£	66,224,217			7 1/2	240,000	4 7/8	36,830	2 7/16	168,830	8 1/4	1,159,275
				8	140,000	5	55,544,945	2 1/2	220,701	8 1/2	13,834,594
	Average rate of Interest on Loans 4·19.			8 3/5	90,780	5 1/2	720,520	2 17/24	550,000	8 13/16	789,202
				9	440,570	6	2,312,489	2 3/4	367,293	9	17,361,558
				10	50,000	6 1/4	308,500	3	355,925	9 1/2	350,000
				10 11/20	200,000	7	1,503,374	3 1/5	6,839,943	10	2,300,920
				11 23/50	87,725	6 1/2	58,108	3 1/4	1,169,840	10 1/2	37,000
				12 1/2	2,000	7 1/4	170,000	3 7/20	228,675	12	290,000
						8	227,500	3 3/8	90,000	12 1/4	2,420,300
				£	63,004,313	10	385,840	3 1/2	8,947,653	12 1/2	905,000
						12 1/2	50,000	3 3/4	324,644	12 17 2	30,000
								3 7/8	1,105,372	18 3/4	40,000
						£	114,760,361	4	7,475,440		
								4 1/20	1,014,000	£	239,039,089
				Total - £177,764,674				4 1/4	8,817,336		
				Average rate of Interest on Guaranteed and Preference Capital 4·49.				4 3/8	175,000		Average rate of Dividend on Ordinary Capital 5·14.
								4 1/2	3,700,065		
								4 3/4	35,000		
									continued.		

The average rate of Dividend or Interest upon the whole, calculated upon the above amounts, and at the above rates as given in the Annual Return, was 4·75.

No. 4.

Per-centage Proportion of Capital Paid up, Per-centage of Net Receipts to Total Capital, and Average Interest on Preference and Loan Capital, 1858 and 1870.

Year.	Per-centage Proportion.					Average Interest on Ordinary Capital.	Average Interest on Preferential Loan, &c., exclusive of Ordinary Capital.	Per-centage of Net Receipts to Total Capital.
	Ordinary Capital.	Preference Capital, Loan, &c.			Total.			
		Guaranteed and Preference.	Loan and Debenture Stock.	Total.				
1858 - -	56	Preference, 19	Loan, 25	44	100		4·63	3·75
1870 - -	43	Guaranteed and Preference, 30	Loan, 17 Debenture Stock, 10	57	100		4·48	4·19
1871 -	42	Guaranteed and Preference, 31	Loan, 15 Debenture Stock, 12	58	100	5·07	4·42	4·43
1872 - -	42	Guaranteed and Preference, 31	Loan, 12 Debenture Stock, 15	58	100	5·14	4·39	4·51

No. 5.

COMPARISON OF RECEIPTS.

I.—From PASSENGER TRAINS.

		Receipts From Passenger Trains.						
		Receipts from Passengers.					Excess Luggage, Luggage, Parcels, Carriages, Horses, Dogs, and Mails.	TOTAL by Passenger Trains.
		1st Class.	2nd Class.	3rd Class and Parliamentary.	Holders of Season and Periodical Tickets.	TOTAL.		
		£	£	£	£	£	£	£
ENGLAND	1858	2,582,163	3,104,726	2,905,439	196,853	8,789,181	1,094,289	9,883,470
	1870	3,329,681	4,364,533	6,177,230	599,520	14,470,964 *4,673	1,856,587	16,332,174
	1871	3,504,124	4,596,317	6,692,971	678,861	15,472,273 *3,853	1,974,321	17,450,447
	1872	3,654,754	3,669,736	8,681,494	777,129	16,783,113 4,961	2,088,690	18,876,764
SCOTLAND	1858	250,203	174,885	472,598	16,804	914,490	117,310	1,031,800
	1870	363,349	268,189	861,932	59,203	1,552,673	227,979	1,780,652
	1871	379,626	268,108	951,413	70,575	1,669,722	249,881	1,919,603
	1872	397,226	228,531	1,106,163	79,683	1,811,603	276,192	2,087,795
IRELAND	1858	170,472	247,766	238,155	16,182	672,575	110,059	782,634
	1870	255,782	292,890	484,565	27,765	1,010,932	178,153	1,189,085
	1871	264,358	303,110	470,920	32,342	1,070,730	181,800	1,252,530
	1872	267,205	299,934	581,104	35,572	1,133,815 *468	188,713	1,322,996
UNITED KINGDOM	1858	3,002,838	3,527,377	3,616,192	229,839	10,376,246	1,321,658	11,697,904
	1870	3,948,812	4,925,542	7,473,727	686,488	17,034,569 *4,673	2,262,669	19,301,911
	1871	4,148,108	5,167,535	8,115,304	781,778	18,212,725 *3,853	2,406,002	20,622,580
	1872	4,319,185	4,198,201	10,318,761	892,384	19,728,531 *5,429	2,553,595	22,287,555

II.—From GOODS TRAINS, and PROPORTION of RECEIPTS from PASSENGER and GOODS TRAINS.

		Receipts from Goods, &c. Trains.				TOTAL from Passenger and Goods, &c. Trains.	Proportion of Receipts from Passenger and Goods Trains.		
		Minerals.	General Merchandise.	Live Stock.	TOTAL Goods, &c. Trains.		Passenger.	Goods, &c.	TOTAL.
		£	£	£	£	£			
ENGLAND	1858	3,335,122	6,637,585	387,918	10,360,625	20,244,095	49	51	100
	1870	8,086,386	11,630,753	641,825	20,358,964	36,691,138	45	55	100
	1871	8,610,713	13,056,770	724,464	22,391,947	39,842,394	44	56	100
	1872	9,680,225	14,073,714	744,489	*24,499,414	43,376,178	44	56	100
SCOTLAND	1858	692,893	765,403	46,887	1,505,133	2,536,933	41	59	100
	1870	1,269,003	1,490,883	112,399	2,872,285	4,652,937	38	62	100
	1871	1,360,513	1,631,585	129,784	3,121,882	5,041,485	38	62	100
	1872	1,482,065	1,808,937	140,254	*3,454,975	5,542,770	38	62	100
IRELAND	1858	18,046	308,398	66,643	393,087	1,175,721	66	34	100
	1870	37,124	688,560	188,226	883,910	2,072,995	57	43	100
	1871	58,027	729,816	183,306	971,149	2,223,679	56	44	100
	1872	63,867	805,179	193,124	1,062,170	2,385,166	56	44	100
UNITED KINGDOM	1858	4,046,061	7,711,386	501,398	12,258,845	23,956,749	49	51	100
	1870	9,392,513	13,810,196	912,450	24,115,159	43,417,070	44	56	100
	1871	10,029,253	15,418,171	1,037,554	26,484,978	47,107,558	44	56	100
	1872	11,226,157	16,687,830	1,077,867	*29,016,559	51,304,114	44	56	100

N.B.—The receipts from rents, tolls, navigations, steamboats, &c. are not included in the above.

* Including receipts not classified.

No. 6.

COMPARISON of RECEIPTS per Mile of Railway open from Passenger Trains, 1858, 1870, 1871, and 1872.

—		1st Class.	2nd Class.	3rd Class and Parliamentary.	Mixed, Season Ticket Holders, and Excess Fares.	TOTAL.	Excess Luggage, Parcels, Carriages, Horses, and Dogs.	Mails.	TOTAL Receipts from Passenger Trains.
		£	£	£	£	£	£	£	£
In ENGLAND -	1858	375	451	422	28	1,276	112	46	1,434
	1870	301	395	559	54	1,309	132	37	1,478
	1871	323	423	617	63	1,426	144	38	1,608
	1872	328	320	779	69	1,507	149	38	1,694
In SCOTLAND -	1858	192	134	363	13	702	45	45	792
	1870	144	106	342	23	615	59	32	706
	1871	149	106	375	27	657	63	36	756
	1872	153	88	427	31	700	69	38	807
In IRELAND -	1858	151	219	211	14	595	40	57	692
	1870	129	149	220	14	512	44	46	602
	1871	133	152	237	16	538	45	47	630
	1872	127	148	254	17	542	45	45	632
In the UNITED KINGDOM -	1858	322	379	386	25	1,112	94	47	1,253
	1870	254	317	481	44	1,096	102	37	1,235
	1871	259	336	528	51	1,184	118	38	1,340
	1872	273	265	652	66	1,254	122	39	1,409

No. 7.

COMPARISON of NUMBERS of PASSENGER-JOURNEYS, and TONNAGE of GOODS and MINERALS conveyed, 1858, 1870, 1871, and 1872.

—		PASSENGERS.					Minerals.	General Merchandise.
		1st Class.	2nd Class.	3rd Class and Parliamentary.	TOTAL.	Holders of Season or Periodical Tickets.		
							Tons.	Tons.
ENGLAND -	1858	15,162,796	36,199,873	64,568,572	115,940,741	26,216	21,687,649	38,298,709
	1870	27,004,386	66,736,823	194,891,712	288,632,921	118,110	—	—
	1871	30,092,538	73,011,105	225,449,303	328,552,946	139,041	*31,412,357	58,978,558
	1872	32,015,513	64,963,939	275,470,771	372,450,223	217,838	88,038,840 23,071,086*	41,363,265 }
SCOTLAND -	1858	1,983,821	2,150,334	10,647,854	14,782,009	6,959	2,895,916	9,040,903
	1870	3,124,350	3,372,288	20,550,276	27,046,864	23,462	—	—
	1871	3,600,786	3,687,070	23,832,018	31,119,874	31,776	20,387,781	5,722,387
	1872	3,721,361	3,324,614	27,051,208	34,097,183	35,233	17,966,430 45,682*	5,754,938 }
IRELAND -	1858	1,155,767	3,343,582	3,929,038	8,428,387	19,387	1,071,055	180,064
	1870	1,710,355	4,044,052	8,750,206	14,324,613	14,831	—	—
	1871	1,948,875	4,323,765	9,275,294	15,547,934	17,575	422,326	2,441,289
	1872	1,941,664	4,171,009	10,214,743	16,327,416	19,271	489,571 496,073*	2,076,236 }
UNITED KINGDOM -	1858	18,302,384	41,693,289	79,145,464	139,141,137	52,562	25,654,620	47,469,676
	1870	31,839,091	74,153,113	224,012,194	330,904,398	156,403	—	—
	1871	35,642,199	81,021,940	258,556,615	375,220,754	188,392	*102,222,464	67,142,234
	1872	37,678,538	72,459,562	312,736,722	422,874,822	272,342	106,494,841 23,612,841*	49,194,439 }

N.B.—The tonnage returned by the Companies was so incomplete that it is impossible to give an accurate total for 1870.
* The tonnage of Minerals in the case of the London and North Western Railway is included in General Merchandise.

No. 8.

COMPARISON of EXPENDITURE and RECEIPTS per Train-Mile for the Years 1858, 1870, 1871, and 1872, of the following Railway Companies.

—	Expenditure per Train Mile.						Receipts per Train Mile.			Proportion per Cent. of Expenditure to Receipts.
	Maintenance of Way.	Locomotive and Rolling Stock.*	Traffic and General Charges.	Rates and Taxes, and Government Duty.	Miscellaneous.	TOTAL.	From Passenger Trains.	From Goods, &c. Trains.	TOTAL.	
	d.	d.	d.	d.	d.	d.	d.	d.	d.	
Bristol and Exeter 1858	9·86	14·79	8·44	4·74	5·18	42·01	79·80	142·52	93·09	46
1870	7·09	11·58	11·91	3·35	1·71	35·59	68·47	86·86	74·25	48
1871	7·22	11·07	11·96	3·25	1·51	35·01	70·01	81·30	73·87	47
1872	6·39	12·89	12·22	3·26	0·69	35·45	69·81	83·75	74·52	47
Caledonian 1858	3·49	10·89	6·24	4·74	1·40	26·76	62·34	61·39	61·74	43
1870	5·29	9·52	7·46	1·58	1·28	25·13	41·21	56·11	49·74	50
1871	5·24	10·01	7·86	1·41	1·36	25·88	45·77	58·67	52·45	49
1872	5·01	12·05	8·57	1·37	2·07	29·07	43·48	64·72	55·55	52
Dublin and Drogheda 1858	5·86	18·06	5·86	4·05	0·96	29·79	66·14	67·68	66·55	45
1870	6·89	9·82	7·69	1·76	0·78	26·95	—†	—†	58·46	46
1871	7·56	10·12	7·91	1·88	1·12	28·59	—†	—†	60·82	47
1872	7·66	11·03	8·43	2·14	1·16	30·47	—†	—†	64·74	47
Great Eastern 1858	5·89	11·37	9·63	2·81	4·23	33·93	63·46	72·56	67·43	50
1870	5·53	11·56	11·29	2·95	1·14	31·77	57·44	70·78	63·55	50
1871	5·85	12·09	11·74	2·28	1·17	33·13	62·18	73·93	67·86	49
1872	5·32	13·12	12·39	2·29	1·11	34·23	58·60	75·31	65·89	52
Great Northern 1858	5·19	11·27	7·69	1·98	3·12	29·25	53·64	58·63	56·29	52
1870	5·22	9·94	9·82	1·76	1·18	27·92	54·39	59·53	57·28	49
1871	5·53	10·54	10·33	1·83	1·07	29·09	58·52	59·33	58·99	49
1872	5·77	11·13	11·08	1·69	0·96	30·63	57·09	62·00	59·71	51
Great Western 1858	6·27	8·62	3·94	3·10	7·28	29·21	68·78	69·91	69·16	42
1870	5·55	10·43	10·24	2·02	1·65	29·89	61·15	65·67	63·43	47
1871	5·57	10·32	9·92	1·90	1·61	29·32	63·26	64·54	63·97	46
1872	5·49	10·76	9·89	1·71	1·63	29·48	63·69	64·46	64·11	46
Great Southern and Western 1858	4·30	13·85	7·02	2·27	1·92	28·86	71·37	78·44	73·55	39
1870	8·32	12·34	8·42	1·82	1·07	31·98	56·72	71·96	62·49	51
1871	8·23	11·83	7·92	1·99	2·24	32·21	57·90	74·24	64·14	50
1872	9·28	12·38	8·58	2·19	1·61	34·04	59·94	80·78	68·00	50
Lancashire and Yorkshire 1858	4·72	9·62	11·62	2·32	3·51	31·79	54·28	95·37	73·24	43
1870	4·62	9·20	12·70	1·75	2·38	30·65	46·24	85·31	64·23	48
1871	4·87	9·46	13·70	1·75	·97	30·75	45·62	86·51	64·27	48
1872	4·55	11·21	15·36	1·56	1·18	33·86	51·01	88·98	69·36	49
London and North Western 1858	5·18	13·66	15·73	2·51	4·73	42·01	65·88	88·56	77·43	54
1870	5·93	10·32	10·54	1·92	2·23	30·94	56·56	75·71	66·31	47
1871	5·72	9·97	10·99	1·91	2·07	30·66	58·26	76·78	67·78	45
1872	5·97	10·24	11·46	1·70	2·18	31·55	58·63	73·98	66·67	47
London and South Western 1858	5·57	10·06	9·31	3·74	1·97	30·65	68·27	58·15	65·45	46
1870	6·36	9·95	11·90	3·13	2·95	34·29	59·56	76·17	63·84	54
1871	6·30	10·19	12·43	3·25	3·19	35·36	61·28	77·98	65·71	54
1872	6·58	10·62	11·56	3·03	3·38	36·12	60·97	77·72	65·46	55
London, Brighton, and South Coast 1858	5·63	13·70	12·17	6·07	1·51	39·08	79·82	105·55	85·53	46
1870	5·70	11·47	11·12	4·01	2·54	34·84	61·64	94·12	66·69	52
1871	5·51	11·86	10·65	4·11	1·40	33·53	62·69	95·49	68·28	49
1872	4·65	13·11	10·47	3·84	1·21	33·28	61·79	91·18	66·83	50
Midland 1858	4·19	11·61	6·38	1·67	2·67	26·47	50·96	70·37	61·67	42
1870	4·60	8·82	8·94	1·37	0·81	24·44	41·59	60·07	52·31	47
1871	5·32	9·06	9·82	1·88	0·98	26·56	46·58	65·85	58·24	46
1872	6·08	10·35	11·22	1·44	1·01	30·10	51·34	70·70	63·55	47
North Eastern 1858	3·09	11·16	4·37	2·31	1·66	22·59	57·17	50·24	52·71	42
1870	6·08	13·99	7·28	1·76	0·76	29·87	49·17	74·70	65·55	46
1871	6·31	13·69	7·65	1·78	1·03	30·41	51·63	74·21	66·46	46
1872	7·44	16·79	9·44	1·86	0·83	36·36	52·48	76·47	67·31	54

* There is no means of knowing in certain of the above cases whether shunting of engines is included by the Companies in their returns from which the above Table is taken.

† Mixed trains in some cases.

COMPARISON of EXPENDITURE and RECEIPTS per Train-Mile and per Mile of open Railway, for the whole of the Railways, and the Proportion per Cent. of EXPENDITURE to RECEIPTS.

PER TRAIN MILE.

	Expenditure per Train Mile.						Receipts per Train Mile.			Proportion per Cent. of Expenditure to Receipts.
—	Maintenance of Way.	Locomotive and Rolling Stock.	Traffic Charges.	Rates and Taxes, *Government Duty.	Miscellaneous.	TOTAL.	From Passenger Trains.	From Goods &c. Trains.	TOTAL.	
	d.	*d.*	*d.*	*d.*	*d.*	*d.*	*d.*	*d.*	*d.*	
In ENGLAND 1858	5·48	12·29	9·29	4·26	2·50	33·82	60·08	73·90	66·44	50
1870	5·73	10·80	10·35	2·13	1·67	30·68	59·92	70·73	63·64	48
1871	5·82	10·77	10·55	2·08	1·59	30·81	57·05	72·64	64·93	47
1872	6·03	11·84	11·27	2·02	1·67	32·83	58·50	74·51	66·21	49
In SCOTLAND 1858	4·21	11·26	7·21	4·00	1·64	28·32	57·30	69·97	64·24	44
1870	5·98	9·17	8·03	1·52	1·16	25·86	45·16	57·42	51·69	50
1871	5·84	9·28	8·28	1·48	1·39	26·22	44·36	59·43	52·58	50
1872	5·65	10·68	8·92	1·40	1·68	28·33	†46·00	†60·86	54·81	51
In IRELAND 1858	4·22	11·04	6·62	3·14	1·29	26·31	‡57·18	‡79·50	63·10	40
1870	8·51	11·24	9·20	1·51	1·08	31·54	‡49·04	‡87·95	60·36	52
1871	8·87	11·22	9·30	1·46	1·81	32·66	‡48·78	‡93·86	61·73	53
1872	9·07	11·85	9·34	1·58	1·46	33·30	§52·42	§87·53	62·02	53

United Kingdom rows with Miscellaneous broken into: Locomotive, Rolling Stock (under Locomotive and Rolling Stock); Traffic Expenses, General Charges (under Traffic Charges); Rates and Taxes, Government Duty (under Rates and Taxes, Government Duty); Compensation {For personal Injury, For damage to Goods}, Legal and Parliamentary Expenses, Miscellaneous (under Miscellaneous).

	Maint. of Way	Locomotive	Rolling Stock	Traffic Expenses	General Charges	Rates and Taxes	Government Duty	For personal Injury	For damage to Goods	Legal and Parliamentary Expenses	Miscellaneous	TOTAL	From Passenger	From Goods &c.	TOTAL	Proportion
	d.	*d.*	*d.*	*d.*	*d.*	*d.*	*d.*	*d.*	*d.*	*d.*	*d.*					
In UNITED KINGDOM 1870	5·89	7·92	2·63	8·64	1·35	1·32	*0·72	0·45	0·17	0·35	0·58	30·02	53·46	70·20	61·63	49
1871	5·98	7·96	2·65	8·92	1·28	1·28	*0·69	0·42	0·19	0·38	0·63	30·33	54·99	71·35	63·13	48
1872	6·13	8·99	2·70	9·53	1·35	1·29	*0·63	0·88	0·23	0·38	0·66	32·27	§56·77	§72·95	64·56	50

* England and Scotland only.
† Exclusive of Highland Railway receipts, the trains of which are mixed.
‡ In many cases goods and passengers are taken by the same trains; the receipts, therefore, per train mile from goods and passenger trains on certain railways are necessarily to some extent inaccurate.
§ Exclusive of receipts on railways in cases where the traffic is conveyed by mixed trains.

PER MILE of OPEN RAILWAY.

	Expenditure per Open Mile.						Receipts per Open Mile.			Proportion per Cent. of Expenditure to Receipts.
—	Maintenance of Way.	Locomotive and Rolling Stock.	Traffic Charges.	Rates and Taxes, Government Duty.	Miscellaneous.	TOTAL.	From Passenger Trains.	From Goods &c. Trains.	TOTAL.	
	£	£	£	£	£	£	£	£	£	
In ENGLAND 1858	248	556	421	113	192	1,532	1,468	1,538	3,006	50
1870	300	567	340	111	87	1,609	1,479	1,942	3,399	48
1871	329	610	597	118	90	1,744	1,609	2,063	3,672	49
1872	355	697	663	118	98	1,931	1,695	2,200	3,895	49
In SCOTLAND 1858	129	348	222	50	123	875	806	1,179	1,985	44
1870	216	331	288	55	42	932	707	1,140	1,847	50
1871	221	351	311	56	51	990	756	1,230	1,986	50
1872	221	418	349	55	65	1,108	807	1,335	2,142	51
In IRELAND 1858	72	189	113	22	53	451	706	354	1,060	40
1870	147	195	159	26	18	548	602	447	1,049	52
1871	161	203	168	27	33	592	630	488	1,118	53
1872	167	218	171	29	27	612	682	508	1,140	53

United Kingdom rows with Miscellaneous broken into: Locomotive, Rolling Stock; Traffic Expenses, General Charges; Rates and Taxes, Government Duty; Compensation {For personal Injury, For damage to Goods}, Legal and Parliamentary Expenses, Miscellaneous.

	Maint. of Way	Locomotive	Rolling Stock	Traffic Expenses	General Charges	Rates and Taxes	Government Duty	For personal Injury	For damage to Goods	Legal and Parliamentary Expenses	Miscellaneous	TOTAL	From Passenger	From Goods &c.	TOTAL	Proportion
	£	£	£	£	£	£	£	£	£	£	£					
In UNITED KINGDOM 1870	260	361	119	391	61	59	36	21	8	15	26	1,357	1,235	1,551	2,786	49
1871	289	386	129	433	61	62	34	20	9	17	31	1,471	1,340	1,724	3,064	48
1872	308	452	136	479	68	64	32	19	12	19	33	1,622	1,409	1,835	3,244	50

No. 10.

COMPARISON of the NUMBER of LOCOMOTIVES, CARRIAGES, and other VEHICLES, 1858, 1870, 1871, and 1872.

		Locomotives.	Carriages used for the Conveyance of Passengers only.	Other Vehicles attached to Passenger Trains.	Waggons of all kinds used for the Conveyance of Live Stock, Minerals, or General Merchandise.	Any other Carriages or Waggons used on the Railway not included in the preceding Columns.	Total of Vehicles excluding Locomotives.
		No.	No.	No.	No.	No.	No.
ENGLAND - · ·	1858	4,427	10,360	2,598	133,312	- - -	146,270
	1870	7,671	16,480	6,719	204,625	5,237	232,061
	1871	8,711	18,432	6,889	218,970	4,400	248,691
	1872	9,110	19,496	7,102	232,558	3,711	262,867
SCOTLAND - -	1858	713	1,724	310	22,749	- -	24,783
	1870	1,241	2,564	801	43,701	475	47,541
	1871	1,297	2,750	861	48,167	945	52,723
	1872	1,325	2,952	908	59,749	956	64,565
TOTAL -	1858	5,140	12,084	2,908	156,061	- -	171,053
	1870	8,912	19,044	7,520	244,326	5,712	276,602
	1871	10,008	21,182	7,750	267,137	5,345	301,414
	1872	10,435	22,448	8,010	292,307	4,667	327,432
IRELAND - · ·	1858	305	858	207	3,689	- - -	4,754
	1870	467	1,077	519	7,544	252	9,392
	1871	482	1,091	513	8,316	93	10,013
	1872	498	1,121	513	8,516	317	10,467
UNITED KINGDOM -	1858	5,445	12,942	3,115	159,750	- - -	175,807
	1870	9,379	20,121	8,039	251,870	5,964	285,994
	1871	10,490	22,273	8,263	275,453	5,438	311,427
	1872	10,933	23,569	8,523	300,823	4,984	337,899
		No. per Mile.	No. per Mile.	No. per Mile.	No. per Mile.	No. per Mile.	No. per Mile.
ENGLAND AND SCOTLAND - .	1858	·62	1·47	·35	18·00	- - -	19·82
	1870	·65	1·40	·56	18·01	·42	20·39
	1871	·74	1·58	·59	19·94	·40	22·51
	1872	·76	1·62	·58	21·30	·34	23·85
IRELAND - · ·	1858	·27	·76	·18	3·30	- - -	4·24
	1870	·28	·54	·26	3·88	·13	4·76
	1871	·24	·55	·26 .	4·19	·04	5·04
	1872	·23	·54	·24	4·07	·15	5·00
UNITED KINGDOM - ·	1858	·58	1·39	·31	17·14	- - -	18·84
	1870	·60	1·29	·51	16·20	·38	18·38
	1871	·68	1·45	·53	17·91	·36	20·25
	1872	·68	1·49	·53	19·02	·32	21·36

LONDON:
Printed by GEORGE E. EYRE and WILLIAM SPOTTISWOODE,
Printers to the Queen's most Excellent Majesty.
For Her Majesty's Stationery Office.

9 781334 347238

 your online bookshop

Your Details

Order date:	05/03/2019
Order reference:	AUK-46636080
Dispatch note:	20190306193101

Your Order

ISBN	Title	Quantity
9781334347238	Railway Returns for England and Wales...	1

For returns information visit wordery.com/returns. Please keep this receipt for your records.

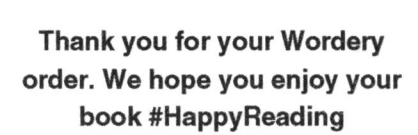

Thank you for your Wordery order. We hope you enjoy your book #HappyReading

wordery
your online bookshop

20190306193101